W9-AKU-098

The STORIES *of* HYMNS

The STORIES *of* HYMNS

The History Behind 100 of Christianity's Greatest Hymns

FR. GEORGE WILLIAM RUTLER

EWTN PUBLISHING, INC.
Irondale, Alabama

Copyright © 2016 by George William Rutler

The Stories of Hymns was formerly published in 1998 by Ignatius Press, San Francisco, under the title *Brightest and Best: Stories of Hymns.*

Printed in the United States of America. All rights reserved.

Cover and interior design by Perceptions Design Studio.

On the cover: detail from an English Book of Hours, ca. 1480.

Unless otherwise noted, all Scripture quotations have been taken from the Catholic Edition of the Revised Standard Version of the Bible (RSV), copyright © 1965 and 1966 by the Division of Christian Education of the National Council of the Churches of Christ in the United States of America. Used by permission. All rights reserved.

No part of this book may be reproduced, stored in a retrieval system, or transmitted in any form, or by any means, electronic, mechanical, photocopying, or otherwise, without the prior written permission of the publisher, except by a reviewer, who may quote brief passages in a review.

EWTN Publishing, Inc.
5817 Old Leeds Road, Irondale, AL 35210

Distributed by Sophia Institute Press, Box 5284, Manchester, NH 03108.

Library of Congress Cataloging-in-Publication Data

Names: Rutler, George W. (George William), editor.
Title: The stories of hymns : the history behind 100 of Christianity's
   greatest hymns / by George William Rutler.
Other titles: Brightest and best.
Description: Irondale, Alabama : EWTN Publishing, Inc., [2016] |
   Originally published: San Francisco : Ignatius Press, 1998. | Includes
   bibliographical references and index.
Identifiers: LCCN 2016039973 | ISBN 9781682780244 (pbk. : alk. paper)
Subjects: LCSH: Hymns, English — History and criticism. | Catholic
   Church — Hymns — History and criticism.
Classification: LCC BV312 .B74 2016 | DDC 264/.2309 — dc23 LC record available at
https://lccn.loc.gov/2016039973

CONTENTS

The
STORIES
of HYMNS

PREFACE

The treasury of sacred song is meant to be plundered by the faithful. In recent times, it has largely been left untouched, and in its stead very poor song has been taken up. Hymns, as individual compositions distinct from the Church's official collective prayer, have always been susceptible to aesthetic lapses, like any other form of art. More than a generation ago, C. S. Lewis complained that most hymns are "fifth-rate poetry set to fourth-rate music." The situation is worse now for two reasons: the degraded state of our culture and the banality of our liturgical life.

My purpose in writing this book was to restore attention to some of the finest hymns, in the hope that they might replace the miserable afflictions that keep cropping up in the baleful "missalettes," which are tokens of failure by their very existence (the Liturgy is not a didactic exercise to be read like a theater program) and appearance (their disposable form reflects the transitory quality of the contents). It seemed to me that hymns might be better appreciated if we knew a little more about the stories behind them: first of all, who wrote them and in what circumstances. In many cases, the background of a single hymn could supply the text for a whole book, so I remain frustratingly aware of the inadequacy of a few paragraphs to account for each. But these pages are offered only as intimations of the vast amount of material that the reader may want to explore on his own.

My choices, I freely admit and even boast, have sometimes been arbitrary, for, by embarking on such a project, one has to omit more than one selects. I have, moreover, been highly prejudiced in what I did choose because, although I have wanted to pick the most excellent in all respects, I have been guided by my own tastes and recollections. If an occasional choice lacks full obedience to the canons of high art, I plead that such was not meant to scandalize; it was the indulgence of a sense that the hymn represented some neglected virtue.

I deliberately call these songs "hymns" to distinguish them from run-of-the-mill songs. We do not often make that distinction now. But there was a time when Catholics and Protestants alike understood the difference, which is why they did not impose secular idioms on music or text. When the distinction is blurred, the Church does not transfigure culture; the Church is usurped by culture. That is not a sacramental economy but its very opposite.

Starting off as the least of choirboys in the 1950s, it has been my good fortune to have had an acquaintance with many kinds of hymns in different places and circumstances. I was brought up as an Anglican—that is, as an Episcopalian—first in New Jersey and then in New York, in a social and moral climate made almost unimaginable for young people now by the radical changes of just a brief generation. It was our practice every Sunday to sit as choirboys in highly starched collars as men in frock coats ushered parishioners into Morning Prayer or Holy Communion. Weekday rehearsals were rewarded with a monthly allowance of $1.25 and an ice cream at the soda fountain across the street. While I have assiduously avoided writing autobiographical books or essays, the stories of one's favorite hymns often bring in strands of one's own story. So where such allusions and reminiscences may appear gratuitously in these following pages, it is because their remembrance was enjoyable to me and may find some sympathetic readers, too.

The hymn tradition is also part of the Church's biography, and so I have tried to show this by listing the hymns chronologically instead of according to their liturgical seasons or themes. Sometimes precise dating is difficult, but a general period can be given. The chronology is based on the texts rather than on the music, for a text may be sung to a tune from a different time, and to more than one tune at that.

Only because I was familiar with most of these hymns from an early age was I able years ago to take offense at their bowdlerization by clumsy editors and ideologues. I came to notice that, in almost every instance of "updating," solid theology was the victim. References to sacrifice, grace, sin, spiritual combat, and Christ's blood were replaced by insistence on kindness, altruism, and social enlightenment. The revisions of old hymns, and most of the inventions substituted for them, are uniformly sentimental: edifying in the worst condescending way, as well as redundant and gauche. This is to be expected of those who have been so unfeeling and rapacious in dismantling the fabric of our churches and the sacred texts used in them, for as selfish ambition has been called the lust of the cleric, so is sentimentalism the indulgence of the cruel.

Very often, people may sing a hymn without any clue as to how reduced the received version is. And, as hymns are poetry, it is decadent to alter their grammatical archaisms instead of rising up to them. We do not do it to Shakespeare, so neither should we do it to the friends of Shakespeare. Like children with sticky hands near fine furniture, a generation that has vandalized the sacred Liturgy should be prevented from laying hands on the great hymns.

The sorry state of hymnody is reflected in the architecture of the buildings in which the hymns are sung. The nervous Prometheanism of so many interpreters of the Second Vatican Council has abused architectural integrity. There are bright signs of classical revival, but these are conspicuous as reactions to the modernist spiritlessness whose dead hand still has executive influence. When it comes to music and architecture, "music in stone," what is particularly discouraging is the way so many in positions of authority seem tone-deaf to the problem; and what bodes particularly ill is the refusal of the few who do sense it to address it.

Whether or not those critics are correct who say that certain ecclesiastical documents of the Vatican II period were anodyne and even naive in their measure of modernity, it cannot be denied that the generation that wallowed in euphoria is now, in old age, littering the landscape with architectural "Muzak in stone" in one last miscalculated attempt to be *au courant*. But it is like the spectacle of an aged man trying to impress the young with jargon he does not realize is already out of date. The Church is not faithful to her prophetic, priestly, and kingly offices if she does not inspire great art. For the Catholic, art is not superficial or extraneous, nor is it peripheral to the sacramental vision. To suppose it is exposes the worst kind of philosophical idealism in opposition to authentic metaphysical realism.

As has always been the case, these philosophical prejudices are rooted in mistaken Christologies. In *Lin neues Lied fur den Herrn* (1995), then-Cardinal Ratzinger contended that "it is no longer Monophysitism that threatens Christianity, but a new Arianism or at least a new Nestorianism, parallel with a new iconoclasm." Since Vatican II, the charismatic movement has tried to redress this theological desolation, but too frequently it has seemed to be trying to do so within the context of its own miswrought idealism. Indeed, often its Manichean subtext has frustrated any attempt to renew worship in an authentically Catholic way. There have been impressive expressions of moral and doctrinal obedience, but the Manichean mood betrayed itself in its total aesthetic failure.

Charismatic enthusiasm has produced no art or music tempting to the iconoclast. And again, in a sacramental Church, this is not a mere defect; it is a radical disorientation. Although there are signs of improvement, the visitor to Rome will have a hard time hearing good music even in the noble churches there. But *Sacrosanctum Concilium* of Vatican II taught that "the musical tradition of the universal Church is a treasure of inestimable value, greater even than that of any other art" (no. 112). In relation to song, even worthy architecture cannot compensate for prosaic liturgies.

Nonetheless, the finest music of worship inspires, and in turn is inspired by, the vaults to which it soars. The self-consciously "modern" church building (usually an acoustical disaster) houses suburbanites who sing like Icarus about rising up on eagles' wings while dashing out to the parking lot. After a generation of synthetic and unrealized "renewal," there remains a reluctance to tell the truth about this situation, while dwindling congregations in their imposed aesthetic squalor sing painful metaphors about satisfying the hungry heart and breaking bread on their knees. Such was not the voice of John Damascene in the desert and Bernard of Clairvaux in the abbey. They knew that Christ makes the soul sing in the brightest and best way. If the following selection of hymns joins to these great orthodox souls a Lutheran such as the war-ravaged Melchior Teschner and the nonconformist John Milton, blind but singing his metrics, this is testimony to the wonders God accomplishes through those who seek His goodness even when they have not fully grasped the truth of it. I do not blush to say that some of these in their day wrote of doctrine more sturdily than nymph-like New Agers strumming guitars on "spirituality weekends."

If there have been no decent hymns written in the last generation, there is still reason to expect great ones in the next. Antiquity is not the justification of greatness; quality is. But if someone gushes that one's taste is as valid as another's, we have to reply with Catholic common sense what the Church has said in her finest moments at the city gates: If you think that, you are a barbarian.

Hymns, when they are worthy and worthily understood, should enhance the classical Liturgy which, by God's grace, will soon rise from its aesthetic stupor. A right understanding of the hymn form means a right understanding of prayer, the psychology of collective song, and the integrity of the Eucharistic action. Properly sung, the Mass has its own liturgical hymns. Sacred hymns were primitively held to be sacrosanct indeed: until the seventh century in the Roman Rite, only the priest sang the Our Father, and it stayed that way in the Mozarabic Rite; the Gloria was generally reserved for bishops until the eleventh century. The Creed was understood as a hymn from the fifth century; Pope Symmachus introduced the Gloria deliberately as a hymn in the early sixth century; and Pope Sergius made the Agnus Dei a hymn intrinsic to the Liturgy in the late seventh century. And all because a hymn was sung in the Upper Room.

The hymns that follow complement the Liturgy but are not part of it. The whole Mass itself is its own gigantic hymn, and it is only by indult that it is said at all instead of being sung. It is liturgically eccentric to "say" a Mass and intersperse it with extraliturgical hymns. Hymns may precede or follow the Mass, but they should never replace the model of the sung Eucharist itself with its hymnodic propers. In the Latin Rite, that model gives primacy of place to the Latin language and Gregorian chant, according to numerous decrees, most historically those of Pope Pius X in *Tra le Sollecitudini* and Vatican II's *Sacrosanctum Concilium*. The Church has normally reserved other hymns for other forms of public prayer, especially the Daily Office. And, of course, all hymns can be part of private prayer, following the Augustinian principle that he who sings prays twice.

HYMNS

O Brightness of the Immortal Father's Face

ST. NICHOLAS

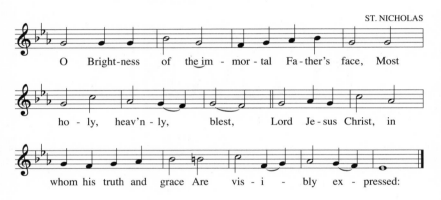

O Bright-ness of the im-mor-tal Fa-ther's face, Most ho-ly, heav'n-ly, blest, Lord Je-sus Christ, in whom his truth and grace Are vis-i-bly ex-pressed:

2. The sun is sinking now, and one by one
   The lamps of evening shine;
   We hymn the eternal Father, and the Son,
   And Holy Ghost divine.

3. Worthy art thou at all times to receive
   Our hallowed praises, Lord.
   O Son of God, be thou, in whom we live,
   Through all the world adored.

O Brightness of the Immortal Father's Face

❧

Electric lighting has obscured a sense of the toil needed to erase darkness. The Latinate idiom of "making the light" has been replaced by the casualness of the modern "turning on the light." If the heightened sensitivity to days and seasons is now left to the lower creatures, man still cannot evade the marvel of light appearing. We prefer the light to the dark because we are creatures of the God of light. Nothing that God made is evil. So His darkness is a good, too, when it is threshold to His day and not the shelter of deprivation and the corner for ill deeds.

God has endowed the human reason with the ability to harness light. This Creator is not like the mythic powers that punished Prometheus for stealing fire from heaven. The true God sent His Holy Spirit as fire for His Church. Every act of true worship is thanksgiving for this brightness. Fire worship among the pagans was an untutored prophecy of Pentecost and the true worship of the Holy Trinity: the Holy Father, who sent the Holy Son into the world as its whole Light, and the Holy Spirit, who enlightens all who obey Him.

Since this hymn is traditionally sung at the lighting of the candles in the Liturgy of Vespers (and not, thank you, the punching of a button on an electric votive light), it is understandably among the oldest of Christian verse, sung at the close of day in tandem with hymns of Matins sung to greet the rising of the sun. It was probably many generations old when Saint Basil the Great (ca. 330–379) quoted it: *Phos hilaron hagias doxes athanatou patros*.

A winding road leads from the arid Greek hills to bucolic New England, where, almost improbably, Henry Wadsworth Longfellow (1807–1882) translated it for his Golden Legend in 1851. The translation given here is even better, published in 1861 in *Hymns for the Use of the Churches* by the learned eccentric Edward William Eddis (1825–1905). The churches for which his hymns were intended were those of the "Catholic Apostolic Church," a sect sometimes known as the "Irvingites" for Edward Irving (1792–1834), a former Church of Scotland minister who founded it in London in 1832 after he was removed from the pastorate of the Regent Square Church. That church would give its name to the famous tune of Henry Smart, published in 1867. Irving's apocalyptic revivalism was based on eclectic sources, including the Jesuit Lacunza and the Tory politician Henry Drummond, who was ordained in 1834 as an Irvingite "angel for Scotland." Should sung Vespers return to parish life, this hymn will be better known, as I remember it in the amber hours floating from choir stalls to the altar, where seven lamps hung.

The author of the tune "St. Nicholas" was an Anglican clergyman of Eton and London, Clement Cotterhill Scholefield (1839–1904), who had been a curate in the Church of St. Peter, Kensington, where he knew the fledgling organist Arthur Sullivan (1842–1900). The inspired Sullivan also served for eleven years as organist and choirmaster of St. Michael's, Chester Square. While we remember Sullivan best for his association with William Gilbert (1836–1911), who remarked that Sullivan concluded a lifetime of composing by decomposing, Sullivan remembered the Rev. Mr. Scholefield for his hymn tune, which, thankfully, he preserved and published. When Queen Victoria knighted Sir Arthur, she let it be known that he was being honored for his sacred music, such as the *Church Hymns with Tunes* (1874), more than for such deathless ephemera as *The Pirates of Penzance* and *Iolanthe*.

Master of Eager Youth

ST. DUNSTAN'S

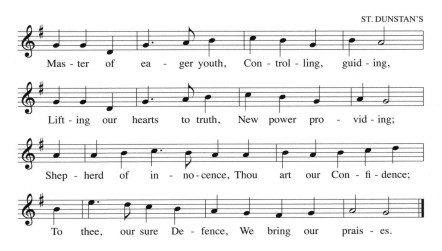

Mas - ter of ea - ger youth, Con - trol - ling, guid - ing,

Lift - ing our hearts to truth, New power pro - vid - ing;

Shep - herd of in - no - cence, Thou art our Con - fi - dence;

To thee, our sure De - fence, We bring our prais - es.

2. Thou art our mighty Lord,
   Our strength in sadness,
   The Father's conquering Word,
   True source of gladness;
   Thy Name we glorify,
   O Jesus, throned on high,
   Who gav'st thyself to die
   For man's salvation.

3. Good Shepherd of thy sheep,
   Thine own defending,
   In love thy children keep
   To life unending.
   Thou art thyself the Way:
   Lead us then day by day
   In thine own steps, we pray,
   O Lord most holy.

4. Glorious their life who sing,
   With glad thanksgiving,
   True hymns to Christ the King
   In all their living:
   Ye who confess his Name,
   Come then with hearts aflame;
   Let word and life acclaim
   Our Lord and Savior.

Master of Eager Youth

———————— ❧ ————————

Saint Clement of Alexandria (ca. 150–ca. 215) recorded these lines in his *Peidagogos* (The tutor) for use in his academy, which was at its height when this was written, around the year 200. Typically, he joined his own poetic praise of Christ with paraphrases of Scripture to dissuade the Gnostics from their heresy, challenging them with some of their own terms and phrases about the divine wisdom. For thirteen years, starting in 190, he headed the catechetical school in Alexandria, where such verse had of course a didactic purpose in the best classical sense, for there can be no true Christian learning that is not also Christian worship. That, in fact, is at the heart of the meaning of "orthodoxy," or "right praise." Origen (ca. 185–ca. 254) might be imagined among his pupils singing these words.

The present version, first published in 1938, is a very free translation by Francis Bland Tucker, an Episcopal clergyman born in 1895 in Virginia, where he served before taking a parish in Washington, D.C. The tune "St. Dunstan's" was composed on December 15, 1917, in a commuter train between Manhattan and Peekskill by Charles Winfred Douglas (1867–1944). Canon Douglas was a principal compiler of the hymnal that, for me, had been *the hymnal*. He was also musical director for a convent of Episcopal nuns in Peekskill, the Community of Saint Mary, whose stately buildings and venerable girls' school enjoyed a splendid prospect from a cliff overlooking the Hudson. The buildings are now gone, and the view is blighted by a nuclear power plant.

As Archbishop of Canterbury, Saint Dunstan (909–988) had been an accomplished musician and a first-rate illuminator of musical manuscripts. Whether Canon Douglas named his tune for the saint or for his cottage in Peekskill called "St. Dunstan's" is a question of the chicken or the egg. Mention of such items prompts one to recall how the Waldorf salad was concocted by a chef of the old Waldorf-Astoria Hotel, on the site of the present Empire State Building, for a luncheon to benefit St. Mary's School.

Master of Eager Youth

Clement would find odder than all these details the world-weariness that has taken from many current youths the youthful joy that outlasts youth when it comes from Christ. When I sang this as a boy, I had not the slightest idea who Clement was or where Alexandria was, but I was glad to be young, with older people telling me that I had a Divine Master. In the full version of the hymn, Clement calls Christ *Stomion Polone Adaone* (Bridle of the untamed colt), and that He was to me.

Let all mortal flesh keep silence

PICARDY

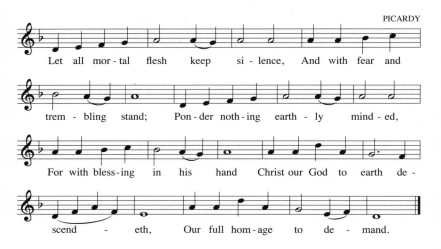

Let all mor-tal flesh keep si-lence, And with fear and
trem-bling stand; Pon-der noth-ing earth-ly mind-ed,
For with bless-ing in his hand Christ our God to earth descend - eth, Our full hom-age to de - mand.

2. King of kings, yet born of Mary,
   As of old on earth he stood,
   Lord of lords, in human vesture,
   In the body and the blood:
   He will give to all the faithful
   His own self for heavenly food.

3. Rank on rank the host of heaven
   Spreads its vanguard on the way,
   As the Light of Light descendeth
   From the realms of endless day,
   That the powers of hell may
        vanish
   As the darkness clears away.

4. At his feet the six-winged seraph;
   Cherubim with sleepless eye,
   Veil their faces to the Presence,
   As with ceaseless voice they cry,
   "Alleluia, alleluia,
   Alleluia, Lord most high!"

LET ALL MORTAL FLESH
KEEP SILENCE

T he Byzantine Liturgy of Saint James of Jerusalem certainly predates
the end of the fifth century, since it is common to the Orthodox
Churches and the Syrian Jacobites who split from them in consequence
of the Council of Chalcedon in 451. The Jacobites' heresy consisted in
their confusion of the two natures of Christ. That Monophysitism notwithstanding, they, as well as the Western Churches and some Protestants
with a relatively high Eucharistic theology, are able to add their voices
to the cherubim with sleepless eye in adoration of the Lord, who vests
Himself in our humanity.

The hymn *Sigasato pasasarx* is sung most poignantly at the Presenta-
tion of the Gifts in the Orthodox celebration of the death of Saint James,
the traditional author, on October 23 in Zante and in Jerusalem on the
Sunday following the Nativity of the Lord. The normative Liturgies are
those of Saint John Chrysostom and, less frequently, Saint Basil.

This tune, "Picardy," of course, is Western, from the mid-seventeenth
century, and typical of the last period of the *chansons de geste*, which, like
the Spanish *romanceros*, were sung by troubadours as narratives of heroic
deeds. Often these were sung in monastic settings for religious edification.
The admixture of the Eastern text with a Western tune that, in all its quiet
beauty, attains to the glory of the Eastern chants is, pray God, a promise
that when the Churches are reunited, the ethereal integrity of Byzantine
worship will transfigure, and not be corrupted by, the present decadence of
the Western rite. But there is no need to wait for the healing of the tragic
schism of the Church Universal in 1054. This hymn may be sung now as
a sublime antidote to the lamentable musical trivia that has so mutilated
the psychology of Catholic worship as it is ordinarily encountered. "Let
all mortal flesh keep silence" is the music of angels—and not the fallen
angels, who must rejoice at the present lowering of Eucharistic sensibility.

There can be no unity of the Church on earth that is not united with the song of the rank on rank of the hosts of heaven.

The familiar translation is the work of Gerard Moultrie (1829–1885), an Anglican clergyman. He learned classics at Rugby and Exeter College, Oxford, whose present chapel is a copy of the Latin Church's unsurpassed architectural achievement, the Sainte Chapelle of Saint Louis IX. Good hearts allow no justification, unless schizophrenia is invoked, for placing arts Latin and Byzantine at enmity, and the singing of this hymn in the West is ecumenism of an honest and fruitful kind.

I bind unto myself today

ST. PATRICK

1 I bind un - to my - self to - day The strong Name
2 I bind this day to me for - ev - er, By pow'r of
3 I bind un - to my - self the pow'r Of the great
4 I bind un - to my - self to - day The vir - tues
5 I bind un - to my - self to - day The pow'r of

of the Trin - i - ty, By in - vo - ca - tion
faith, Christ's In - car - na - tion; His bap - tism in the
love of cher - u - bim; The sweet "Well done" in
of the star - lit heav'n, The glo - rious sun's life -
God to hold and lead, His eye to watch, his

of the same, The Three in One, and One in Three.
Jor - dan riv - er; His death on cross for my sal - va - tion;
judg - ment hour; The ser - vice of the ser - a - phim;
giv - ing ray, the white - ness of the moon at ev'n.
might to stay, His ear to heark - en to my need.

2 His burst - ing from the spi - céd tomb; His rid - ing
3 Con - fess - ors' faith, a - pos - tles' word, The pa - triarchs'
4 The flash - ing of the light - ning free, The whirl - ing
5 The wis - dom of my God to teach, His hand to

up the heav'n - ly way; His com - ing at the
prayers, the proph - ets' scrolls; All good deeds done un -
wind's tem - pes - tuous shocks, The sta - ble earth, the
guide, his shield to ward; The word of God to

day of doom: I bind un - to my - self to day.
to the Lord, And pu - ri - ty of vir - gin souls.
deep salt sea, A - round the old e - ter - nal rocks.
give me speech, His heav'n - ly host to be my guard.

DIERDRE

6 Christ be with me, Christ with - in me, Christ be - hind me, Christ be - fore me,
  Christ be - neath me, Christ a - bove me, Christ in qui - et, Christ in dan - ger,

Christ be - side me, Christ to win me, Christ to com - fort and re - store me,
Christ in hearts of all that love me, Christ in mouth of friend and stran - ger.

ST. PATRICK

7 I bind un - to my - self the Name, The strong Name

of the Trin - i - ty, By in - vo - ca - tion

of the same, The Three in One, and One in Three.

Of whom all na - ture hath cre - a - tion; E - ter - nal

Fa - ther, Spir - it, Word: Praise to the Lord of

my sal - va - tion, Sal - va - tion is of Christ the Lord.

I BIND UNTO MYSELF TODAY

———————— ❧ ————————

The Apostle to the Gaels, fierce and wonderful in his fire-lighting zeal for the Faith, is heard through the stormy Irish centuries courtesy of the congenial wife of the Protestant Archbishop of Armagh. A rare proponent in Ireland of the Oxford movement, Cecil Frances Alexander (1818–1895), looking from her Victorian parlor window toward Down Patrick and the saint's grave, was persuaded that her lace and lavender circumstance was the authentic inheritance of what the saint had intended for Eire.

She is the one who paraphrased the words attributed to Patrick as the "Faeth Fiada," or "Deer's Cry," so named because it was thought that he had intoned it as he trod the stony way to Tara, hunted by the fierce hidden scouts of the Druid high king Loegaire mac Neill. The Latin annals of the seventh-century Irish monk Muirchú recreate the scene. And all this as Saint Augustine was singing hymns of his own on the shores of North Africa. It is possible that the words, sonorously beginning *atomriug indiu*, of which the first complete records date only to the eleventh century, followed the form of Druid incantations cast as spells. An early description of this transparent allusion to Ephesians 6:13–17 calls it "a lorica [shield] of faith for the protection of body and soul against demons and men and vices: when any person shall recite it daily with pious meditation on God, demons shall not dare to face him."

So Patrick brought something good and holy out of something superstitious and profane, planting the Faith beyond the southeast of Ireland, where it had been brought by his predecessor Palladius, "the first bishop of the Irish who believe in Christ." The incantation may even have drawn from the Druid attention less to meter than to the symbolic designs of the words when written: it seems that these were illuminated in the manuscript in the circular form of a Celtic breastplate. "St. Patrick's Breastplate" is the more common title for the verses. The shrine of one tooth from the mouth that incanted the "Breastplate" is in the National

Museum of Dublin. The saint's ardently expressed trinitarianism should confound the recent effrontery of those who would deconstruct him into some sort of post-Christian theosophical shaman. And one may also be edified by Patrick's insistence on celebrating the Eucharist in Latin instead of Gaelic.

Mrs. Alexander, using the clout of her marital rank, along with a prolific talent, published her version for use in the parishes of the Church of Ireland on Saint Patrick's Day in 1889. It soon spread to Catholics, reminding them of what was theirs, just as the Norman invaders had intensified the cult of Saint Patrick in their own day, when the Celts of Armagh were in danger of losing their traditions to the Danes who had settled principally in alien strongholds around Dublin.

The tune "St. Patrick" was an older Irish tune included in a collection edited by Charles Villiers Stanford (1852–1924), friend of Brahms, collaborator with Tennyson, and teacher of Ralph Vaughan Williams. The sixth stanza is set to "Deirdre," an even older Irish melody preserved by the Dublin-born professor of music for forty years at Cambridge University. Many of Stanford's own rhapsodic variations on such old tunes are particularly stunning. His talent was precocious: it is a fact, and not a legend, that he composed a piece at the age of eight that was performed two years later in the Dublin Royal Theatre for a children's pantomime. He has given us that rare thing, an Irish opera, called *Shamus O'Brien*, besides an Irish symphony, six Irish rhapsodies, and arrangements for *Songs of Erin*, all in addition to nine more operas and half a dozen other symphonic works.

As a model for the highest liturgical Victoriana, few specimens can match his Prayer Book service commonly called "Stanford in B flat." He died in the month following George Gershwin's first performance of "Rhapsody in Blue" with the Paul Whiteman Orchestra, and the canyon between the styles has inclined captious critics to install Stanford in the contemptible loggia reserved by them for audacious Victorian romantics. For his distinguished musical services, not least of which is his recollection of a glorious Celtic heritage, Stanford was given burial in Westminster Abbey.

This hymn was sung in procession at my ordination as an Anglican priest on December 20, 1969, by Bishop Horace William Baden Donegan, whose Anglo-Irish parents had been contemporaries of Mrs. Alexander. The long ambulatories and aisles of the Cathedral of St. John the Divine in New York City, which then was a blatantly Christian place, permitted ample opportunity to do justice to all the stanzas.

Among the ambulatory chapels there is one in exquisite Celtic style dedicated to St. Columba, or Colmcille, spiritual brother and worthy heir of Patrick, whose foundation at Iona was second in reputation only to Armagh itself. The admixture of architectural idioms in that succession of chapels, and indeed throughout that Romanesque-Gothic structure, is as thrillingly eclectic as Stanford was himself. After all, his Irish repertoire was woven through a vaster portfolio that included works that have become almost the definition of Englishness, and among these has to be mentioned the dramatic score he composed to accompany the Lyceum Theater debut of Tennyson's *Queen Mary*.

Early Welsh missionaries in Ireland created a fictitious ancestor for the whole population of Hibernia and called him "Gwyddel," which became Goídel in Irish and Gael when Anglicized. So G. K. Chesterton was prompted to write in the *Ballad of the White Horse*:

> For the great Gaels of Ireland
> Are the men that God made mad,
> For all their wars are merry,
> And all their songs are sad.

Patrick, like Palladius before him, and all his successors, was engaged in a different kind of war when he marched against the grim idol Crom Cruach, whose shadow some would want to conjure up in our own fraction of history. Patrick's song was neither merry nor sad, for his battle brought the sound known only to those who conquer idols, and that is the sound of joy.

Hail thee, festival day!

SALVA FESTA DIES

Hail thee, fes - ti - val day! blest day that art hal - lowed for ev - er;

1st time / *2nd time*

Day where - on Christ a - rose, break - ing the king - dom of death. death.

Stanzas

1 Lo, the fair beau - ty of earth, from the death of the win - ter a - ris - ing!
3 Dai - ly the love - li - ness grows, a - dorned with the glo - ry of blos - som;
5 God the All - Fa - ther, the Lord, who rul - est the earth and the heav - ens,
7 Spir - it of life and of pow'r, now flow in us, fount of our be - ing.

repeat Refrain

Ev - 'ry good gift of the year now with its Mas - ter re - turns:
Heav - en her gates un - bars, fling - ing her in - crease of light:
Guard us from harm with - out, cleanse us from e - vil with - in:
Light that dost light - en all, life that in all dost a - bide.

2 He who was nailed to the cross is Lord and the
4 Rise from the grave now, O Lord, who art au - thor of
6 Je - sus the health of the world, en - light - en our
8 Praise to the Giv - er of good! Thou Love who art

rul - er of all men; All things cre - at - ed on
life and cre - a - tion. Tread - ing the path - way of
minds, thou Re - dee - mer, Son of the Fa - ther su -
au - thor of con - cord, Pour out thy balm on our

repeat Refrain

earth sing to the glo - ry of God.
death, life thou be - stow - est on man.
preme, on - ly be - got - ten of God.
souls, or - der our ways in thy peace.

HAIL THEE, FESTIVAL DAY!

In a long processional hymn, we can bend the canon that would allow no caesura, or break in meter. It happens here in "Salve festa dies," composed in 1906 by Ralph Vaughan Williams. Bear in mind that a processional hymn needs a procession: not a quick traipse up the aisle but a little pilgrimage of its own, around the church, even perhaps going outside. If the church is fortunate enough to have side altars and shrines, and possibly an ambulatory to ambulate through, the procession pauses at the several "stations," where a prayer is sung (not said), and the way resumes. Banners and incense are part of it.

Music serves the words, if we want to conform to Catholic logic. So it does here. Grand as the music is, grander is the text of Venantius Honorius Fortunatus (ca. 535–ca. 600). He was born in Italy, not far from Traviso, and was combed and groomed in the elaborate protocols of the court of Metz, which would later be made even more splendid in its baroque embellishments. Thus he cuts a fine figure of the universality of Christendom before there were nations enough for the lesser thing we call internationalism. From Metz in the northeast of France, he moved to the west central city of Poitiers, whose anti-Arian saint, Hilary (315–367), the "Athanasius of the West," he often praised in song.

In Poitiers Venantius resided near the Abbey of the Holy Cross, which had been founded by his personal friend and wife of Clothar I, Saint Radegund (518–587). Having sincerely consecrated to God his talents as the leading Latin poet of his generation, he was ordained and, shortly before his sixtieth birthday, became Bishop of Poitiers, dying a year or two later. His chief poetic theme was the Holy Cross, a fragment of which had been obtained by the saintly queen from Emperor Justin II in 569. The last decade of Venantius's life was during the pontificate of the Latin Doctor and "Father of the Medieval Papacy," Saint Gregory the Great, who decidedly encouraged veneration of legitimate relics.

There is not a festival of the Church that is not a veneration of the Cross, by which all feasts come. Attached to this Easter hymn are alternate lines for Ascension Day, Pentecost, Corpus Christi, the Dedication of a Church, and so forth. It is hard to say how many of these interpolations are the work of Venantius, but he provided the literary framework and expected adaptations. There were no copyrights or public jealousies when hymns were made anonymously, like cathedrals, for God's glory, and romantic individualism was odd and uncouth.

In the sixteenth century, egregious Thomas Cranmer, Henry VIII's puppet Archbishop of Canterbury, recommended an already extant translation of this hymn for his sovereign's carefully crafted public devotions. For at least two centuries before the Protestant schism, versions had appeared in various languages for popular use. In England, where the climate made the arrival of spring an especially vivid Paschal icon, the hymn appears to have been translated separately for the rites of Sarum (Salisbury) in the south and York in the north. Sung in their wondrous cathedrals, the sound could persuade anyone of a longer procession to the shadowless vaults of paradise.

O come, O come, Emmanuel

VENI, VENI, EMMANUEL

O come, O come, Em-man - u - el, And ran-som cap-tive
Is - ra-el, That mourns in lone-ly ex - ile here
Un-til the Son of God ap-pear. Re-joice, re-joice!
Em-man - u - el Shall come to thee, O Is - ra-el.

2. O come, thou Wisdom from on high,
Who orderest all things mightily;
To us the path of knowledge show,
And teach us in her ways to go.
Refrain

3. O come, O come, thou Lord of Might,
Who to thy tribes, on Sinai's height,
In ancient times didst give the law
In cloud, and majesty, and awe.
Refrain

4. O come, thou Rod of Jesse's stem,
From every foe deliver them
From depths of hell thy people save
And give them vict'ry o'er the grave.
Refrain

5. O come, thou Key of David, come,
And open wide our heav'nly home;
Make safe the way that leads on high,
And close the path to misery.
Refrain

6. O come, thou Day-spring from on high,
And cheer us by thy drawing nigh;
Disperse the gloomy clouds of night,
And death's dark shadows put to flight.
Refrain

7. O come, Desire of nations, bind
In one the hearts of all mankind;
Bind thou our sad divisions cease,
And be thyself our King of Peace.
Refrain

O COME, O COME, EMMANUEL

To "keep your O" was a medieval monastic expression, referring to the great O Antiphons of Advent. From December 17 (or, in present usage, from December 18 if the seventeenth is a Sunday) through December 23, these praises of the Messiah, drawn from scriptural typology, are still sung at the Magnificat in Evening Prayer. It once was the custom for officers in the monastery, starting with the abbot and proceeding in descending order of rank, to intone their "O" and later supply some token gift to the brethren. The pleasant custom followed a rather elaborate system in the Benedictine house of Fleury (now Saint-Benoît-sur-Loire), whose Romanesque abbey sheltered the relics of Saint Benedict and Saint Scholastica during the Lombard pillaging of Italy; and the Romanesque glory of England, Durham, had equally careful specifications, including the furnishing of a hogshead of wine for each "O."

An antiphon is usually attached to an office hymn, frequently as a Christian eisegesis of an Old Testament text, as in the case of this hymn, which has become nearly synonymous with what is left of Advent observance in our culture. Gradually, antiphons were lengthened for use on their own, which explains the root of "anthem" in "antiphona," referring to lines sung to music especially composed for them rather than to plainchant.

What may be an oblique reference by Boethius (ca. 480–524) in part 3 of *De Consolatione Philosophiae* would suggest a very early date for the great Os, and they were part of the Roman Liturgy by the eighth century, although they may not have originated in Rome. In a radio broadcast on the death of Patrick Cardinal Hayes (1867–1938), Monsignor Fulton J. Sheen (1895–1979) likened the late Archbishop of New York to Saint Augustine in his frequent recourse to the exclamation "O"; the rhetorical flourish unsettled many who knew the sedate cardinal well. But more

O come, O come, Emmanuel

problematic has been the occasional citation of the exclamation, as old as speech itself, as evidence that Augustine was the author of the antiphons.

They remain fully intact in the revised breviary: O Sapientia, O Adonai, O radix Jesse, O clavis David, O Oriens, O Rex gentium, O Emmanuel. Typical of the Marianism of the medieval English Church, which was known as "Mary's Dowry," an eighth antiphon, " O Virgo virginum," was sung last, with the sequence beginning on December 16. The form of the hymn most familiar to us, based on numerous English translations beginning with one by John Mason Neale in 1851, has the last antiphon first, recasting it for the refrain, which is an invention. It is a singularly beautiful Latinity: "O Emmanuel, Rex et legifer noster, exspectatio gentium, et Salvator earum: veni ad salvandum nos Domine Deus noster."

The radical English paraphrases are inspired by German metrical versions published in Cologne in 1710 as an addition to the main text of *Psalteriolum Cantionum Catholicarum*. The tune is a compilation, a "pasticcio" or "cento," of several plainchant melodies, the work of Thomas Helmore (1811–1890). A clergyman and master of choristers at the Chapel Royal, St. James's Palace, he did much to promote plainchant in Anglican worship and died exactly one month before the death of Cardinal Newman.

Sing, my tongue, the glorious battle

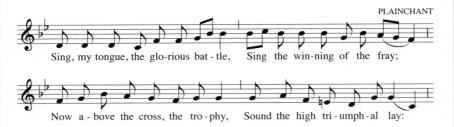

Sing, my tongue, the glo-rious bat-tle, Sing the win-ning of the fray;

Now a-bove the cross, the tro-phy, Sound the high tri-umph-al lay:

Tell how Christ, the world's Re-deem-er, As a vic-tim won the day.

2. Thirty years he dwelt among us,
   His appointed time fulfilled;
   Born for this, he met his passion,
   This the Savior freely willed:
   On the cross the Lamb was lifted,
   Where his precious blood was
      spilled.

3. He endured the nails, the spitting,
   Vinegar, and spear, and reed;
   From that holy body broken
   Blood and water forth proceed:
   Earth, and stars, and sky, and ocean,
   By that flood from stain are freed.

4. Faithful cross! above all other,
   One and only noble tree!
   None in foliage, none in blossom,
   None in fruit thy peer may be:
   Sweetest wood, and sweetest iron!
   Sweetest weight is hung on thee.

5. Bend thy boughs, O tree of glory!
   Thy relaxing sinews bend;
   For awhile the ancient rigor
   That thy birth bestowed, suspend;
   And the King of heavenly beauty
   On thy bosom gently tend!

6. To the Trinity be glory
   Everlasting, as is meet
   Equal to the Father, equal
   To the Son, and Paraclete:
   God the Three in One, whose
      praises
   All created things repeat.

SING, MY TONGUE, THE GLORIOUS BATTLE

%

Seven hundred years are the span of these lines, for Saint Thomas Aquinas (1225–1274) wrote his Eucharistic hymn bidding his tongue to praise the mystery of the glorious Body — "Pange, lingua, gloriosi/ Corporis mysterium" — after having long meditated on this poem of Venantius Honorius Fortunatus, ordering his tongue to sing the tale of the glorious battle won on the Cross — "Pange, lingua, gloriosi/ Proelium certaminis." Although the dates of his birth and death are only approximate, we know that Venantius wrote these words for the nineteenth of November in 569. They were used, as were so many of his hymns, for a procession escorting the relic of the True Cross, but these particular lines were used for the actual arrival of the relic in Poitiers from Tours, where it had been brought from the East, and were sung in the presence of Queen Radegund, the Saint Helena of her day, when she donated it to her new abbey. Gregory of Tours described the procession, which included the Bishop of Tours, Eufronius, attended by his clergy "with much singing and gleaming of tapers and fragrance of incense."

The indefatigable John Mason Neale (1818–1866) translated the text for publication in 1851 with the tune that originated in the Use of Sarum, which modification of the Roman Rite was codified by Bishop Richard Poore of Salisbury, and later of Durham, early in the thirteenth century and revised a century later. By the mid-fifteenth century, it was common throughout England, as well as Wales and Ireland. Neale, a Church of England clergyman and a man of advanced Tractarian principles, from time to time was allegedly obliged to "translate" texts of his own Greek and Latin composition, an enterprise that enabled the mild-mannered scholar to insert Catholic doctrine into Anglican worship on the authority of ancient credentials. He did not have to invent this text. Not only is the source impeccable for primitivists, but the words harken back to the beginning of creation.

There was a convoluted medieval legend, suggested in the second stanza's "De Parentis protoplasti," in which Adam's son Seth was able to comfort his dying father with a medication made from seeds he had recovered from the Tree of Life in the Garden. After Adam's death, these seeds grew into the tree from which the Cross of Christ was rudely fashioned. The tale is intertwined with the pious tradition that had Adam buried under Golgotha and the blood of Christ trickling down to revive Adam's bones. The skull and crossbones portrayed at the foot of crucifixes to this day allude to this story. The supercilious would ridicule such beautiful conceits, but it would certainly be out of place to do so in our generation, which rightly esteems similarly fertile symbolism in Negro spirituals and, less exaltedly, in pseudo folk-songs and rock ballads.

How much of this appeared in the original texts of Venantius is uncertain. Even by the later Middle Ages, the full hymn, usually sung for part of the Divine Office, was familiar only to the Mozarabic Rite, as it was preserved through the efforts of the archbishop of Toledo, Francisco Cardinal Jimenez de Cisneros (1436–1517).

O Trinity of blessed light

PLAINCHANT

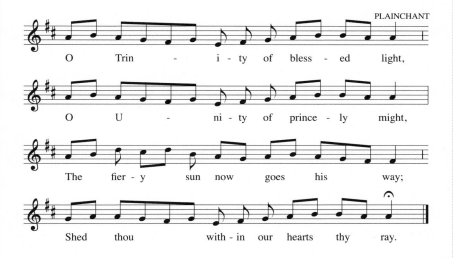

O Trin - i - ty of bless - ed light,

O U - ni - ty of prince - ly might,

The fier - y sun now goes his way;

Shed thou with - in our hearts thy ray.

2. To thee our morning song of praise,
To thee our evening prayer we raise;
O grant us with thy saints on high
To praise thee through eternity.

3. All laud to God the Father be,
All praise, eternal Son, to thee,
All glory, as is ever meet,
To God the holy Paraclete.

O TRINITY OF BLESSED LIGHT

Saint Augustine may have heard this hymn, for it was almost certainly written by Saint Ambrose, the spiritual father of Augustine's conversion, although this particular hymn does not occur in the Liturgy named for the Bishop of Milan. As in the late nine hundreds the emissaries of Vladimir, Emperor of the Rus, were dazzled to conversion by the splendor of the worship in Santa Sophia, and in the late nineteenth century the poet Paul Claudel was reconverted by the Song of Our Lady in her cathedral in Paris, so was Augustine ravished by the music he heard around the altar and throne of Ambrose in Milan. A dozen hymn texts are said to be from the pen of Ambrose, and surely one can confidently say that in syntax, style, and valiant assertions of authentic trinitarianism against the Arianism of the fourth century, this one functions as a kind of Ambrosian theme song.

If Ambrose is tentatively connected to the Ambrosian Rite only eponymously, everything about that rite accords with the mystical clarity of expression and action that convinced Augustine to embrace the Catholic beauty "ever ancient, ever new." In a similar way, Gregorian chant, to which this hymn is traditionally sung, is less the invention of Pope Gregory the Great than it is a gradual development named in honor of the saint whose principles of music are symbolized by his promotion of the Roman *schola cantorum* in the sixth century. The Gregorian tune for "O lux beata, Trinitas" has been attached to it since the eleventh century.

Safely assuming that Bishop Ambrose was familiar with many of the characteristic usages later identified as the Ambrosian Rite, we might imagine this being sung before the Creed in the solemn offertory procession, all as part of an anti-Arian polemic. Ambrose was a pontifex in more ways than one, using his knowledge of Greek to build a bridge between East and West. The tune he used quite probably had Byzantine antecedents, especially if there is substance to the theory that the Milanese Liturgy incorporated usages from the ten Greek bishops who preceded

O Trinity of blessed light

him in his See. While his immediate predecessor, Auxentius, was an Arian, there is no reason to think that the Church of Milan purged his Oriental chant when it purged any heresies that had been sung to it. Or perhaps the hymns inherited by Auxentius were left untouched by his erroneous hand, out of fear of the multitude, for whom conservatism is most jealously evident in matters of song.

Saint Ambrose joins Saint Jerome, Saint Augustine, and Saint Gregory the Great in the quartet of Latin Doctors of the Church. Poetry and song were essential to the intellectual economy of these men, even for the blunt Jerome. Thought that does not begin and end in acts of praise is sterile speculation. Thus Ronald Knox explained why the Modernists do not compose hymns: "Birds of prey have no song." Saint Ambrose, by his life of daylong praise, was granted his petition: "Te nostra supplex gloria/ Per cuncta laudet saecula." Or, in the masterful translation of John Mason Neale, who in his lifetime of forty-eight years became the greatest hymn translator of the nineteenth century: "To thee our morning song of praise/ To thee our evening prayer we raise."

Blessèd city, heavenly Salem

ORIEL

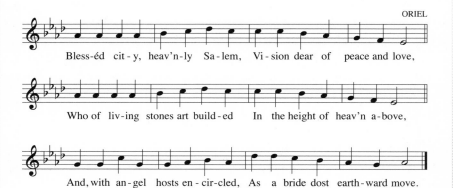

Bless-éd cit-y, heav'n-ly Sa-lem, Vi-sion dear of peace and love,

Who of liv-ing stones art build-ed In the height of heav'n a-bove,

And, with an-gel hosts en-cir-cled, As a bride dost earth-ward move.

2. From celestial realms descending,
   Bridal glory round thee shed,
   Meet for him whose love espoused
      thee,
   To thy Lord shalt thou be led;
   All thy streets and all thy bulwarks
   Of pure gold are fashioned.

3. Bright thy gates of pearl are shining;
   They are open evermore;
   And by virtue of his merits
   Thither faithful souls do soar,
   Who, for Christ's dear Name, in
      this world
   Pain and tribulation bore.

4. Many a blow and biting sculpture
   Polished well those stones elect,
   In their places now compacted
   By the heavenly Architect,
   Who therewith hath willed for
      ever
   That his palace should be decked.

5. Laud and honor to the Father,
   Laud and honor to the Son,
   Laud and honor to the Spirit,
   Ever Three, and ever One,
   Consubstantial, co-eternal,
   While unending ages run.

Blessèd city,
heavenly Salem

Everyone wants to go to heaven, even those who consciously deny its existence, and certainly those who would lengthen their earthly years; for heaven as the state of perfection is the soul's ultimate good and, in the stubborn conundrum of the Scholastic theologians, it is impossible not to will one's good. Were a man so perverse as to want to kill himself, that would be his twisted notion of what is good for him in that moment; and were he to desire hell, he would want to go there because his infernal imagination gave hell the quality of heaven. The prophet promises "woe unto them that call evil good" (Isa. 5:20), knowing that there are those who do precisely that, and they do it not only because evil is the opposite of the good but because that opposition postures as good itself. The Serpent in the Garden did not tell our first parents that they would be as serpents.

In the seventh century, possibly even a century earlier, Christians were singing the anonymous "Urbs beata Jerusalem, dicta pacis visio," and there is no hymn older than the variations on the theme of the Heavenly City. The book of Revelation is its own hymn. Its architectural imagery is flaunted in confidence of the Jerusalem on High being a cogent, solid place—so much more substantial than what passes for solidity in this wooden world that it seems opaque to wooden minds. But saints seem that way, too, to those who are not saints.

Orthodox belief in heaven is an "inscape" to the escapism of those who claim there is no heaven. Brave souls are eager for heaven, at least souls brave enough to reorder their minor pleasures and temporary affections, while one of the world's most abiding sadnesses is the suspicion that death would deprive us of loved ones. I have never met a man melancholy at the prospect of death robbing him of his dentist or his dry cleaner. But in heaven, the noblest and most endearing loves will seem like vapid northern lights and gossamer compared with the Love who is there. It does take a very strong lover to desire eternal life in the place where there is no "marrying and giving in marriage" (Matt. 24:38). Only a valiant lover understands that sometimes, and always in the most important matters, loss is gain.

John Mason Neale's version is quite exact line by line, needing little artifice to make the exalted images attractive to the ordinary taste. The pearly gates are there in the third stanza, saved by him from the indignity of cliché: "Portae nitent margaritas, adytis patentibus...." And the fourth stanza's laud for the Architect is a tour de force of difficult, but not strained, architectural rhyme.

The congregational alternative to the traditional plainchant tune is, in spite of its name, "Oriel," the composition of a Bavarian Catholic, Caspar Ett, born in 1788. He was trained in voice by the Benedictines and served as organist of St. Michael's Church in Munich for more than thirty years, until his death on May 11, 1847. A particularly splendid anthem setting for the text was written by Edward Bairstow (1874–1946), organist of York Minster, and based on an old Sarum melody.

Christ is made the sure foundation

WESTMINSTER ABBEY

Christ is made the sure foun-da-tion, Christ the head and cor-ner-stone;

Cho-sen of the Lord, and pre-cious, Bind-ing all the Church in one;

Ho - ly Si - on's help for ev - er, And her con - fi - dence a-lone.

2. All that dedicated city,
   Dearly loved of God on high,
   In exultant, jubilation
   Pours perpetual melody:
   God the One in three adoring
   In glad hymns eternally.

3. To this temple, where we call thee,
   Come, O Lord of Hosts, today;
   With thy wonted loving-kindness
   Hear thy servants as they pray,
   And thy fullest benediction
   Shed within its walls alway.

4. Here vouchsafe to all thy servants
   What they ask of thee to gain;
   What they gain from thee, for ever
   With the blessed to retain,
   And hereafter in thy glory
   Evermore with thee to reign.

CHRIST IS MADE THE
SURE FOUNDATION

─────────────── ❧ ───────────────

Recite the strong meter of the first verse, and you have built a strong foundation indeed: "Angularis fundamentum lapis Christus missus est." John Mason Neale's text is just as sturdy. Recollection of these lines should move charitable souls to thankfulness that Neale and the anonymous author of the original verses from around the seventh century, which form a second part of nine stanzas of the "Urbs beata" hymn previously mentioned, did not live to see the great many mean churches built since the 1960s, decorated minimally and so miserably. The paramount effrontery of such architecture to Christ and culture does not consist in its vulgarity, since it lacks the panache needed for real vulgarisms; it most offends in its bourgeois contentment. I cannot envision anyone who is content with such banality being made happy by the prospect of heaven.

While much cultural sensibility has moved beyond the sterility of these structures that resemble the lounges of highway motels, limited faith and monetary selfishness have kept many ecclesiastical bureaucracies a generation behind the present reawakening to a nobler idiom in architecture. If the new classicists have put the remnant minimalists on the defensive, modern architectural hacks still get contracts from local church committees. Every time some suburban horror is built to look like sloth in stone, I hope Abbe Suger and Saint Louis and Borromini are permitted to call down to the perpetrators of such misery, "Shame, shame, shame on you."

"Angularis fundamentum" is typically sung at the dedication or consecration of a church and on church anniversaries. For constructions too numerous to list in recent generations, it would be more appropriate to sing that Christ had been made a temporary foundation. A dispirited generation built temporary housing for its Lord, and in the next millennium, the ease of its removal may be looked back upon as its chief virtue.

Christ is made the sure foundation

While Americans who grew up with this hymn are probably most accustomed to singing it to the tune "Regent Square," that fine setting is possibly overused. Equally stately and monumental is "Westminster Abbey," from an anthem of Henry Purcell (1659–1695). The only problem with it is its office as a sad reminder that the composer died in his thirty-sixth year, like Mozart. Purcell had been an organ tuner in the abbey and eventually became its organist. He got into a bit of trouble for charging admission to the organ loft at the coronation of William and Mary in 1689. But he was forgiven by the Chapter, who voted him burial in the abbey and publicly resolved that they would attend "with their vestments; together with all the Lovers of that Noble Science, with the united Choyres of that and the Chappel Royal, when the Dirge composed by the Deceased for her late Majesty of Ever Blessed Memory will be played by Trumpets and other Musick; And his place of Organist is disposed of to that great Master, Dr. Blow."

The day of resurrection

ALL HALLOWS

The day of res-ur-rec-tion! Earth, tell it out a-broad;

The pass-o-ver of glad-ness, The Pass-o-ver of God.

From death to life e-ter-nal, From earth un-to the sky,

Our Christ hath brought us o-ver With hymns of vic-to-ry.

2. Our hearts be pure from evil,
   That we may see aright
   The Lord in rays eternal
   Of resurrection light;
   And, listening to his accents,
   May hear so calm and plain
   His own "All hail!" and, hearing,
   May raise the victor strain.

3. Now let the heavens be joyful,
   Let earth her song begin,
   The round world keep high triumph,
   And all that is therein;
   Let all things seen and unseen
   Their notes together blend,
   For Christ the Lord is risen,
   Our joy that hath no end.

THE DAY OF RESURRECTION

From the Holy Sepulcher at midnight in the Greek Easter Liturgy, candles flood fire from the Paschal Candle, filling the church and spreading through the surrounding courtyards and streets. Jerusalem then is what Jerusalem was when the Resurrection broke the moral darkness of man. In the middle of the eighth century, the Greek Father Saint John Damascene (ca. 675–ca.749) wrote this first part of his "Golden Canon." Saint John had been influenced in musical taste by adopted brother Saint Cosmas, who had learned from their common tutor, also named Cosmas. Both removed to the laura of St. Sabas outside Jerusalem, where the monks grew jealous of their talent and, more understandably, distressed by their constant singing. All this was complicated by imperial politics and theology, which were not inseparable; but Patriarch John V intervened, and John thrived in his monastery, while Cosmas became bishop of Majuma, where he sang to his heart's content. Saint John championed the veneration of images in a long struggle with the iconoclastic emperor Constantine Copronymus, his eloquence earning him the sobriquet Chrysorrhoas, or "gold-flowing." The English text is a fair specimen of what John Mason Neale produced when he decided upon a broader kind of translation, almost a paraphrase.

George Clement Martin (1844–1916) published his setting "All Hallows" in 1888. Few musical careers were as radiantly Victorian as his. A comparatively late bloomer, he is said to have never touched a keyboard until, as a sixteen-year-old, he heard a Bach fugue performed by the grand Herbert Stanley Oakley (1830–1903). His conversion to a life of music happened as Stephen Foster in America was copyrighting "Old Black

Joe." There is no record that Martin ever remarked the coincidence. He began lessons with the grander John Stainer (1840–1901), often riding twenty-two miles by horse for classes. Having completed studies at Oxford, Martin went to Scotland as personal organist for the fifth Duke of Buccleuch and seventh Duke of Queensbury, Walter Francis Scott (1806–1884), who maintained five enormous country houses, three lesser ones, and two palatial London houses. The status symbol of having one's own organist spread to America: Henry C. Frick hired Archer Gibson, and Walter Gale played every morning as Andrew Carnegie bathed and shaved. Martin succeeded Stainer as head organist of St. Paul's Cathedral, London, in 1888. Five years before his appointment, he received a Lambeth degree in music; that is, an honorary degree that the archbishops of Canterbury, as papal legates, had been able to confer since the thirteenth century, and which right was maintained by decree of Henry VIII. In celebration of the Diamond Jubilee in 1897, he was knighted in seemly succession to his first mentor, Oakley, who in equally Victorian fashion had been knighted by the queen in 1876 on the occasion of the dedication in Edinburgh of the memorial to the Prince Consort.

"The Day of Resurrection," *Anastaseos haemera*, joins light and sound. "The Lord in rays eternal/ Of resurrection light" is the efficient cause for bidding "all thing seen and unseen/ Their notes together blend." In the angelology of Saint Gregory Nazianzen and Pseudo-Dionysius, with which Saint John Damascene was imbued, there is no distinction between light and sound for the holy angels, as they are pure spirit. For us, the combination is more difficult; in a world of sin, attempts to unite them can be catastrophic as, for example, in a discotheque.

O blest Creator of the light

BROMLEY

O blest Cre - a - tor of the light, Who mak'st the day with ra - diance bright, And o'er the form - ing world didst call The light from cha - os first of all;

2. Whose wisdom joined in meet array
   The morn and eve, and named them day:
   Night comes with all its darkling fears;
   Regard thy people's prayers and tears,

3. Lest, sunk in sin, and whelmed with strife,
   They lose the gift of endless life;
   While thinking but the thoughts of time,
   They weave new chains of woe and crime.

4. But grant them grace that they may strain
   The heavenly gate and prize to gain:
   Each harmful lure aside to cast,
   And purge away each error past.

5. O Father, that we ask be done,
   Through Jesus Christ, thine only Son,
   Who, with the Holy Ghost and thee,
   Doth live and reign eternally.

O BLEST CREATOR
OF THE LIGHT

$\mathcal{S}$

Saint Gregory the Great is piously, if gratuitously, given credit for this praise of the Creator of light. One certainty is that it was written before the eighth century, and, using critical canons, it is almost as evident that an expression so compact must have been the work of a single author. John Mason Neale rarely surpasses anywhere his couplet: "While thinking but the thoughts of time/ They weave new chains of woe and crime." He published this in 1851 as Herman Melville was publishing the first American edition of *Moby Dick, or The Whale* — incongruous works save for the classic status they share.

Romance unguided by theology inevitably lapses into naturalism, not all of which is as harmless and satisfying as love songs to the harvest moon and paeans to the lucky old sun. The liturgical context of traditional evening hymnody roots the creation of life in its divine source and makes a play of moral rays and physical shades in the contest of grace and original sin. It is all here in this little "Summa of the Soul."

Historically sung to plainchant, of course, this poem was not ill served by the innovative tune "Bromley," by Jeremiah Clark, who was born about 1670. This unfortunate man's brilliant career as composer for stage and keyboard and organist of the Chapel Royal had its own shadows. Disappointed in love, Clark killed himself on December 1, 1707, in his house right next to St. Paul's Cathedral, where he had been appointed organist in 1695. His tomb is in its crypt. He might have killed himself a second time if he had known that his great trumpet voluntary written in honor of Queen Anne's consort, Prince George of Denmark, would be widely misattributed since the 1870s to Henry Purcell (1659–1695).

The manuscript for "Bromley" was uncovered in the Foundling Hospital in London, which reminds me that I slept my first night as a priest as an overaged guest of the Foundling Hospital in New York City. The location was convenient for celebrating my First Mass the next morning in St. Patrick's Cathedral. Everyone would be an eternal foundling if the sun and moon were our parents; and that melancholy notion is the new pagan suspicion of ersatz "creation spirituality." But each person is a child of the Creator, who joined our first parents in paradise after he "joined in meet array/ The morn and eve, and named them day." And by baptismal regeneration, we become sons of adoption, able to call the Creator "Abba," "Father" (cf. Gal. 4:5; Eph. 1:5). What the soul discerns of the day and night in the moral life depends on the free will's affirmation of the most classical stanza for concluding sacred song, as it concludes this Vespers hymn:

> Praesta, Pater piisime,
> Patrisque compar unice,
> Cum Spiritu Paraclito,
> Et nunc et in perpetuum.

Stars of the morning

TRISAGION

Stars of the morn - ing, so glo - rious - ly bright,

Filled with ce - les - ti - al splen - dor and light,

These that, where night nev - er fol - low - eth day,

Raise the "Thrice Ho - ly" song ev - er and aye.

2. These are thy ministers, these dost thou own,
    God of Sabaoth, the nearest thy throne;
    These are thy messengers, these dost thou send,
    Help of the helpless ones! man to defend.

3. These keep the guard amid Salem's dear bowers,
    Thrones, principalities, virtues, and powers,
    Where, with the living ones, mystical four,
    Cherubim, seraphim bow and adore.

4. "Who like the Lord?" thunders Michael the chief;
    Raphael, "the cure of God," comforteth grief,
    And, as at Nazareth, prophet of peace,
    Gabriel, "the light of God," bringeth release.

5. Then, when the earth was first poised in mid space,
    Then, when the planets first sped on their race,
    Then, when were ended the six days' employ,
    Then all the sons of God shouted for joy.

6. Still let them succor us; still let them fight,
    Lord of angelic hosts, battling for right;
    Till, where their anthems they ceaselessly pour,
    We with the angels may bow and adore.

STARS OF THE MORNING

The faddishness of so-called New Age theosophy, as a kind of rehashed Gnosticism, has illuminated our generation by the religious equivalent of swamp gas. The Gnostic always got his angels wrong, confusing them with gods or fantastic energies. So caution is needed: the current renewal of interest in angelology widely trivializes the choirs of angels. The holy angels that commonly come to us are of the lowest ranks but still immeasurably higher than the reach of human imagination. They do not contradict matter, as Gnostic dualism would think they do; they guide the human race, which is made "a little lower than the angels," to an awareness of its "glory and honor" (cf. Heb. 2:7). The worthiest human boast is of our Blessed Mother as Queen of angels and of men. In the present cultural meltdown, maudlin dilettantishness with the angels is the reverie of human intellects not sufficiently informed by grace really to believe in them. And, in ironic juxtaposition, the faithful who should know better may neglect them, even as they invoke them at the Sanctus of Holy Mass with "all the company of heaven."

Michaelmas Day, September 29, originally commemorated the dedication to the Archangel Michael of a Roman basilica on the Salerian Way. As of 1970, Gabriel and Raphael were joined to the feast. This hymn for Saint Michael and All Angels, honestly weepy in affective splendor, is suitable for any Christian assembly and would be so until that impossible time when God took our angels from us. The constant tutor in ancient hymnody John Mason Neale ascribed this particular text to the ninth-century Saint Joseph the Hymnographer, though later commentary has produced Greek manuscripts fixing it on Saint John Damascene, the last of the Greek Fathers, who was declared a Doctor of the Church by Pope Leo XIII in 1890. Probability opts for the opinion of John Julian (1839–1913), the Anglican clergyman and author of *The Dictionary of Hymnology* in 1892: Neale had no particular hymn in mind when he produced this text in 1862 but was presenting a digested version of the entire Greek Canon for the feast of the Holy Angels.

Julian is not to be gainsaid. The Cornishman was honored in 1895 with honorary degrees at Howard University in Washington, D.C., and at Durham University by the Archbishop of Canterbury, Edward White Benson (1829–1896). Dr. Benson wrote a biography of Saint Cyprian and persecuted the saintly Bishop of Lincoln Edward King (1829–1910) for ritualist excesses. He also fathered the convert apologist Monsignor Robert Hugh Benson and E. F. Benson, whose many novels included the series about Lucia, the Auntie Mame-ish pianist of limited talent.

In the best sense is this hymn didactic, training the human intelligence on the nine angelic choirs with their explosive IQs and frightening beauty. The three archangels hymned are, of the seven "who stand before the Lord," the only ones named in the Bible. Michael, captain of the angelic hosts, appears twice in the Old Testament (Dan. 10:13ff.; 12:1) and twice in the New (Jude v. 9; Rev. 12:7–9). Raphael the healer appears in Tobit (12:12, 15) and is identified with the angel in Enoch 10:7 and (in some versions) John 5:1–4. Gabriel the messenger carries announcements in Daniel (8:16–26; 9:21–27) and heralds the Incarnation in the birth narrative of Luke (1:11–21, 26–38). "Amid Salem's dear bowers" the three are accurately assigned their typologies as an antidote to sentimentalism and skepticism. "Trisagion" was composed for Neale in 1868 by Henry Thomas Smart.

Hark! a thrilling voice is sounding

MERTON

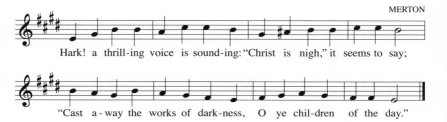

Hark! a thrill-ing voice is sound-ing: "Christ is nigh," it seems to say;

"Cast a-way the works of dark-ness, O ye chil-dren of the day."

2. Wakened by the solemn warning,
   Let the earth-bound soul arise;
   Christ, her sun, all sloth dispelling,
   Shines upon the morning skies.

3. Lo! the Lamb, so long expected,
   Comes with pardon down from heaven;
   Let us haste, with tears of sorrow,
   One and all to be forgiven;

4. So when next he comes with glory,
   And the world is wrapped in fear,
   May he with his mercy shield us,
   And with words of love draw near.

5. Honor, glory, might, and blessing
   To the Father and the Son,
   With the everlasting Spirit
   While unending ages run.

HARK! A THRILLING VOICE IS SOUNDING

I took an Anglican Bishop of Lincoln to an American college where, at the conclusion of his lecture, he was asked the age of Lincoln Cathedral. The cathedral was begun in 1086, but the rafters cut before its completion at the end of the thirteenth century were from trees already hundreds of years old and from forests long since disappeared. When an undergraduate suggested that the cathedral could be considered well over a thousand years old if one took into account the age of the wood, the man replied that it would be much older than that if such logic were applied to the stones. So, too, with the hymn piously but wrongly ascribed to Saint Ambrose. Its age is an ambiguous and vexing consideration.

It is very likely older than the first evidence of it in the tenth century, when it was used for the Office of Lauds on the First Sunday of Advent; it is even older if you factor in the biblical texts it paraphrases. The second stanza clearly alludes to Romans 13:11, which was the Epistle for the First Sunday of Advent, where Saint Paul says that it is high time to awake out of sleep. And Luke 2:25, from what was then the Gospel for the Second Sunday of Advent, in which Simeon waited for the consolation of Israel, provides an image more subtly invoked in the third stanza. What matters most is that the haunting beauty of Advent has produced some of the best hymns, and this particular one is in the first rank of the musical literature for the season.

"Merton," the alternative tune to the plainsong, is the work of the prolific William Henry Monk (1823–1889), organist in numerous London parishes and music teacher in several academies, including a school for the indigent blind. His contemporary Edward Caswall (1814–1878), who paraphrased the Latin, learned classical languages at Marlborough School and Oxford. The young Anglican clergyman converted to Roman Catholicism and, when he became a widower, joined the Oratory of St.

Hark! a thrilling voice is sounding

Philip Neri under John Henry Newman, near whose grave at Rednall he was buried. Out of respect for the sensibilities of overreaching choristers, whose number is legion, Caswall's opening verse was altered for its second printing in 1852 from the line first published three years before: "Hark, an awful voice is sounding ..."

Christian, dost thou see them

ST. ANDREW OF CRETE

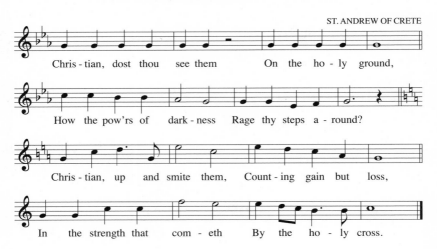

Chris - tian, dost thou see them On the ho - ly ground,

How the pow'rs of dark - ness Rage thy steps a - round?

Chris - tian, up and smite them, Count - ing gain but loss,

In the strength that com - eth By the ho - ly cross.

2. Christian, dost thou feel them,
   How they work within,
   Striving, tempting, luring,
   Goading into sin?
   Christian, never tremble;
   Never be downcast;
   Gird thee for the battle,
   Watch and pray and fast.

3. Christian, dost thou hear them,
   How they speak thee fair?
   "Always fast and vigil?
   Always watch and prayer?"
   Christian, answer boldly:
   "While I breathe I pray!"
   Peace shall follow battle,
   Night shall end in day.

4. "Well I know thy trouble,
   O my servant true;
   Thou art very weary,
   I was weary too;
   But that toil shall make thee
   Some day all mine own,
   And the end of sorrow
   Shall be near my throne."

CHRISTIAN, DOST
THOU SEE THEM

———————— ⸭ ————————

A*sticheron* in the Greek liturgy is a kind of trope, or poetic elaboration of a verse of Scripture, often a verse of a psalm, that functions as a hymn. In the small Church of England academy in East Grinstead, where he was warden, the chronically ill John Mason Neale translated these verses, which he called "*sachem* for the second week of the great fast." His diligent archeology brought him laurels from the Patriarch of Moscow, and, in their own inscrutable way, the Unitarians at Harvard made him an honorary Doctor of Divinity. As a prophet is not without honor save in his own country, the High Church ritualism he fostered, beginning as a member of the Cambridge Camden Society, also brought him censure from his own Anglican Bishop of Chichester, who put him under canonical inhibition from 1847 to 1863.

It may be that this is a good case of Neale's tendency to compose in Greek or Latin and then translate his own achievement, to get approval on the claims of antiquity for his Catholic sentiments. There is no record of the hymn having been written by Saint Andrew of Crete (ca. 660–740) to whom he attributed it. The saint, originally from Damascus, did indeed write many hymns in celebration of orthodoxy after a brief surrender to the Monothelitic heresy, which denied that Christ had two wills, divine and human. This heresy was formally condemned in Saint Andrew's early years by the Council of Constantinople in 680. None of this figures in the present lines, nor is there anything so overtly classical about their doctrine to make us think that Neale invented them to test and try the Evangelical tastes of his ecclesiastical superiors. So the authorship remains up for grabs.

The less well known of two tunes for it, entitled "St. Andrew of Crete," composed by John Bacchus Dykes in 1868, is especially stolid and sober and particularly good for male voices. The opening monotone has a drumbeat quality about it, just right for marching against the devils, and I should not be surprised if it was in the back of Sir Arthur Sullivan's mind when he wrote the music for Sabine Baring-Gould's "Onward Christian soldiers" three years later.

All glory, laud, and honor

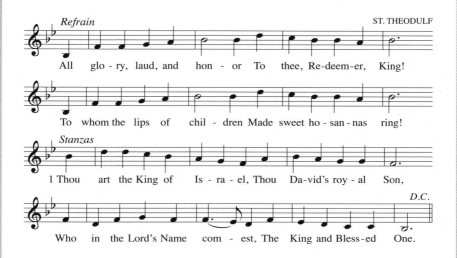

ST. THEODULF

Refrain

All glo-ry, laud, and hon-or To thee, Re-deem-er, King!

To whom the lips of chil-dren Made sweet ho-san-nas ring!

Stanzas

1 Thou art the King of Is-ra-el, Thou Da-vid's roy-al Son,

D.C.

Who in the Lord's Name com-est, The King and Bless-ed One.

2. The company of angels
   Are praising thee on high;
   And mortal men, and all things
   Created, make reply. *Refrain*

3. The people of the Hebrews
   With palms before thee went
   Our praise and prayers and anthems
   Before thee we present. *Refrain*

4. To thee before thy passion
   They sang their hymns of praise:
   To thee, now high exalted,
   Our melody we raise. *Refrain*

ALL GLORY, LAUD, AND HONOR

§§

Here the "Golden Gate" of our Lord's entry into Jerusalem is sealed, a mute sign that part of the world awaits the return of none but him in hope, and another part dreads it. Neither attitude terribly occupied my fellows and me in my boyhood parish. There was just the distracting fun of the Palm Sunday procession around the block, all the Sunday School classes with banners, and the choristers dueling with palm branches as swords before assuming faces appropriate to the solemn entrance into the church. I doubt that the children on the walls of Jerusalem were much different when the Son of David rode through the gates.

Kaiser Wilhelm II scandalized many, especially those prepared to be scandalized for political interests, when he entered Jerusalem on a horse. But it would have been far more presumptuous to have used an ass. The ass was the royal beast and a signal that Messiahship was being claimed. True kings see no contradiction between the beast of burden and royalty and no incongruity between humility and majesty. When John Mason Neale published the translation in 1851, he remarked the pleasant "quaintness" of one stanza that was retained until well after the Middle Ages: "Be thou, O Lord, the Rider,/ And we the little ass;/ That to God's Holy City/ Together we may pass."

Generals and princes may enter Jerusalem however they choose, but no one can enter Jerusalem on High without singing that stanza and meaning it. This was the symbolism of the procession with palms that the Spanish nun Etheria witnessed on her pilgrimage to Jerusalem at the end of the fourth century. The custom had spread from the East to become well established in Europe by the time Bishop Theodulf of Orléans (ca. 750–821) wrote this hymn for the procession. What a marvelous endowment this Spanish Goth left to the Church's dowry of beauty: poetry, liturgical refinements, patronage of architecture and art, especially

All glory, laud, and honor

manuscript illumination. Exactly one thousand years before Robert Raikes (1735–1811) established the English Sunday Schools, Theodulf fathered the original system of parish schools. All of this was nurtured by his theology. He confounded Adoptionism and promoted the Filioque phrase in the Creed, which Frankish monks in Jerusalem began to sing in his lifetime. Pope Saint Leo III refrained from officially incorporating this term, out of consideration for its Greek opponents, and it did not gain complete ascendancy in the West until about two centuries later. In the year of the coronation of his patron Charlemagne, Theodulf was one of the theologians who vindicated Pope Leo of charges of heresy, which had been brought by jealous relatives of his predecessor, Pope Adrian I. These creatures, the year before, had actually tried to mutilate the new Pope during another liturgical procession in honor of Saint Mark. When Leo III visited Paderborn in 799, Charlemagne bid the populace welcome him with the "Gloria in excelsis," which, until the eleventh century, was reserved to Masses sung by bishops, although priests could intone it on Easter. One account says that it was the loveliness of "Gloria, laus, et honor" that won Theodulf release after he was imprisoned on charges of treason against King Louis the Pious.

The tune, named for Theodulf, is by the Lutheran Melchior Teschner (1584–1635) of Silesia, who became Pastor of Oberpritschen in 1614, just four years before the start of the Thirty Years' War. After the carnage that devastated German industry and saw the loss of three-fourths of the German population, this is the only composition of Teschner to have survived.

O come, Creator Spirit, come

GRACE CHURCH

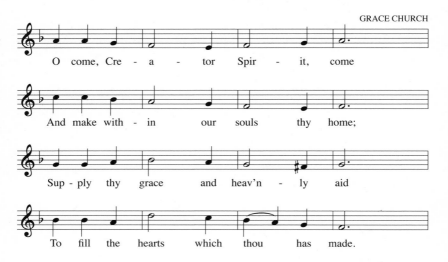

O come, Cre - a - tor Spir - it, come

And make with - in our souls thy home;

Sup - ply thy grace and heav'n - ly aid

To fill the hearts which thou has made.

2. O Gift of God, most high, thy name
   Is Comforter; whom we acclaim
   The fount of life, the fire of love,
   The soul's anointing from above.

3. The sevenfold gift of grace is thine,
   Thou finger of the hand divine;
   The Father's promise true, to teach
   Our earthly tongues thy heavenly
   speech.

4. Thy light to every sense impart;
   Pour forth thy love in every heart;
   Our weakened flesh do thou restore
   To strength and courage evermore.

5. Drive far away our spirit's foe,
   Thine own abiding peace bestow;
   If thou dost go before as guide,
   No evil can our steps betide.

6. Through thee may we the Father
   learn,
   And know the Son, and thee discern,
   Who art of both; and thus adore
   In perfect faith for evermore.

O COME, CREATOR
SPIRIT, COME

———————— ❧ ————————

A priest has hallowed memories of this hallowing hymn, which has been an intrinsic part of the Rite of Ordination since the eleventh century. The phrasing is so instinctive that one may presume numerous antecedents to its composition traditionally attributed to Rabanus Maurus (ca. 784–856), who is not to be confused with Saint Maurus, the sixth-century patron of charcoal burners and sufferers from gout. As Archbishop of Mainz, where he was enthroned in 847, this great Benedictine must have intoned it himself at many ordinations. Before that he had spent many years as a pilgrim in the Holy Land and twenty years as abbot of Fulda.

The seven gifts of the Holy Spirit are versified as a little catechism, just as the *Catechism of the Catholic Church* summarizes them by quoting Saint Ambrose (no. 1303). Rabanus had studied the gifts at Tours as a student of Charlemagne's theologian, Alcuin. It was Alcuin, an associate of the hymn writer Theodulf, who gave Rabanus the name of Maurus, perhaps after Saint Maurus because of his own gout. Back in his original monastery at Fulda, Rabanus began to amass the vast literary corpus that has left us sixty-four extant homilies, acrostic poems, and numerous commentaries on Scripture, which employed his Syriac, Greek, and Hebrew. His exemplary combination of intellect rightly used, discernment vigorously applied (especially against the heretical abuses of Saint Augustine on grace), and charity zealously shown the poor made his life its own hymn to the spiritual gifts.

It would be miserable to think of divorcing the text from the Sarum plainchant, Mode VIII, so long used with it for ordinations and church consecrations and which fits it like a shoe, or a sanctuary sandal. But the tune "Grace Church" is fine for other occasions and devotions. The composer is unknown, although the tune was familiar enough to have been published in 1815. It became more widespread after 1858, when it was recommended for general use among Episcopalians by a music commission that included the pioneer in the reform of hymn singing, William Augustus Muhlenberg (1796–1877). Of an old line of Lutheran clergymen in Pennsylvania, Muhlenberg read for the Anglican priesthood with the support of Bishop William White, chaplain of the Continental Congress, and Bishop Jackson Kemper, missionary to the West (that is, Ohio). He founded St. Luke's Hospital in Manhattan, as well as the first religious order for women in the Episcopal Church, which he formed in 1852, only nineteen years after the symbolic start of the Oxford movement. His committee edited the translation of Rabanus's text by Edward Caswall, the Anglican convert who joined Newman's Oratory.

In all likelihood, the tune was named for Grace Church on lower Broadway, whose architect, James Renwick (1818–1895), designed the present church in 1843 and, later, St. Patrick's Cathedral. As it became the most fashionable parish in the city, its verger, Mr. Brown, was said to decide the social fate of the population by the pews he assigned them. My one contact there, as an Episcopalian seminarian, was to explain the Holy Trinity in forty-five minutes to a fifth-grade class in the parish school.

O sacred head, sore wounded

PASSION CHORALE

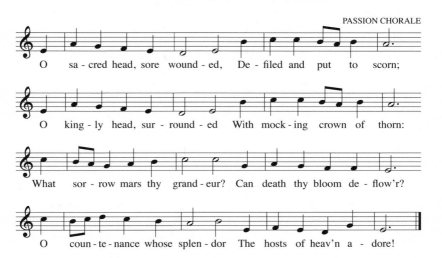

O sa - cred head, sore wound - ed, De - filed and put to scorn;

O king - ly head, sur - round - ed With mock - ing crown of thorn:

What sor - row mars thy grand - eur? Can death thy bloom de - flow'r?

O coun - te - nance whose splen - dor The hosts of heav'n a - dore!

2. Thy beauty, long-desirèd,
   Hath vanished from our sight;
   Thy power is all expirèd,
   And quenched the light of light.
   Ah me! for whom thou diest,
   Hide not so far thy grace:
   Show me, O Love most highest,
   The brightness of thy face.

3. In thy most bitter passion
   My heart to share cloth cry,
   With thee for my salvation
   Upon the cross to die.
   Ah, keep my heart thus movèd
   To stand thy cross beneath,
   To mourn thee, well-belovèd,
   Yet thank thee for thy death.

4. My days are few, O fail not,
   With thine immortal power,
   To hold me that I quail not
   In death's most fearful hour:
   That I may fight befriended,
   And see in my last strife
   To me thine arms extended
   Upon the cross of life.

O SACRED HEAD,
SORE WOUNDED

$\mathcal{S}$

While the *St. Matthew Passion* of Johann Sebastian Bach (1685–1750) is universally regarded as the closest the Passion chorale form has attained to perfection, the antecedents of this particular chorus, which Bach uses five times in the Passion, are not widely appreciated. The fact is that Bach knew how to make the best of a good thing, and he did that here by using what was actually a love song of the fifteenth century, which he got from an edition of Hans Leo Hassler (1564–1612). In it a lovesick swain, with a lack of imagination typical of that state, cites a maid as the cause of his confusion: "Das macht ein Magdlein zart." The words substituted by Bach were the work of Henrici, a postal official in Leipzig, who, under the pen name "Picander," often supplied material for his composer friend, as a kind of upscale Ira Gershwin to Bach's George.

The tune is used fittingly for this sublime love song, which extracts the last of the seven parts of a mystical love poem of the Cistercian reformer and ascetic Saint Bernard of Clairvaux (1090–1153). The long "Salve Mundi Salutate," which takes its name from the first part, is genuinely his writing, unlike the "Jesu Dulcis Memoria," known as the "Rosy Sequence." His profound love for Christ on the Cross has vivid expression in his long metrical prayer to the Lord's feet, knees, hands, side, breast, heart, and face. There is nothing abstract about this commitment of Bernard's devotion, just as there was nothing vague or unreal about his severe austerities and corporal mortifications. These were a real prayer of Bernard's senses, and their intensity provoked his friend William of Champeaux to caution him against excess. If his pure ardor made him overly strict in judging the faults of more wayward lovers such as Abelard, it had happy issue in his radiant treatise on grace and free will, *De Diligendo Deo*, and bore social fruit in his protection of Jews persecuted by the extravagant monk Rudolf and in his desire for the sanctification of the laity as well as clerics.

This hymn to the Holy Face draws on a long history of devotion typified in the story of Veronica's veil and heightened by pilgrimages to the Holy Shroud. The perpetuation of this devotion in modern times was perhaps intensified by the romantic interest in portraiture, which was rare in earlier literature (Christ's appearance is not mentioned in the Gospel narratives of the Passion) and takes a decidedly modern tone in the development of photography. It will be remembered that that most popular modern saint, the Carmelite Saint Thérèse of Lisieux, had a deep devotion to and was consecrated to the Holy Face.

Other translations already existed, principally German and notably that of the Lutheran pastor Paulus Gerhardt (1607–1676), whose verse forms a bridge between strict confessional and freer pietist hymnody. Gerhardt's poetic diction is especially striking in light of the background of the Thirty Years' War, which traumatized his years. But all of what we have here was done directly from the Latin by Robert Seymour Bridges (1844–1930), who was poet laureate of England from 1913 to 1930, all through the war years and social trials that must have made him long for the lovely vision of Saint Bernard. As a student in New England, I sang this often in a chorale with flinty Yankees, far removed from the Clairvaux and Cistercian ways, but mindful of the words addressed to all who looked upon the Face when the Face could be seen in the flesh: "He who has seen me has seen the Father" (John 14:9).

Come sing, ye choirs exultant

PRAETORIUS

Come sing, ye choirs ex - ult - ant, Those mes-sen-gers of God,

Through whom the liv-ing Gos - pels Came sound-ing all a - broad!

Whose voice pro-claimed sal - va - tion That poured up-on the night,

And drove a-way the shad - ows, And filled the world with light.

2. In one harmonious witness
   The chosen four combine,
   While each his own commission
   Fulfils in every line;
   As, in the prophet's vision,
   From out the amber flame
   In form of visage diverse
   Four living creatures came.

3. Foursquare on this foundation
   The Church of Christ remains,
   A house to stand unshaken
   By floods or winds or rains.
   O glorious happy portion
   In this safe home to be,
   By God, true man, united
   With God eternally!

COME SING, YE
CHOIRS EXULTANT

Praetorius is the Latinized version of the name Schultz, and several German composers used it, the most celebrated of whom was Michael (1571–1621). This music is attributed to that author of the three-volume collection of all the chief works known to his age, the *Syntagma Musicum*. The evidence is, however, that it was being sung at least a half century before his birth.

The words sometimes attributed to Adam of Saint Victor (d. ca. 1192) are probably not his, although they well bespeak an idiom he perfected. Adam was a Breton poet, educated in Paris, and particularly distinguished for the many sequences he wrote, sequences being the verses chanted between the Gradual (or what is now commonly called the "Alleluia verse") and the Gospel. This normally involved a procession of the Gospel Book, customarily embellished and often decorated with the symbols of the Evangelists, the "four living creatures" (Rev. 4:6–10) hymned by our anonymous author. In cathedral or monastic use, the deacon takes the book to the bishop or the abbot for a blessing first and, after the singing of the Gospel, returns for the prelate to kiss it. The sequence upon which this hymn is based was in regular use at Paris in the late twelfth century for feasts of the Evangelists. Thus it could have been sung in the earliest days of the Cathedral of Notre-Dame, which was consecrated in 1182. The only evidence of its medieval use in England was at York. The basilica built there by King Edwin, who was baptized in 627 by Saint Paulinus, was destroyed during the Norman conflict in 1069, but the present York Minster may have echoed with the sound of the Latin source of this sequence from the thirteenth century. Whoever the actual imitator was who composed the verses adopted for York in this instance, there is a satisfying symmetry in the fact that the modern translator, Jackson Mason (1833–1889), was a Yorkshire vicar who took an interest in the legacy of Adam of Saint Victor. In old style he might be called Jackson of Settle, for that was the parish he was serving when this was first published, in the year of his death.

Liturgical ceremonial and music accompanying ancient singing of the Gospel should dispel any latent suspicion that the Scriptures were hidden between Pentecost and the Protestant discovery of them. The anonymous sequence honoring Matthew, Mark, Luke, and John has always been the Catholic boast: "Foursquare on this foundation/ The Church of Christ remains." The "Foursquare Gospel Church" is the Church that built Notre-Dame in Paris and York Minster.

Blessèd feasts of blessèd martyrs

ALTA TRINITA BEATA

Bless - èd feasts of bless - èd mar - tyrs, Ho - ly days of ho - ly men, With af - fec - tion's re - col - lec - tions Greet we your re - turn a - gain. Wor - thy deeds they wrought, and won - ders, Wor - thy of the Name they bore; We, with meet - est praise and sweet - est, Hon - or them for - ev - er - more.

2. Faith prevailing, hope unfailing,
   Loving Christ with single heart,
   Thus they, glorious and victorious,
   Bravely bore the martyr's part,
   By contempt of every anguish,
   By unyielding battle done;
   Victors at the last, they triumph,
   With the host of angels one.

3. Therefore, ye that reign in glory,
   Fellow-heirs with Christ on high,
   Join to ours your supplication
   When before him we draw high,
   Praying that, this life completed,
   All its fleeting moments past,
   By his grace we may be worthy
   Of eternal bliss at last.

BLESSÈD FEASTS OF
BLESSÈD MARTYRS

───────────── ❧ ─────────────

An illuminated page of a fourteenth-century copy of this sequence, anonymously written in the twelfth century, is in the collection of the Morgan Library in New York City. John Pierpont Morgan (1837–1913), as vestryman of St. George's Episcopal Church at Gramercy Park, had particular interest in ecclesiastical artifacts since his early days of study in Switzerland and Germany. John Mason Neale, in translating the sequence, thought it German, more by intuition than by hard evidence. The music is more definitively Florentine of the fourteenth century, a reduced version of a form known as a "laude spirituali." This special kind of spiritual song, written in the vernacular, was meant for the popular use of a musical confraternity in Florence known as the "Laudisti." From the end of the thirteenth century, such songs spread to many confraternities throughout Italy. The concept of this popularized form inspired Saint Philip Neri's development of the oratorio and has an English equivalent in the Christmas carols. It finds far earlier echoes in the troubadour tradition of Saint Francis of Assisi and songs of his like the "Canticle of Brother Sun," written in 1225 with fervent joy in the midst of excruciating physical pain.

The music as we have it here, "Alta Trinita Beata," is taken from the masterly *General History of Music*, published in 1782 by the polymath Charles Burney (1726–1814). Praise from Dr. Johnson is praise indeed, and the great man gladly acknowledged the influence of "that clever dog" Burney's musical study tours through Germany, the Low Countries, Italy, and France. Burney also enjoyed the eclectic friendships of Garrick the actor, Reynolds the painter, and Burke the historian. He was an astronomer, art collector, poet, organist, and composer of incidental music for the Drury Lane Theatre. One wishes he might have spent time matching notes with Thomas Jefferson. Oxford made him a Doctor of Music, and this Englishman was made a Member of the Institute of France at the height of the war with Napoleon. More than that, he gave the world his novelist daughter Fanny, his anthropologist son James, who sailed with Captain Cook, and another son, the classicist Charles, whose library is now a treasure of the British Museum.

Old as this hymn is, "affection's recollections" have never been more inspiring than in the wake of the twentieth century, which offered God more martyrs than all other centuries combined. It is a preparation and encouragement for this uncharted millennium.

Jerusalem the golden

EWING

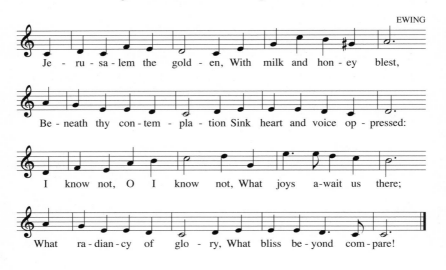

Je - ru - sa - lem the gold - en, With milk and hon - ey blest,

Be - neath thy con - tem - pla - tion Sink heart and voice op - pressed:

I know not, O I know not, What joys a - wait us there;

What ra - dian - cy of glo - ry, What bliss be - yond com - pare!

2. They stand, those halls of Sion,
   All jubilant with song,
   And bright with many an angel,
   And all the martyr throng:
   The Prince is ever in them,
   The daylight is serene;
   The pastures of the blessed
   Are decked in glorious sheen.

3. There is the throne of David;
   And there, from care released,
   The shout of them that triumph,
   The song of them that feast;
   And they who with their Leader
   Have conquered in the fight,
   For ever and for ever
   Are clad in robes of white.

4. O sweet and blessed country,
   The home of God's elect!
   O sweet and blessed country
   That eager hearts expect!
   Jesus, in mercy bring us
   To that dear land of rest,
   Who art, with God the Father,
   And Spirit, ever blest.

JERUSALEM THE GOLDEN

In 909, when the Church in the West was entering a period of breath-taking corruption, Duke William of Aquitaine founded the monastery of Cluny in Saône-et-Loire, which would become the fountainhead of monastic and cultural reform. At its height in the twelfth century, the Congregation of Cluny regulated some two thousand monasteries. Blessed Peter the Venerable (ca. 1092–1156) became abbot at the age of thirty and provided constitutions for Cluny's own reform after the desultory years of misrule by the abbot haplessly named Pontius. The thirty years of Blessed Peter's abbacy were a golden time and framed his own splendid virtues. His equanimity was such that he was able to mitigate the rigorism of his friend Saint Bernard of Clairvaux when he was at Cîteaux. Condemning the Saracens, he also sponsored the first translation of the Koran and various Arabic astronomical texts into Latin; and while publishing complaints against Jews, he defended them against persecution. This was the man to whom Bernard of Morval (fl. ca. 1140), more often called Bernard of Cluny, dedicated the three thousand lines of his poem "De Contemptu Mundi," of which this hymn is the fourth part.

Bernard of Cluny is often mistakenly referred to as Saint Bernard. He was never canonized, but a man who wrote about heaven the way he did would seem to belong there; and if a miracle is needed, something close to one is his complex scheme of dactylic hexameters and internal rhyme. John Mason Neale does not reproduce the rhyme scheme, but what we have is unsurpassed by anything from his pen. Alexander Ewing (1830–1895), who wrote the tune as an amateur musician, was a Scottish diplomat who served the Crown in Constantinople, Australia, and China. His wife, Juliana, wrote many stories for children, including *The Brownies* and *Jan of the Windmill*, and his brother-in-law, Alfred Scott-Gatty (1847–1919), wrote the operetta version of *Rumpelstiltskin*. Ewing took his music seriously enough to object to the present alteration of his melody's meter by William Henry Monk, who wrote the music for

"Hark! a thrilling voice is sounding," above. The change is very slight and more flowing.

Neale thought the tune most suitable and found it especially appealing to children. It was certainly appealing to me, and I still have clear recollection of singing it as a choirboy, facing a great Tiffany-style window of an opulent heaven full of people in luminous togas. Decades of distracting information have not changed my tastes, I am flagrantly happy to say. Bernard's Romanesque monastery of Cluny, once the greatest church of Christendom, was destroyed in the French Revolution in 1790, and the Huguenots seized the moment to ransack one of civilization's most important libraries. The sturdy neo-Romanesque church of my boyhood has suffered other trials, and I think this hymn is not sung there now. But destructions and demolitions are only rumbling tremolos beneath grand golden halls that are forever. This was and is and will be my favorite hymn.

Daily, daily sing to Mary

DAILY, DAILY

Dai - ly, dai - ly sing to Mar - y, Sing, my soul, her prais - es due:

All her feasts, her ac - tions hon - or With the heart's de - vo - tion true.

Lost in won - d'ring con - tem - pla - tion, Be her maj - es - ty con - fessed:

Call her Moth - er, call her Vir - gin, Gra - cious Moth - er, Vir - gin blest.

2. She is mighty in her pleading,
Tender in her loving care;
Ever watchful, understanding,
All our sorrows she will share.
Gifts of heaven she has given.
Noble Lady, to our race;
She the Queen, who decks her subjects
With the light of God's own grace.

3. Sing, my tongue, the Virgin's trophies,
Who, for us, her Maker bore;
For the curse of old inflicted,
Peace and blessings to restore.
Sing in songs of praise unending.
Call upon her lovingly:
Seat of wisdom, Gate of heaven,
Morning star upon the sea.

4. All my senses, heart, affections,
Strive to sound her glory forth:
Spread abroad the sweet memorials
Of the Virgin's priceless worth.
Where the voice of music thrilling,
Where the tongues of eloquence,
That can utter hymns beseeming
All her matchless excellence?

5. All our joys do fall from Mary,
All then join her praise to sing;
Trembling sing the Virgin Mother,
Mother of our Lord and King.
While we sing her aweful glory,
Far above our fancy's reach,
Let our hearts be quick to offer
Love the heart alone can teach.

DAILY, DAILY SING TO MARY

❧

"Daily, daily sing to Mary" is a marvelously raucous hymn to our Lady, especially so when set to a tune like "Deus Tuorum Militum," used here for the fifteenth-century Latin hymn "Apparuit benignitas," as translated in 1854 by Benjamin Webb. The music was erroneously believed to have been taken from a French parish hymnal, or *paroissien*. Possibly the misattribution is due to a reluctance on the part of English editors during World War I to locate German sources. One would be hard pressed to find anything of Grenoble or of France at all in what is actually an alteration of the hymn "Maria zu lieben" as it appeared in 1765 in the *Paderborn Gesangbuch*. There is a statelier melody, quite majestic even, that purists prefer: "Landes Mariae," which was written expressly for it by Henri Frederick Hemy, who also wrote the most popular melody, "St. Catherine," for Father Faber's "Faith of our Fathers." But, unquestionably, popular sentiment is with the alternative to Hemy's tune, which, in fact, is superior to his "St. Catherine."

At the height of the Anglo-Catholic ritualist movement at the start of the twentieth century, with its congresses described nostalgically by the likes of John Betjeman, this was the sort of hymn that separated the "extreme" wing of the Church of England from the run-of-the-mill, old-fashioned High Churchmen. So potent was the music that Sabine Baring-Gould, author of "Onward Christian soldiers," supplied a tamer text, which replaced all references to Mary with lines such as "There the meadows green and dewy/ Shine with lilies wondrous fair." But those lines about the eternal paradise have already proven themselves less than eternal, while the Marian lines translated by the classicist Henry Bittleston (1818–1886) perdure, although they are much in need of recovery by authentically Catholic voices. Bittleston's ascription of the original text to Bernard of Cluny in the twelfth century is quite shaky; at best, it is a very free translation, but then everything about the lyrics and melody is marked with the very freedom enjoyed by devout children of so great

Daily, daily sing to Mary

a Mother. The monks of Cluny would have been innocently delighted with the updated version, which is especially suitable for processions. The staid 1933 edition of the *English Hymnal* contented itself with Baring-Gould's version, but there it designated the hymn for mission services, thus acknowledging the force of its music. In the near future of Christianity, Mary herself, far from being a chief obstacle to Church unity, will be better understood as the indispensable means for reconciling all God's children, for they are also hers by the mission mandate from the Cross.

Protect us while telling

LOURDES

Pro - tect us, while tell - ing Thy prais - es we sing,

In faith - ful hearts dwell - ing, Christ Je - sus, our King,

Refrain

A - ve, a - ve, a - ve Ma - ri - a;

A - ve, a - ve, a - ve Ma - ri - a.

2. Thou cam'st to redeem us,
   A pure Maiden's Child;
   Pure bodies beseem us,
   And hearts undefiled. *Refrain*

3. And thou, ever glorious
   'Midst children of Eve,
   God's Mother victorious,
   Our praises receive. *Refrain*

4. By God's visitation
   Thy chaste womb did bear
   The King of creation,
   King David's true heir. *Refrain*

5. Whose glory in heaven
   And earth is confessed,
   To thee it was given
   To nurse at thy breast. *Refrain*

6. On thy bosom playing
   From Bethlehem brought,
   His own law obeying,
   His temple he sought. *Refrain*

7. While thou didst embrace him,
   The Magi adored
   With gifts brought to praise him,
   Their King and their Lord. *Refrain*

8. Then Egypt received him,
   Its idols o'erthrown;
   And strangers believed him,
   Denied by his own. *Refrain*

9. With Joseph, thou losing
   The joy of mankind,
   His Father's house using
   Thy Truant didst find. *Refrain*

10. The prayer from him earneth
    A mystical sign,
    When water he turneth
    To life-giving wine. *Refrain*

11. Thy heart, ever truest,
    Is pierced by the sword,
    As dying thou viewest
    Thy King and thy Lord.
    Refrain

12. His thunders he sends thee,
    While life doth endure;
    To John he commends thee,
    The pure to the pure. *Refrain*

13. Day breaks; he is risen,
    Thy Lord and thy Son,
    Set free from death's prison;
    His glory is won. *Refrain*

14. Heaven's true Light returning
    To heaven thou didst see,
    Who once, heaven spurning,
    Came down unto thee. *Refrain*

15. When Pentecost crowned thee
    What praises were thine,
    While star-like around thee
    Apostles did shine! *Refrain*

16. Through thee, who all graces
    Canst win from thy Son,
    For these our poor praises
    Acceptance be won. *Refrain*

17. And while we revere her,
    Chaste Mother and Maid,
    Emmanuel, hear her,
    And lend us thine aid. *Refrain*

PROTECT US WHILE TELLING

───────────── ❧ ─────────────

Saint Bernadette Soubirous (1844–1879) would never succumb to the nervous and fatuous suggestion that "the real miracle of Lourdes is the faith of its pilgrims." Faith is a virtue, and a virtue is not a miracle. Besides, the definitive miracle of Lourdes was the series of apparitions of the Blessed Virgin; and the subsequent miracles are the supernatural healings. Saint Bernadette was remarkably adverse to flaccid sentimentality, and in this she was a true daughter of her Holy Mother, who is honored in this hymn, which must be among the most widely sung in the world.

The long nightly processions at the actual shrine, following upon the afternoon procession of the Blessed Sacrament, give full space for lots of stanzas, which may be otherwise altered according to circumstance. Texts vary, and the different languages sung together without any incongruity make each of the Lourdes processions like the day "When Pentecost crowned thee."

Many versions have been written to this tune traced to Grenoble in 1882. Some are so cloying in diction and distressing in rhyme that only a Mother could love them, but that is precisely the point. The words I like are paraphrases of a hymn by Saint Bede (673–735), the "Father of English History," whom Pope Leo XIII declared a Doctor of the Church in 1899 and who taught practically to the moment he died. His shrine remains in the "Bethlehem" chapel of Durham Cathedral. The author of the paraphrase, Monsignor Ronald Arbuthnott Knox (1888–1957), was probably the most original and eloquent preacher of the century. Before his conversion, he was a daring "Anglo-Catholic," when his entertaining opinions as Chaplain of Trinity College in Oxford were preached in rambunctious defiance of the Evangelical tradition of his father and grandfather, Church of England bishops. As an Anglican, Knox informed his own bishop that Mary was the Mother of God and not, as the bishop gave the impression, "a dead Roman Catholic."

In his *Retreat for Priests*, Knox wrote:

Protect us while telling

Protestants sometimes laugh at us because we address ourselves, now to our Lady of Perpetual Succour, now to our Lady of Good Counsel, now to our Lady of Lourdes, and so on, as if they were so many different people. But the case is much worse than that, if they only knew; every individual Catholic has a separate Our Lady to pray to, His Mother, the one who seems to care for Him individually, has won Him so many favours, has stood by Him in so many difficulties, as if she had no other thought or business in heaven but to watch over Him.

Perhaps because of the way English speakers inflect the Latin "Ave," the chorus is generally sung in the United States with a plodding repetition of the first note, but it is far more Gothic and fine to use the original double notation with the accent on the second syllable.

There is a traditional ritual practice of conducting festal procession clockwise and penitential processions counterclockwise. The latter would include the singing of litanies in Advent and Lent and the old pattern of Ember days and Rogationtide. Some maintain that the Stations of the Cross should follow the same pattern. Knox's paraphrase is clearly celebratory, but Bede and he follow liturgical form in invoking a blessing for protection to begin — for the Devil does not like any kind of processions; he is all for recessions.

When looking at her calm features in the glass coffin in Nevers, we have to remember that, to the very end, Bernadette was aware of the Devil's attempts to block life's heavenly progress. Racked with pain, she often murmured: "Heaven, heaven . . ." But as death came closer, she also cried out: "Go from me, Satan, go!" Ronald Knox's magisterial erudition on the subject of religious neuroses and delusions makes especially appealing his confidence in the integrity of Bernadette. Her practicality was polished by supernatural events to a luster that philosophical pragmatism has never attained. Above the singing at Lourdes, her words form a descant: "When you are done with a broom, you put it behind a door, and that is what the Virgin has done with me. While I was useful, she used me, and now she has put me behind the door." The man who was known by thousands of Oxford undergraduates as "Ronnie" would remind them, with studied nonchalance, that the "door," by the way, was the Gate of Heaven.

O what their joy and their glory must be

O QUANTA QUALIA

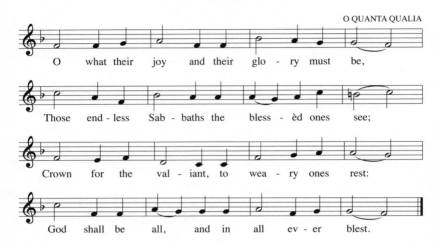

O what their joy and their glo - ry must be,

Those end - less Sab - baths the bless - èd ones see;

Crown for the val - iant, to wea - ry ones rest:

God shall be all, and in all ev - er blest.

2. Truly Jerusalem name we that shore,
   Vision of peace that brings joy evermore;
   Wish and fulfillment can severed be ne'er,
   Nor the thing prayed for come short of the prayer.

3. There, where no troubles distraction can bring,
   We the sweet anthems of Sion shall sing;
   While for thy grace, Lord, their voices of praise
   Thy blessed people eternally raise.

4. Now, in the meanwhile, with hearts raised on high,
   We for that country must yearn and must sigh,
   Seeking Jerusalem, dear native land,
   Through our long exile on Babylon's strand.

5. Low before him with our praises we fall,
   Of whom, and in whom, and through whom are all;
   Of whom, the Father; and in whom, the Son;
   Through whom, the Spirit, with them ever One.

O WHAT THEIR JOY AND THEIR GLORY MUST BE

Among the gracious acts of Peter the Venerable, that man so admired by Bernard Cluny, was to send the body of Abelard (1079–1142) to his former wife, Heloise (ca. 1095–1164) for burial. Abelard, or, more accurately, Abailard, had difficulty tempering his intellect and is, of course, more notorious for not having kept his own vessel in honor. Having fathered a child by the niece of Canon Fulbert of Paris, he secretly married this Heloise, which was not totally unconscionable, since he was still only in minor orders. The canon's agents mutilated Abelard, and Heloise eventually became prioress of the abbey at Argenteuil and then abbess of the Benedictine abbey of the Paraclete, in the Diocese of Troyes, which had been built by her suitor and lover. Heloise went on to live an exemplary life.

Abelard tried to do the same, but he was to controversy as a fish is to water. Having become a Benedictine monk at St. Denis, he immediately proceeded to prove that its founder was not really Dionysius the Areopagite, and this little endeared him to his new brethren. The brain that outran prudence was a vital one. Stunning confrontations with William of Champeaux laid the foundations for a philosophy of the very concept of concepts (the subject of "universals") that has animated every great epistemologist from Albert the Great to Newman and marked the dawn of the whole Scholastic system. Blessed Peter's favorable comparison of Abelard with Aristotle was strained, especially as Abelard had no information of Aristotle, but the extravagance was one of grace. Typically, Peter performed the amazing feat of reconciling Abelard and Bernard of Clairvaux. When with magnificent courtliness he had the body sent to Heloise from the Cluniac priory, where Abelard had died, he sent with it assurance that the tempestuous genius had died with the sacraments.

The bodies of Abelard and Heloise lie side by side in the Parisian cemetery of Père-Lachaise (named for Louis XIV's confessor), where they were taken from the Paraclete in 1817 for entombment in a neo-Gothic sarcophagus that has fascinated me on more than one visit. Nearby are the earthly remains of the illegitimate son of the apostate bishop Talleyrand, known to us as the painter Delacroix; Chopin at rest from the keyboard; the chef Escoffier; the deathbed convert Oscar Wilde; the chanteuse Edith Piaf; and the rock star Jim Morris. Death quiets the moral cacophony of it all, and Divine Mercy resolves it. Possibly after his "long exile on Babylon's strand," Abelard can sing something even finer than this hymn of his, "O quanta, qualia sunt illa sabbata." The present melody, of unknown origin, was adapted from an 1808 critical work on plainchant by François de La Feillée, where it accompanied the poem "Regnatur orbis summus." John Mason Neale translated Abelard's resplendent exclamation that we have here. All about it is heavenly, although a sullen clergyman once opined to me that the prospect of an eternity of Sundays may appeal to anyone more than to a parish priest.

Humbly, I adore thee

ADORO TE DEVOTE

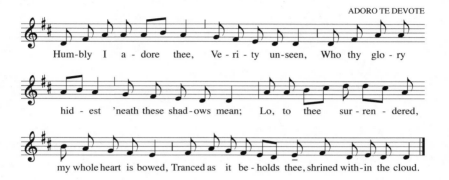

Hum-bly I a - dore thee, Ve - ri - ty un-seen, Who thy glo - ry hid - est 'neath these shad-ows mean; Lo, to thee sur - ren - dered, my whole heart is bowed, Tranced as it be - holds thee, shrined with-in the cloud.

2. Taste, and touch, and vision, to discern thee fail;
   Faith, that comes by hearing, pierces through the veil.
   I believe whate'er the Son of God hath told;
   What the Truth hath spoken, that for truth I hold.

3. O memorial wondrous of the Lord's own death;
   Living Bread, that givest all thy creatures breath,
   Grant my spirit ever by thy life may live,
   To my taste thy sweetness never-failing give.

4. Jesus, whom now veiled, I by faith descry,
   What my soul doth thirst for, do not, Lord, deny,
   That thy face unveiled, I at last may see,
   With the blissful vision blest, my God, of thee.

HUMBLY I ADORE THEE

❧

More than one biographer has applied to Saint Thomas Aquinas (1225–1274), the words from the book of Wisdom 4:13–14: "He lived a long life in a short time, and because God loved him, he took him." One of the greatest intellects who ever lived loved his God, too, and was taken by him in gladness. William of Tocco records: "The aforesaid doctor died in the year of our Lord 1274, in the fourth year of the reign of Pope Gregory X, in the forty-ninth year of his life, during the second (imperial) indiction, on the seventh day of March in the morning." In his last days the Angelic Doctor expounded on the Song of Songs, for he knew that the highest speech is music; and only humility, as the ground of all the virtues, makes the soul a perfect instrument for the highest songs.

In Paris in 1269 he placed on the altar his treatise on the Real Presence of Christ in the Eucharist and saw our Lord, who told him: "You have written well of the sacrament of my Body." Heroic humility enabled him to tell that without self-consciousness, and the same detachment saved him from the arid fate of many theologians who dissect the truth without living it. In this hymn, Saint Thomas deliberately refers to his Lord as "latens veritas," and not even the brilliantly nervous translation by Gerard Manley Hopkins (1844–1889) captures the theological subtlety of the saint's diction here: the "Adoro te" does not speak of the "hidden God" but of the "hidden truth" that is God. After Plato in his cave approached divinity "'neath these shadows mean," and Moses better approached the Living Presence "shrined within the cloud," the Eucharistic Church discerns the Lord Himself really present, by an activity of faith upon reason. Saint Thomas sings the intricate economy of substance and accident at the heart of the "sacrament of sacraments." The present version is a slight improvement of the 1932 *Monastic Diurnal*.

So deep was Saint Thomas's vision of the Eucharistic Sacrifice that he understood the priesthood as the highest of the sacramental orders.

Humbly, I adore thee

Once, a priest about to be ordained a bishop had to be corrected when he spoke of an ontological change about to be conferred by episcopal ordination: Saint Thomas taught that episcopacy is the fullness of the priestly character but not separate from the priestly order. And this he held because of the unsurpassed dignity of the authority to offer the Holy Sacrifice.

Benedictine plainchant of the thirteenth century is used for this Dominican text. Residual questions about the Doctor's authorship are strongly, if not absolutely, dispelled by allusions to it found in the literature of Aquinas's Franciscan contemporary Jacopone da Todi (ca. 1228–1306), who wrote the "Stabat mater dolorosa." Although the first extant manuscript did not appear until more than fifty years after the saint's death, it would seem to have been in circulation well before 1280.

Even when my early sacramental theology was formed by the *Book of Common Prayer*, this hymn outsang all the interpolations of Thomas Cranmer (1489–1556). Later on, it was my privilege to stand in the cell of the guest house at the former Cistercian abbey of Fossa Nuova, where the holy Doctor made his profession of faith when receiving Viaticum two days before he went to heaven: "I am receiving you, Price of my soul's redemption: all my studies, my vigils, and my labors have been for love of you. I have taught much and written much of the most sacred body of Jesus Christ; I have taught and written in the faith of Jesus Christ and of the holy Roman Church, to whose judgment I offer and submit everything."

Now, my tongue, the mystery telling

ST. THOMAS

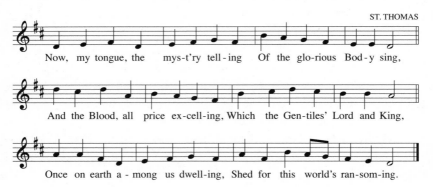

Now, my tongue, the mys-t'ry tell-ing Of the glo-rious Bod-y sing,

And the Blood, all price ex-cell-ing, Which the Gen-tiles' Lord and King,

Once on earth a-mong us dwell-ing, Shed for this world's ran-som-ing.

2. Given for us, and condescending
   To be born for us below,
   He with men in converse blending
   Dwelt, the seed of truth to sow,
   Till he closed with wondrous ending
   His most patient life of woe.

3. That last night at supper lying
   Mid the twelve, his chosen band,
   Jesus, with the Law complying,
   Keeps the feast its rites demand;
   Then, more precious food supplying,
   Gives himself with his own hand.

4. Word-made-flesh, true bread he
       maketh
   By his word his Flesh to be,
   Wine his Blood; when man partaketh,
   Though his senses fail to see,
   Faith alone, when sight forsaketh,
   Shows true hearts the mystery.

5. Therefore we, before him bending,
   This great Sacrament revere;
   Types and shadows have their
       ending,
   For the newer rite is here;
   Faith, our outward sense befriending,
   Makes our inward vision clear.

6. Glory let us give and blessing
   To the Father and the Son,
   Honor, thanks, and praise addressing,
   While eternal ages run;
   Ever too his love confessing
   Who from both with both is One

NOW, MY TONGUE, THE MYSTERY TELLING

Saint Thomas Aquinas deftly plundered the treasury of the saints in the opening words of his "Pange, lingua, gloriosi," which are a quotation of Venantius Honorius Fortunatus. From then on, his own words endow his Holy Mother the Church with a most blessed hymn in honor of the Most Blessed Sacrament. The final stanzas, beginning "Tantum ergo," form the standard fixture for Exposition and Benediction.

This extraliturgical act of devotion to the Eucharistic Victim is the most direct instruction in the greatest human privilege—adoration. I knew a Calvinist professor at Oxford who was converted by attending Benediction, and he was typical of many who take the shortcut through catechesis by beginning with adoration. Adoration can precede edification as readily as it issues from it. In the Latin Rite, nothing is more evangelical than Benediction, which has so wrongly been the puzzlement of self-professed Evangelicals.

The Feast of Corpus Christi was instituted for the universal Church in 1264 by Pope Urban IV (1261–1264), who was born Jacques Pantaléon, the son of a shoemaker in Troyes, and who went on to became Patriarch of Jerusalem. The extension of the feast established in Liège in 1246 by Bishop Robert de Thorete is said to have been a response to the Miracle of Bolsena in 1263. A German priest on pilgrimage to Rome had his doubts about the Real Presence resolved when, in the Umbrian church of Santa Cristina, blood flowed from the Host and marked the corporal. Although the Pope, in nearby Orvieto (where he had taken refuge from Manfred, the illegitimate son of Emperor Frederick II), was shown the altar cloth, there is no mention of the incident in the bull for the Feast. But the Church's recognition of the miracle is attested in the painting of it in Raphael's stanze in the Vatican. The prime moral influence for the devotion was the effort of Saint Juliana of Liège (1193–1258), the city where Pope Urban had been archdeacon.

The Pope ordered Thomas Aquinas to compose hymns for the proper Mass and Office, as the reliable record of Tolomeo da Lucca attests, and this hymn was written for Vespers and is still in the revised breviary. The plainchant for it is the same as that for Fortunatus's processional. The melody "St. Thomas" was most likely written by the English Catholic John Francis Wade, who published it in 1751. This translation, superior to the ones that often afflict missalettes, is a conflation of John Mason Neale, an Anglican, and Edward Caswall, a Catholic convert. Only such a rare achievement can justify — and only occasionally — replacing the incomparable Latin.

In the Church of England, Eucharistic Benediction was forbidden by Article XXVIII of the Articles of Religion, which exacted mental gymnastics for Newman to reinterpret: "The Sacrament of the Lord's Supper was not by Christ's ordinance reserved, carried about, lifted up or worshipped." The saints did not speak thus. Saint John Vianney, in his last years, carried the Sacrament on Corpus Christi, saying, "He who has carried me all my life will give me strength to carry him." And near his life's end, in Salerno, Saint Thomas was praying before a crucifix when a sacristan heard a voice from the cross say a final time: "You have written well of me, Thomas; what reward would you have?" The author of this hymn replied: "Nothing but yourself, Lord."

O saving victim, opening wide

ST VINCENT

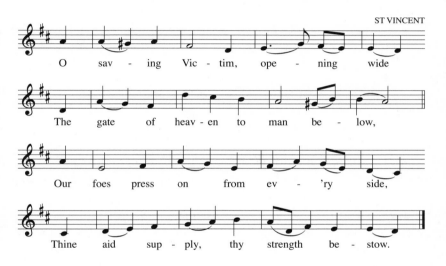

O sav – ing Vic – tim, ope – ning wide
The gate of heav-en to man be – low,
Our foes press on from ev – 'ry side,
Thine aid sup – ply, thy strength be – stow.

2. All praise and thanks to thee ascend
    For evermore, blest One in Three;
    O grant us life that shall not end,
    In our true native land with thee.

O SAVING VICTIM,
OPENING WIDE

———————— ✄ ————————

Saint Thomas Aquinas wrote this for Lauds of Corpus Christi, among his Eucharistic poems of 1263. Just as "Tantum ergo" is the last part of "Pange, lingua," what we are accustomed to as traditional parts of Benediction of the Blessed Sacrament are the concluding stanzas of a hymn that is retained in the morning office of the new Liturgy of the Hours:

> Verbum supernum prodiens
> nec Patris linquens dexteram,
> ad opus suum exiens
> venit ad vitae vesperam.

And as the opening line of "Pange, lingua" quotes Fortunatus, so the first line of this, "O Word proceeding on high," is from an Ambrosian hymn for Advent. This translation by the reliable Edward Caswall is measurably superior to most and is very useful as a private prayer, although, as with similar Eucharistic hymns, it will always be a poor second to the Latin.

One of these verses' most ardent and unlikely admirers was the humbug romantic Jean-Jacques Rousseau (1712–1778), who published a *Dictionary of Music* in 1767 and said, in what is quite an amazing admission from him, that all his works combined were not worth these few lines of the Angelic Doctor. Other bits of his musical criticism had not been so pious: in 1753 he was burned in effigy for his *Letter upon French Music*. Only the year before that, his opera *Le Devin du village* was performed before King Louis XV and was then translated by Charles Burney, publisher of the hymn "Blessed feasts of blessed martyrs." All of which information may be placed in the "small world" file.

In that file, too, may be deposited the information about the composer of the alternative to the hymn's venerable plainchant, Sigismund

O saving victim, opening wide

Neukomm (1778–1858). James Uglow (1814–1894), a musician of Cheltenham, usually gets the credit for the tune "St. Vincent," but he only arranged what he received from his teacher at Gloucester Cathedral, the Austrian Neukomm, who visited England many times. Uglow was thus in a succession going back to the well-beloved Franz Joseph Haydn (1732–1809), with whom Neukomm had studied in Vienna. The peripatetic Neukomm also spent five years in Brazil as capellmeister for the Emperor Pedro I and frequently traveled as court pianist to Charles-Maurice de Talleyrand-Périgord (1754–1838), latterly prince of Benevento and formerly bishop of Autun. After the Concordat of 1801, Pope Pius VII restored the apostate to communion, but the ex-bishop did not mend all his ways until his deathbed profession in the presence of the Abbé Dupanloup.

At the Congress of Vienna in 1815, Neukomm entertained Talleyrand's guests, including the papal secretary of state Ercole Cardinal Consalvi (1757–1824). On more informal occasions, this composer of a hymn that has become the emblem of things true and Catholic was situated to provide background music for the favorite mistress of Talleyrand, who was uncle to her husband, the Duke of Dino.

Jesus Christ is risen today

EASTER HYMN

Je - sus Christ is ris'n to - day, Al - le - lu - ia!

Our tri - um-phant ho - ly day, Al - le - lu - ia!

Who did once up - on the cross, Al - le - lu - ia!

Suf - fer to re - deem our loss, Al - le - lu - ia!

2. Hymns of praise then let us sing, Alleluia!
   Unto Christ, our heav'nly king, Alleluia!
   Who endured the cross and grave, Alleluia!
   Sinners to redeem and save. Alleluia!

3. But the pains that he endured, Alleluia!
   Our salvation have procured; Alleluia!
   Now above the sky he's king, Alleluia!
   Where the angels ever sing. Alleluia!

4. Sing we to our God above, Alleluia!
   Praise eternal as his love; Alleluia!
   Praise him, all ye heav'nly host, Alleluia!
   Father, Son, and Holy Ghost, Alleluia!

Jesus Christ is
Risen Today

$$ \text{\textsection} $$

There are Easter carols as well as Christmas carols, for a carol is a hymn on a joyful occasion, and Easter is the most joyful day of all. This Easter hymn qualifies as a carol if we want to define the carol precisely as a vibrant song with popular appeal, lending itself to dancing. When this is sung to a stately cadence, it may seem grander than a carol, but the lilt is only subdued, like a child trying to act grown-up on a formal occasion. The Liturgy is a sacred dance, although the static and puritanized new rites may obscure that, and such a dance is as joyful as any cavorting in the street. At a formal dinner in a club frequented by Anglo-Saxons, I told a guest of different ancestry that the members seemed subdued and even somnolent, but such was their way of expressing ecstasy. That is a little like the way of the Church when she is faithful to herself: there are some celebrations too joyful for ordinary happiness. To be solemn is not necessarily to be sad; it can be a very high happiness. When that is forgotten, the sacred dance can be twisted by touchy-feely affectation into superficial hugging and self-conscious cuteness. And so it is in the "Church of What's Happening Now." But it cannot be so in the Church Catholic.

A long series of textual alterations has not muted the sonorous thrill—like a heavy bourdon bell—of the original fourteenth century Bohemian carol: "Surrexit Christus hodie, Alleluia!/ Humano pro solamine, Alleluia!" In the Resurrection faith, *Alleluia* needs no translation. The present hymn opened every Easter of my youth. Only on that day did we choirboys wear white bows instead of black ones, and the rector gave us all white chocolate. What we sang is a translation by the poet laureate Nahum Tate (1652–1715), who had a rather sad life himself, and the Anglican clergyman Nicholas Brady (1659–1726). Charles Wesley's doxology to the Holy Trinity, at the end, is a recent addition.

Tate and Brady's version first appeared in 1749 in the *Compleat Psalmodist* of John Arnold (1720–1792), which enjoyed seven editions, the second of which introduced this. This hymn, then, is representative of an important expansion of English congregational singing. In 1539, Miles Coverdale (1488–1568) had tried to broaden the English repertoire by embellishing the psalms with some German tunes he had evidently heard as a visiting pastor in Bergzabern. King Henry VIII forbade the use of these "Goostly Psalms," thinking that kind of singing too Protestant. After the introduction of the *Book of Common Prayer*, settings for Coverdale's translations of the psalms multiplied, of which Arnold's was most prominent, with provision for four-voice harmony and instrumentation. This was quite unlike the Church of Scotland, which was barebones and only reluctantly admitted a pitch pipe in the eighteenth century. A pitch pipe might have been welcome after Arnold's influence; and congregations still suffer from some of his directives on quavering the voice and the use of trills and shakes "to slur or break the Note, to sweeten the Roughness of a Leap." But even voices hard at such work cannot mitigate the objective joy of Easter.

O love, how deep, how broad, how high

DEUS TUORUM MILITUM

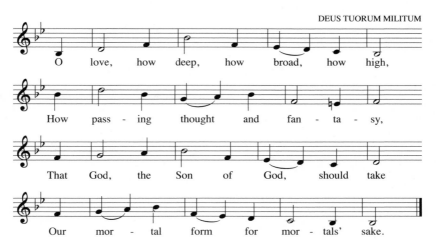

O love, how deep, how broad, how high,

How pass - ing thought and fan - ta - sy,

That God, the Son of God, should take

Our mor - tal form for mor - tals' sake.

2. For us baptized, for us he bore
   His holy fast, and hungered sore;
   For us temptations sharp he knew;
   For us the tempter overthrew.

3. For us he prayed, for us he taught,
   For us his daily works he wrought,
   By words and signs and actions, thus
   Still seeking not himself, but us.

4. For us to wicked men betrayed,
   Scourged, mocked, in purple
       robe arrayed,
   He bore the shameful cross and
       death;
   For us gave up his dying breath.

5. For us he rose from death again,
   For us he went on high to reign;
   For us he sent his Spirit here
   To guide, to strengthen, and to
       cheer.

6. All glory to our Lord and God
   For love so deep, so high, so
       broad;
   The Trinity whom we adore
   For ever and for evermore.

O LOVE, HOW DEEP, HOW BROAD, HOW HIGH

───────────── ✂ ─────────────

The name Thomas Hemerken (ca. 1380–1471) probably rings no more bells than the titles of his books *Hospitale Pauperum* and *Vallis Liliorum*. Few, however, would not recognize the name by which he went after entering, in 1399, the house of the Canons Regular at Agnieten-berg. Fewer would fail to have heard of Thomas à Kempis's *Imitation of Christ*, the most widely read spiritual book after the Bible. As it was published anonymously in 1418, the perennial fidget of doctoral students has proposed alternative possibilities as the true author, including a saint, Bonaventure, and a pope, Innocent III. The practical mysticism of the school of piety known as the *devotio moderna*, inspired by the Canons of Windesheim, who established the daughter-house at Agnietenberg, depended on Thomas more than anyone for its earliest motions and successes among the "Brethren of the Common Life." The *Imitation* is its virtual charter.

It would be nearly as churlish, although rather more plausible, to question Thomas's authorship of this hymn, which, in its entirety, was of twenty-three stanzas. The English version's opening line copies more than adequately the sweeping sense of affective piety that the author raises in his first breath and sustains throughout:

> Apparuit benignitas
> Dei nec non humanitas
> Ex caritate nimia
> Ad nos atque gratuita.

Benjamin Webb (1819–1885) was the translator. Along with John Mason Neale, he started the Cambridge Camden Society, which provided the artistic and ritualistic complement to the theological developments of the Oxford movement. After 1846 it was known as the Ecclesiological

O love, how deep, how broad, how high

Society and lasted until 1863, publishing *The Ecclesiologist*, a monthly review. The society was a principal force behind the ritualism and Gothic revival in art and architecture that is widely, if rashly, linked with the Tractarians of Oxford. The Tractarians, like Pusey and Keble, were themselves a rather austere lot. Webb was a model Cambridge scholar with a zeal that outran his imagination, and therefore he was very unlike his Oxford counterparts. Only a second generation carried his ritualism to the lengths that provoked the legal authorities of the day. He was more given to speculation than experiment, and his admiration for things medieval did not extend to his own services. In days when a surplice was considered Romish, he never wore a chasuble.

Webb's rectorship of St. Andrew's parish, Wells Street, London, was a model of pastoral solicitude for Christ in others and quite what Thomas à Kempis had prescribed as a spiritual director in his Germanic Latin. The *devotio moderna* had incalculable influences beyond German Catholics. John Wesley carried the *Imitation* with him in his preaching tours, as he tried to dispel the aridity of the eighteenth-century deists, and its spirited piety was not lost on consequent hymnodists in the English-speaking world. To emphasize the universal appeal of such devotion, the tune is from a French parish source in the region of Grenoble, which produced many simple and durable settings.

Light's abode, celestial Salem

REGENT SQUARE

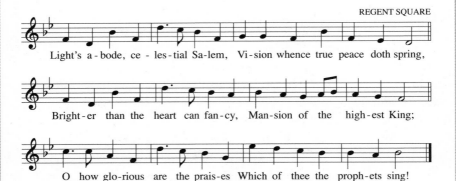

Light's a-bode, ce-les-tial Sa-lem, Vi-sion whence true peace doth spring,

Bright-er than the heart can fan-cy, Man-sion of the high-est King;

O how glo-rious are the prais-es Which of thee the proph-ets sing!

2. There for ever and for ever
   Alleluia is outpoured;
   For unending, for unbroken
   Is the feast-day of the Lord;
   All is pure and all is holy
   That within thy walls is stored.

3. There no cloud nor passing vapor
   Dims the brightness of the air;
   Endless noonday, glorious noonday,
   From the Sun of suns is there;
   There no night brings rest from labor,
   For unknown are toil and care.

4. O how glorious and resplendent,
   Fragile body, shalt thou be,
   When endued with heavenly beauty,
   Full of health, and strong, and free,
   Full of vigor, full of pleasure
   That shall last eternally!

5. Now with gladness, now with
         courage,
   Bear the burden on thee laid,
   That hereafter these thy labors
   May with endless gifts be paid,
   And in everlasting glory
   Thou with brightness be arrayed.

6. Laud and honor to the Father,
   Laud and honor to the Son,
   Laud and honor to the Spirit,
   Ever Three, and ever One,
   Consubstantial, co-eternal,
   While unending ages run.

LIGHT'S ABODE,
CELESTIAL SALEM

Stained glass was the most conservative of Gothic art forms; but in painting, and especially in sculpture, the eye can easily trace the dramatic shift to naturalism and portraiture from the beginning of the fourteenth century. It was already evident on the façade of Reims in the middle of the thirteenth century. The shading needed for more natural representation appears in the modeling of the figures for the illuminations of the Breviary of Philip the Fair about 1300. The Germany of Thomas à Kempis had inherited the mannerism of Gothic "international" idiom in sculpture principally from France, through journeymen such as the Master of Naumburg in the thirteenth century. From the early fourteenth century, Germany quickly led the way in more adventurous, even extravagant, expressionism from Strasbourg to Freiburg and Cologne, whose cathedral choir provides a brilliant example.

The humanism of the piety of Thomas à Kempis and the *devotio moderna* was a fertile climate for artistic experiments. Its combination of naturalism and mysticism, which was the volatile glory of such spirituality before it lapsed into individualism and sentimentalism, found classic expression in those Flemish painters Hubert Van Eyck (ca. 1366–1426), who began *The Adoration of the Lamb* in Ghent, and his brother Jan (ca. 1390–1441), who finished it in 1432. This was exactly when *The Imitation of Christ* appeared. A similar spirit in France was called the "St. Louis style" and is clearly evident in the portrait sculpture, now in the Louvre, of Charles II (1365–1431) actually posing as St. Louis; this too was being carved as the *Imitation* was being published.

The scene of the saints worshipping the *Agnus Dei* is the Apocalypse in paint, just as this hymn, "Ierusalem luminosa/ Verae pacis visio," is the Apocalypse in song. John Mason Neale's translation freezes in enameled words the lush combination of sensual imagery and transcendent wistfulness that makes it an emblem of the fifteenth-century German spirit. One could easily imagine it as a sound track for the Ghent altarpiece. Enough contemporary evidence exists to accept the standard attribution to Thomas à Kempis of all its seventeen original stanzas, as recorded earliest in a contemporary Karlsruhe manuscript. The tune here is "Regent Square," dated 1867, by Henry Smart (1813–1879), the organist of St. Philip's, Regent Street, London, who collaborated with Dr. Hamilton of the Regent Square Church. It was intended for "Glory be to God the Father," by Hamilton's fellow Presbyterian Horatius Bonar (1808–1889), who wrote three series of hymns, all under the title *Hymns of Faith and Hope* (1857–1866). It is nice to think of Smart sitting in his bored youth as an "articled clerk," like the one in *H.M.S. Pinafore*, and spending his spare hours in a London organ factory owned by a Mr. Robson. He flourished as an organist and organ builder in England and Scotland and went blind in the last year of his life while working on an organ in Dublin.

A case against the canonization of Thomas à Kempis was once made on the basis of an exhumation of his body. The poor man, it seems, had been buried alive, and scratch marks were found on the inside of his coffin. The evidence of panic on the part of Kempis was taken by some as token that he lacked the virtue of hope. It was rather, I should think, proof of right reason. Wanting to get out of your coffin when you should not be in it is the mark of the sensible mystic who wants to get to the Celestial Salem — in due time.

Praise to the living God

LEONI

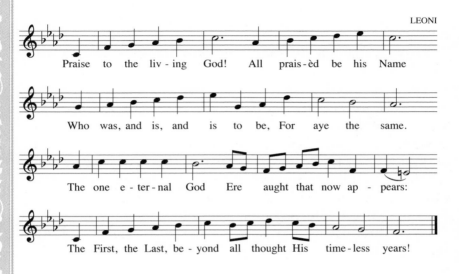

Praise to the liv - ing God! All prais - èd be his Name

Who was, and is, and is to be, For aye the same.

The one e - ter - nal God Ere aught that now ap - pears:

The First, the Last, be - yond all thought His time - less years!

2. Formless, all lovely forms
   Declare his loveliness;
   Holy, no holiness of earth
   Can his express.
   Lo, he is Lord of all.
   Creation speaks his praise,
   And everywhere, above, below,
   His will obeys.

3. His Spirit floweth free,
   High surging where it will:
   In prophet's word he spake of old;
   He speaketh still.
   Established is his law,
   And changeless it shall stand,
   Deep writ upon the human heart,
   On sea, on land.

4. Eternal life hath he
   Implanted in the soul;
   His love shall be our strength
      and stay
   While ages roll.
   Praise to the living God!
   All praisèd be his Name
   Who was, and is, and is to be,
   For aye the same.

PRAISE TO THE LIVING GOD

———— ✄ ————

There is an unlikely congruity between the thirteenth-century Pope Urban IV, promoter of the Corpus Christi devotions, and this hymn's reviser, Thomas Olivers (1725–1799) of Montgomeryshire, in that the pope was the son of a French shoemaker and the orphaned Olivers was a shoemaker's apprentice. Their mutual patrons, the third-century shoemaker brothers Crispin and Crispinian, of course, shine in the speech Shakespeare gave his Henry V at Agincourt. That is about all that this eclectic group had in common, save for their saving devotion to Jesus Christ. Olivers came about it a hard way, having been expelled from his town of Tregonan for delinquency and then converting, not on the Damascus Road, but in Bristol, upon hearing George Whitefield preach. He became a Methodist preacher himself and is buried with John Wesley in London.

The Methodists proposed themselves for the mantle of the new prophets of the New Israel, and Olivers quite comfortably paraphrased the Jewish Creed he heard in the Great Synagogue around 1770, sung in dialogue between the men and the rich baritone of a *chazzan*. The cantors, or *chazzanim*, in the different Ashkenazic (German) and Sephardic (Iberian) forms, have passed to our age the cantillations not at all unlike the way our Lord must have sung from the scrolls in the synagogue at Nazareth. The Creed, or *Yigdal*, was a formalized version of the thirteen articles of Moses Maimonides (1135–1205), introduced at the turn of the fifteenth century, much as the Niceno-Constantinopolitan Creed summarizes earlier professions of faith. And as our Creed finds its place in the Ordinary of the Mass, so is the *Yigdal* proper to the close of the Sabbath service.

The present text is only part of the original metrical translation of Olivers, who, anticipating Pope Pius XI's declaration to the Fascists that Christians are spiritually Semites, climaxed the stanzas with a doxology to the Blessed Trinity. The arranger of this ancient melody was the cantor whom Olivers heard singing in the synagogue at Duke's Place in London. In a venerable tradition, Meyer Lyon (1751–1797) wandered much, combining liturgical and theatrical careers, went to Dublin in 1772, and died in Jamaica.

In my Sunday School, I received a prize in the form of a Bible paid for by a local rabbi, a friend of the rector. And when a family friend, a Jewish undertaker, took me, still a choirboy, to his synagogue, I sat in my yarmulka very taken by the music and surprised to hear them singing what I thought was an Episcopalian hymn.

Years later, in a Right-to-Life march in Manhattan, a group of pro-abortionists tried to drown out our speeches by banging drums and blowing whistles. An elderly Jewish woman who had become a Catholic remarked to me that she had heard that sound many times in her native Germany. The Hitler Youth used to bang and whistle outside the synagogues at prayer time. There is a "whole triumphant host" that cannot be drowned out. Perhaps someday the noisemakers will quit trying.

Wake, awake for night is flying

SLEEPERS, WAKE

Wake, a - wake, for night is fly - ing: The

watch - men on the heights are cry - ing, A -

wake, Je - ru - sa - lem, a - rise! Mid - night's sol - emn

hour is toll - ing, His char - iot wheels are

near - er roll - ing, He comes; pre - pare, ye

vir - gins wise. Rise up, with will - ing feet

Go forth, the Bride - groom meet: Al - le - lu -

ia! Bear through the night your well - trimmed light,

Speed forth to join the mar - riage rite.

2. Sion hears the watchmen singing,
   Her heart with deep delight is springing,
   She wakes, she rises from her gloom:
   Forth her Bridegroom comes, all glorious,
   In grace arrayed, by truth victorious;
   Her star is risen, her light is come!
   All hail, Incarnate Lord,
   Our crown, and our reward!
   Alleluia!
   We haste along,
   In pomp of song,
   And gladsome join the marriage throng.

3. Lamb of God, the heavens adore thee,
   And men and angels sing before thee,
   With harp and cymbal's clearest tone.
   By the pearly gates in wonder
   We stand, and swell the voice of thunder
   That echoes round thy dazzling throne.
   No vision ever brought,
   No ear hath ever caught
   Such rejoicing:
   We raise the song,
   We swell the throng,
   To praise thee ages all along.

WAKE, AWAKE FOR
NIGHT IS FLYING

---------------- ℀ ----------------

If Confession has become the lost sacrament of our age, Advent has become its lost season. These absences are the unholy hollows of the Culture of Death: if man does not confess his sins, he cannot live eternally; and if he has no promise to await, he will find no reason to confess. As a nocturne indicates beauty in what coarse perception registers only as an absence of day, so Advent is the sign that our present life is greater than incidental existence. The season of anticipating the coming of the Savior who is also our Judge is the calendar's tribute to the Beatitude of Purity. The pure in heart are blessed for they shall see God; and the heart's purity consists in moral focus on God as the purpose of all living. Dead men keep no Advent. Secularized Christians have let themselves be swept into this swirl of obscurity and denial by "rushing" Christmas at the expense of Advent—which is like rushing birth by eliminating pregnancy.

Advent became widely observed by the seventh century in Spain and has a longer history and length in the Eastern Church. While its penitential nature is less stated than that of Lent, its tone and liturgical customs are clear about its sobriety. I recall the folded chasubles of Advent and Lent, symbols of austerity like draping statues and covering altar paintings. If a soul sorely tried does not yield to cynicism out of pride, it can return to anticipation out of humility. The author of one of the most euphonious hymns of any season kept hoping while horror spread around him.

This Lutheran pastor of trying times, Philip Nicolai (1556–1608), shared a name with a German Enlightenment writer of very different religious views, Christoph (1733–1811), and the composer Otto (1810–1849). But he was nothing if not a man of the Book, and its verses permeate his manuscript with imagery from Matthew 25:1–13 and Revelation

Wake, awake for night is flying

19:6–9 and, first of all, the Messianic prophecy of Isaiah 52:8, with which he opens the hymn in paraphrase:

> Wachet auff, rufft uns die Stimme
> Der Wächter sehr hoch auff der Zinnen,
> Wach auff, du Statt Jerusalem!

And all this poured from his mind and heart, not in spite of, but because of the plague that killed more than a thousand of his parishioners in Westphalia in the second half of 1597 and scores more in the beginning of 1598. "To comfort other sufferers," as he wrote, and to console himself with the prospect of triumph over death, he entitled what he had written *Mirror of Joys*.

Our translation comes from Catherine Winkworth (1827–1878), a sensible English promoter of women's causes and an equally measured Germanophile. Much of her life was occupied with running and funding educational institutes for women and improving their labor conditions in England and Germany, but not to the neglect of translating German choral works. Her volumes went into dozens of editions. As she was given to revising, the present text is considerably altered by herself (and others) from its first form in her *Lyra Germanica* in 1858. In the hundred-plus years since, it has been virtually unchanged.

Nicolai published the tune we know as "Sleepers, Wake" in 1599, in his *Freuden-Spiegel des ewigen Lebens*, and wrote in the preface, "Day by day I wrote out my meditations, found myself, thank God, wonderfully well, comforted in heart, joyful in spirit, and truly content." Given the depredations of the epidemic all around him, his practice of the virtues makes any technical critique of his work almost pedantic. But in Nicolai we have an instance, and a rare one, of an author who was his own composer and who excelled as both. The tune is better known for having come to the attention of Johann Sebastian Bach, who typified the minuscule population of the empyreal heights of true greatness by not disdaining the amateur. He harmonized Nicolai's melody and, in so doing, added passing notes to improve its singability, the way Corot added a few strokes to a student's painting to their mutual delight.

Bach also paid Nicolai the compliment of making this chorale the climactic chorus of his Cantata no. 140, first performed in 1731, when he was forty-six and director of music in the University of Leipzig. Here he exercised a degree of liturgical liberty, using Advent music for the Twenty-Seventh Sunday after Trinity Sunday; but, whereas the Lutherans were committed to a liturgical calendar, it is unlikely that Nicolai meant his hymn to be only seasonal. Because Bach completely lost his remnant eyesight in 1750, the biographies often say that he spent his last months in Leipzig in total darkness. That cannot have been so, at least not grimly so, if he was able to hear "Wachet auff, rufft uns die Stimme."

Come, my soul, thou must be waking

CARMAN

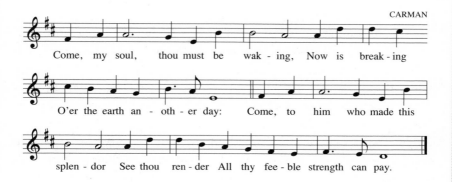

Come, my soul, thou must be wak-ing, Now is break-ing

O'er the earth an-oth-er day: Come, to him who made this

splen-dor See thou ren-der All thy fee-ble strength can pay.

2. Gladly hail the sun returning,
   Ready burning
   Be the incense of thy powers;
   For the night is safely ended,
   God hath tended
   With his care thy helpless hours.

3. Pray that he may prosper ever
   Each endeavor,
   When thine aim is good and true;
   But that he may ever thwart thee,
   And convert thee,
   When thou evil wouldst pursue.

4. Mayest thou on life's last morrow,
   Free from sorrow,
   Pass away in slumber sweet;
   And, released from death's dark
      sadness,
   Rise in gladness
   That far brighter sun to greet.

5. Only God's free gifts abuse not,
   Light refuse not,
   But his Spirit's voice obey;
   Thou with him shalt dwell,
      beholding
   Light enfolding
   All things in unclouded day.

COME, MY SOUL, THOU
MUST BE WAKING

———————————— ⨷ ————————————

This elegant paraphrase, which first appeared in the nineteenth century, is of a considerably longer poem by the German diplomat Friedrich Rudolf Ludwig von Canitz (1654–1699). It is the work of Henry James Buckoll (1803–1871), an Anglican clergyman and very much a "Mr. Chips," who taught German to the boys of Rugby for forty-five years. Baron von Canitz was groom of the bedchamber to Frederick William (1620–1688), elector of Brandenburg, for his last forty-eight years. In many ways Frederick William was the greatest of all Brandenburg's rulers, and his military successes over the Poles, and later over his former Swedish allies at Fehrbellin, did not surpass his educational and financial reforms, which reclaimed lands from the devastation of the Thirty Years' War. As von Canitz's office as groom of the bedchamber was honorific, and as he was a diplomat, it is improbable that he would have awakened his ruler with this morning hymn: "Seele! du musst munter werden."

The music was written by the founding dean of the School of Music at Northwestern University, Peter Christian Lutkin (1858–1931). He also was a founder of the American Guild of Organists, which began with 145 members in 1896. Although of Danish ancestry, Lutkin was organist and choirmaster principally in Episcopal churches and edited Episcopal and Methodist hymnals. Reflecting a year before his death on the low estate of hymnody, he said, "We are years behind England, where the best hymnals make little or no concession to popular taste and yet enjoy a considerable sale." He may have been a bit naïve to assume that the large purchases of these hymnals by parishes meant wide use of their contents. The tune's title, "Carman," was the maiden name of his wife, whose family also produced William Bliss Carman (1861–1929), the Canadian poet who collaborated in *Songs from Vagabondia* with Richard Hovey (1864–1900), the author of Dartmouth's most famous college songs.

Come, my soul, thou must be waking

Hymns for the morning have been especially popular in those Anglican parishes of more "low church" emphasis, where Holy Communion was celebrated less frequently than Morning Prayer at the principal hour of worship. Certain personalities may find hymn singing at an early hour to be a test of virtue. Before any song, a Morning Offering prayer is a Catholic custom for the first moment of rising:

O Jesus, through the Immaculate Heart of Mary, I offer You my prayers, works, joys, and sufferings of this day for all the intentions of Your Sacred Heart, in union with the Holy Sacrifice of the Mass throughout the world, in reparation for my sins, for the intentions of all my relatives and friends, and in particular for the intentions of the Holy Father. Amen.

Let us, with a gladsome mind

MONKLAND

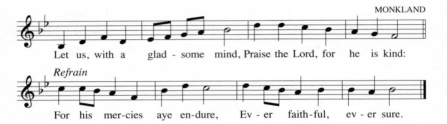

Let us, with a glad - some mind, Praise the Lord, for he is kind:

Refrain

For his mer-cies aye en-dure, Ev - er faith-ful, ev - er sure.

2. Let us blaze his Name abroad,
   For of gods he is the God: *Refrain*

3. He with all-commanding might
   Filled the new-made world with light: *Refrain*

4. He the golden-tressed sun
   Caused all day his course to run: *Refrain*

5. The horned moon to shine by night,
   'Mid her spangled sisters bright: *Refrain*

6. All things living he doth feed,
   His full hand supplies their need: *Refrain*

7. Let us, with a gladsome mind,
   Praise the Lord, for he is kind: *Refrain*

LET US, WITH A
GLADSOME MIND

※

At the age of fifteen, John Milton (1608–1674), himself the son of a "scrivener and composer of musique," paraphrased Psalm 136 in the exuberant way we have here. Two years later he wrote in a more melancholy vein "On the Death of a Fair Infant." The present hymn neglects some eighteen other standards, not all of which are of the same quality, but one of which, from his teenaged hand, I especially like: "The ruddy waves he cleft in twain,/ Of the Erythraean main." A close second goes: "He foiled Seon and his host/ That ruled the Amorrean coast." But the boy knew his Scripture. He knew it better than I did when, at approximately the same age, I set off for Dartmouth College. Because Eleazar Wheelock (1711–1779), a true disciple of Milton, established it so far north in New England, and because of mixed political sympathies, the college was not unduly distracted by the American Revolution and thus has the longest uninterrupted history of commencement ceremonies in the nation. This hymn was long a part of those ceremonies, until the world of academia was brutalized by the philistinism of political correctness. My last recollection of the college was singing this with the hundreds of fellows in my class among the pines of the Hanover Plain. It was also sung at my ordination in St. Patrick's Cathedral, the first recorded instance of its having been heard there.

This solid tune, which would not have displeased the tried and trying Milton, became familiar to its arranger, John Bernard Wilkes (1785–1869), when he was organist of an Anglican church near Leominster, in Monkland, whence is derived its name. The music is of the Moravians, who had a chapel in Leominster. John Wesley had come into contact with the Moravian Brethren on his passage to Georgia in 1735, and in 1738 he visited the Moravian center established by Count von Zinzendorf. The music of the Moravians was congregational, and their influence on him, which grew especially after his visits to the chapel established by Peter Böhler in 1738 at Fetter Lane in London, went worldwide with his Methodism. The Moravians parted from the severity of their Hussite forebears in Bohemia by tolerating instruments. In their earlier period, the violoncello supported the bass voices as the single liturgical instrument, as was quite common earlier even in continental Catholic churches. Eventually the choral societies, long a feature of Bohemian culture, promoted concerts in the New World. One continuing evidence of this is the annual Bach Festival in Bethlehem, Pennsylvania. Although it began only in 1900, it is a reminder of the musical consciousness of those Moravians who settled there in 1741 and immediately set up a "Collegium Musicum."

As an alteration of the original, the first stanza has come to be repeated as a refrain. The *aye* is to be pronounced as a long *a* and not a long *i*, because in this use it means "ever" and not "yes."

Teach me, my God and King

SANDYS

Teach me, my God and King, In all things thee to see;
And what I do in an-y-thing, To do it as for thee.

2. All may of thee partake;
Nothing can be so mean,
Which with this tincture, "for thy sake"
Will not grow bright and clean.

3. A servant with this clause
Makes drudgery divine:
Who sweeps a room, as for thy laws,
Makes that and the action fine.

4. This is the famous stone
That turneth all to gold;
For that which God doth touch and own
Cannot for less be told.

TEACH ME, MY GOD AND KING

⅋

The music for this deceptively innocent-sounding poem was an old English melody published by a London lawyer, William Sandys (1792–1874), who had a firm at Gray's Inn. He spent much of his time pursuing his love of music, which had been cultivated when he was a choirboy in Westminster Abbey. Much of what we associate with Dickensian Christmas caroling is the product of his archival research. He is the one who preserved for the world the carol "The First Nowell," among other items in his somewhat dauntingly titled anthology, *Christmas Carols, Ancient and Modern; including the Most Popular in the West of England; and the Airs to Which They Are Sung*. The tune for this hymn, now named for him, appeared in that volume in 1933 for the carol "A child this day is born."

The author may have been one of the kindliest men who ever lived: George Herbert (1593–1633), who had attended the same Westminster School as Sandys, although in more volatile times. The High Anglican archbishop William Laud of Canterbury (1573–1645), beheaded by the Puritans, had presented him with a parish in Wiltshire, where he wrote his most famous book of spiritual direction, *A Priest to the Temple: or, the Country Parson*. His poetry was preserved by Nicholas Ferrar (1592–1637), the Church of England deacon who established a lay community with a set rule of life at Little Gidding in Huntingdonshire. Having had a considerable impact on domestic piety, and honored by a visit of King Charles I, this community was dispersed by the Puritans in 1646 for its alleged popishness. Herbert's works were printed there and beautifully bound, for such was one of the community's means of making a living, as was the case of a similar settlement of German Baptist Brethren begun at Ephrata Cloister outside Philadelphia in 1735. The Rev. A. L. Maycock, brother of a principal of mine, wrote a book about

Ferrar in 1938; T. S. Eliot's poem about Little Gidding gave the name wider recognition.

On his deathbed, Herbert handed his volume of some 160 poems, which included this one in longer form under the title "The Elixir," to Ferrar for publication. Some of it has been dismissed for bathos and excessive mannerism, but it was in fact quite understated for the tastes of the age. The philosopher's stone alluded to "for thy sake" in the second stanza and explicit in the fourth is typical Caroline imagery. By the seventeenth century, metaphysicians thought they had advanced beyond medieval alchemy, but the wistful world will always be home to Midas and Quixote and questers of lost arks and holy grails. Little Gidding was not far from the real treasure.

Now thank we all our God

NUN DANKET

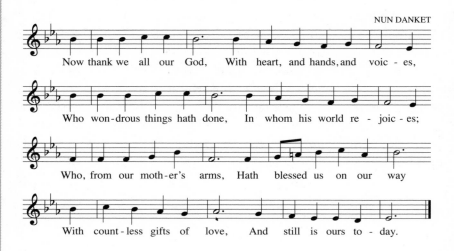

Now thank we all our God, With heart, and hands, and voic - es,

Who won - drous things hath done, In whom his world re - joic - es;

Who, from our moth - er's arms, Hath blessed us on our way

With count - less gifts of love, And still is ours to - day.

2. O may this bounteous God
   Through all our life be near us!
   With ever-joyful hearts
   And blessed peace to cheer us;
   And keep us in his grace,
   And guide us when perplext,
   And free us from all ills
   In this world and the next.

3. All praise and thanks to God
   The Father now be given,
   The Son, and him who reigns
   With them in highest heaven,
   Eternal, Triune God,
   Whom earth and heaven adore;
   For thus it was, is now,
   And shall be, evermore.

Now Thank We All Our God

Like Melchior Teschner, who wrote the music for "All Glory, Laud and Honor," the author of these verses, Martin Rinkart (1586–1649), archdeacon of Ellenburg, wrote this encompassing doxology, which has become a universal standard, during those miseries of the Thirty Years' War whose destructions were not surpassed until the twentieth century. He may in fact have authored it around the start of the third and most violent part of the war, initiated when Cardinal Richelieu backed the Swedish invasion of Pomerania. Its presence in the 1663 edition of *Jesu, Hertz-Buchlein* makes it reasonable to assume that it was in the original 1636 volume, of which no copy is extant. The inspiration is far older, for when Rinkart bids that we thank God "Der uns von Mutterlieb/ Und Kindesbeinen an/ Unzahlig viel zu gut/ Bis hieher hat getan," he does it consciously with the voice of Jesus ben Sirach, who wrote by inspiration, although Protestant canons call his writing apocryphal:

> And now bless the God of all.
> who in every way does great things;
> who exalts our days from birth,
> and deals with us according to his mercy.
> May he give us gladness of heart,
> and grant that peace may be in our days in Israel,
> as in the days of old.
> May he entrust to us his mercy!
> And let him deliver us in our days! (Sir. 50:22–24)

Rinkart is quoted in a work of 1647, the *Praxis Pietatis Melica* of Johann Crüger (1598–1662), who also supplied the music. Crüger, a writer of chorales that influenced Catholics and Lutherans alike, first studied under the Jesuits in Moravia at Olmutz. The indefatigable Catherine Wink-worth supplied the popular translation. Felix Mendelssohn (1809–1847), who was as ardent an Anglophile as Winkworth was a Germanophile, harmonized Crüger's melody for his *Lobgesang* in 1840. Like the father of his contemporary Disraeli, Mendelssohn's father had converted from Judaism. Nevertheless, the Nazis banned the work of his son, along with that of Mahler and others, because of their Jewish blood. The Nazis were less successful in banning the non-Aryan source and subject of the hymn.

Ye holy angels bright

DARWALL

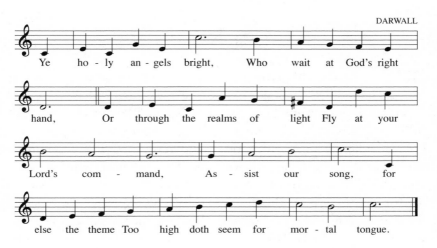

Ye ho-ly an-gels bright, Who wait at God's right hand, Or through the realms of light Fly at your Lord's com - mand, As - sist our song, for else the theme Too high doth seem for mor - tal tongue.

2. Ye blessed souls at rest,
   Who ran this earthly race
   And now, from sin released,
   Behold the Savior's face,
   God's praises sound, as in his sight
   With sweet delight ye do abound.

3. Ye saints, who toil below,
   Adore your heavenly King,
   And onward as ye go
   Some joyful anthem sing;
   Take what he gives and praise him still,
   Through good or ill, who ever lives!

4. My soul, bear thou thy part,
   Triumph in God above:
   And with a well-tuned heart
   Sing thou the songs of love!
   Let all thy days till life shall end,
   Whate'er he send, be filled with praise.

YE HOLY ANGELS BRIGHT

⸱§⸱

The two figures behind this glorious hymn were separated by a century and united by a tendency to political adventure. It does not take a vivid imagination to picture its author, Richard Baxter (1615–1691), in hot water with his government, for that was his frequent posture. He was ordained an Anglican priest and ministered in Kidderminster among the ill-favored hand-loom workers. His Puritanism may have been encouraged by what he saw as a student in London, where his patron was Sir Henry Herbert, Master of Revels. He soon rejected the tenets of Episcopalianism and joined up with the Roundheads, preaching a fiery sermon on October 23, 1642, at the Battle of Edgehill; but soon again he took umbrage against Oliver Cromwell for being so heavy-handed and thought he might help work out a compromise between the Anglicans and the Presbyterians. He was active in restoring the monarchy and played a prominent part at the Savoy Conference (April 15–July 24, 1661), through which the restored and congenial Charles II sought to smooth out religious differences. But most of Baxter's proposed compromises, including his hopeless suggestion that clergymen not ordained by a bishop be accepted without reordination, were disregarded.

For all his fluctuations, he cannot be typed as an opportunistic "Vicar of Bray"; in fact, he refused appointment by the king to the bishopric of Hereford for the logical reason that he disapproved of episcopacy. In 1685 he went before the appalling hanging judge George Jeffreys (1644–1689), whose brutality as chief justice and lord chancellor did not increase popular affection for the Established Church. Jeffreys was solicitor general to the Duke of York at the time of the martyrdom of Saint Oliver Plunket (1629–1681), and his rough trials of the Duke of Monmouth's men who had resisted James II gave the nickname to the "Bloody Assizes." Baxter was fortunate in being released after two years in prison on inflated charges of libel against the Church of England and outlived Jeffreys' death in the Tower of London on April 18, 1689.

Ye holy angels bright

Among the books he wrote extolling moderation in piety and zeal in the cure of souls were *Gildas Salvianus, or The Reformed Pastor* of 1656 and his autobiography, *Reliquiae Baxterianae*. The hymn to the angels, dated 1672, after he had been deprived of his parish, was much revised sometime before 1838 by the Anglican clergyman and historian John Hampden Gurney (1802–1862) when he was curate of Lutterworth in Leicester.

The tune by John Darwall (1731–1789), whose politics were no more fortunate than Baxter's, was intended as a setting for Psalm 148. The son of a rector in Staffordshire and an Oxonian, Darwall ignored the wiser American policies of Fox and Burke and encouraged the ruinous policies of George III's champion of the colonial stamp and tea taxes, Lord North, the second Earl of Guilford. To him, Darwall dedicated some turgid poetry on the American situation.

Praise to the Lord, the Almighty

HAST DU DENN, JESU

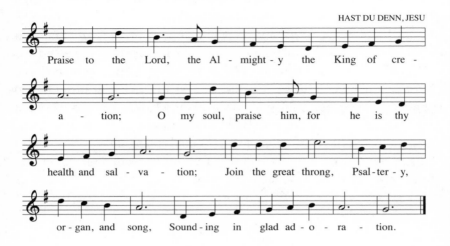

Praise to the Lord, the Al - might - y the King of cre - a - tion; O my soul, praise him, for he is thy health and sal - va - tion; Join the great throng, Psal - ter - y, or - gan, and song, Sound - ing in glad ad - o - ra - tion.

2. Praise to the Lord;
   Over all things he gloriously
      reigneth:
   Borne as on eagle-wings,
   Safely his saints he sustaineth.
   Hast thou not seen
   How all thou needest hath been
   Granted in what he ordaineth?

3. Praise to the Lord,
   Who doth prosper thy way and
      defend thee;
   Surely his goodness and mercy
   Shall ever attend thee;
   Ponder anew
   What the Almighty can do,
   Who with his love doth befriend
      thee.

4. Praise to the Lord,
   O let all that is in me adore him!
   All that hath breath join
   With Abraham's seed to adore
      him!
   Let the "Amen"
   Sum all our praises again
   Now as we worship before him.

PRAISE TO THE LORD,
THE ALMIGHTY

―――――――――――――― ❦ ――――――――――――――

Numerous hands were involved in this translation, which is substantially that of Catherine Winkworth, while both text and tune are by the representative poet of the German Reformed Church, Joachim Neander (1650–1680). The influence of his brief life on subsequent hymnody in both German and English-speaking worlds is indelible, principally through his *Geistreiche Bundes-und-danck-lieder*. The majority of his writing was done during his five years as head of the Latin School in Dusseldorf. His piety did not come as a natural intuition. Like King David, who composed his psalms after an unreflective career, Neander passed a reckless youth in his native Bremen. Given the primitive pursuits of his formative years, it is ironic that his family name is taken from the Neanderthal, that area near Dusseldorf where the remains of the early Stone Age man from the end of the third glacial period would be discovered in 1856. He may have come close to discovering those bones himself, for he was a spelunker, and a cave in the region was named for him.

In any case, he came under Lutheran influences unknown to Neanderthal man through a pastor of St. Mark's Church in Bremen. After his conversion, he became a disciple of Philipp Jakob Spener (1635–1705), who sought to revivify and reform the legacy of the Reformers, which had grown arid under the deadweight of official sanction. His brand of affective piety, held suspect by the Lutheran establishment, came to be called "Pietism," Neander soon was the movement's hymnodic propagandist. As such, he did at least as much as Spener for the advancement of lay spirituality. Spener needed someone with Neander's artistic gifts. It is difficult to imagine, even among the Germans, popular spirits being rekindled by tomes such as the one Spener published the year Neander died: *Die allgemeine Gottesgelehrtheit aller glaübigen Christen und rechtschaffenen*

Theologen. Spener's godson, Count von Zinzendorf (1700–1760), became a Moravian, influenced John Wesley, and took to America hymns of his pietistic revivalism, including this one by Neander, which broadly paraphrases parts of Psalms 103 and 150.

Who are these like stars appearing

ALL SAINTS

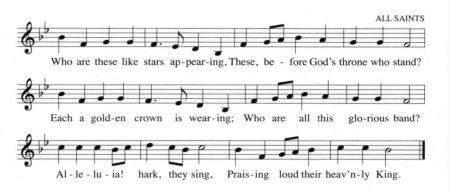

Who are these like stars ap-pear-ing, These, be - fore God's throne who stand?

Each a gold-en crown is wear-ing; Who are all this glo-rious band?

Al - le - lu - ia! hark, they sing, Prais-ing loud their heav'n-ly King.

2. Who are these of dazzling brightness,
   These in God's own truth arrayed,
   Clad in robes of purest whiteness,
   Robes whose luster ne'er shall fade,
   Ne'er be touched by time's rude
      hand?
   Whence comes all this glorious band?

3. These are they who have contended
   For their Savior's honor long,
   Wrestling on till life was ended,
   Following not the sinful throng:
   These, who well the fight sustained,
   Triumph by the Lamb have gained.

4. These are they whose hearts were
      riven,
   Sore with woe and anguish tried,
   Who in prayer full oft have striven
   With the God they glorified:
   Now, their painful conflict o'er,
   God has bid them weep no more.

5. These, like priests, have watched
      and waited,
   Offering up to Christ their will,
   Soul and body consecrated,
   Day and night they serve him still.
   Now in God's most holy place,
   Blest they stand before his face.

WHO ARE THESE LIKE
STARS APPEARING

─────────── ❧ ───────────

In 1539 a large number of hymns burst forth upon the Protestant lands of Europe, clearly for the propagation of Protestant alternatives to Catholic worship. The emphasis was less on theological innovations (for the doctrinal expressions of the texts were for the most part basic and orthodox) and more on the encouragement of congregational singing. The previous year, in Strasbourg, Calvin had published in French a collection of metrical psalms that he had translated with the help of Clément Marot (ca. 1496–1544), a poet formerly in the court of Francis I. The Dutch book of 1539, *Little Spiritual Songs* (*Gheesltelijke Liedekens*), consisted of 259 hymn texts with their tunes. Miles Coverdale (1488–1568), the Augustinian priest who later led the Puritan party in the Church of England as Bishop of Exeter, published the *Great Bible* with the help of the printer Richard Grafton (d. ca. 1572) while exiled on the Continent for his Reformationist views. The Psalter of the *Great Bible*, and not that of the later King James Bible, was used in the *Book of Common Prayer*, thus becoming the source for so many hymn references. In 1539, Coverdale drew on his translations to produce his *Goostly Psalms*, which made use of many tunes and paraphrases from German hymnbooks, including the *Geistliche Lieder auffs new gebessert*, published in Wittenberg ten years earlier. Henry VIII, considering himself a Catholic and rejoicing in the title "Defender of the Faith," conferred on him by Pope Leo X in 1521, promptly suppressed Coverdale's hymnal.

A Lutheran pastor in Giessen, Theobald Heinrich Schenck (1656–1727) was a respected, if not prolific, contributor to the German hymn movement. In 1719, his meditation on Revelation 7:13–17, the same passage metricized by Isaac Watts in 1707 and set to music by Barthelemon, made its debut in a collection printed in Frankfurt as *Neuvermehrtes Gesangbuch*. Schenck's hymn had twenty stanzas, but the reduced version

Who are these like stars appearing

is lengthy enough for singing in festal procession. The tune, now called "All Saints," dates to 1698, when it was included in the *Geistreiches Gesang-buch*. We are indebted to the inspired scholarship of Frances E. Cox (1812–1897) for the English. A contemporary of that other German translator Catherine Winkworth, she led a far more retiring life, in Oxford, producing two English editions of German verse. Nothing of the majesty in Schenck's lines is lost in her equivalent, as is clear, for example, in the incipit: "Wer sind die vor Gottes Throne? Was ist das für eine Schaar?" In 1864 she revised slightly some of her original texts, which she had produced twenty years earlier for *Psalms and Hymns*, a popular collection by William Alford, of the family that also produced another hymn writer and distinguished Greek scholar, Henry Alford, dean of Canterbury. Schenck and Cox have produced by their own lights a marvelous glimpse of the Apocalyptic revelation. Especially on the Feast of All Saints, it serves as an adequate earthly descant to the song sung by the "great multitude, which no man could number, of all nations, and kindreds, and people, and tongues" (Rev. 7:9).

Now from the altar of my heart

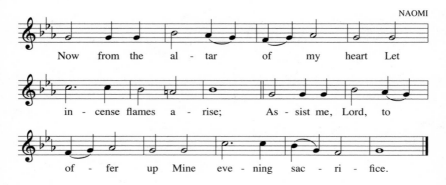

Now from the al – tar of my heart Let
in – cense flames a – rise; As – sist me, Lord, to
of – fer up Mine eve – ning sac – ri – fice.

2. Minutes and mercies multiplied
   Have made up all this day;
   Minutes came quick, but mercies were
   More fleet and free than they.

3. New time, new favor, and new joys
   Do a new song require;
   Till I shall praise thee as I would,
   Accept my heart's desire.

NOW FROM THE
ALTAR OF MY HEART

———————— ✄ ————————

Benjamin Franklin (1706–1790) began his career as a printer in Boston, apprenticed to his brother James, and indicated by the epitaph he wrote for his remains buried in the grounds of Christ Church, Philadelphia, that he never ceased being a printer; his desiccated frame was "the cover of an old book, its contents torn out, and stript of its lettering and gilding." As a high-school student competing in an oratorical competition in the Franklin Club of Philadelphia, I saw a copy of those words but did not know then that they were probably Franklin's revision of a stanza of John Mason (d. 1694).

Mason, the unbalanced son of a Dissenter, took Anglican orders to little effect and proceeded from the theological mire of Cambridge eventually to the rectorship of Water-Stratford in Buckinghamshire. There, later, the salubrious influence of his prodigious output of hymns on the Wesley brothers was ill matched by his suggestion that he was an immortal prophet. A large retinue flocked to his parish, where they sang in gibberish and danced and fainted. It is strange that Ronald Knox's *Enthusiasm* neglected this group of millenarians, for they anticipated the Jansenist convulsionaries of the eighteenth century whom he describes so vividly, gathering in the Parisian cemetery of Saint-Médard to speak in tongues and eat human waste. As with such vaulting neurotics, the clients of Mr. Mason continued in their ways for at least the next sixteen years, even though the new rector of Water-Stratford produced the decayed remains of his predecessor as evidence that he was dead.

John Mason is not to be confused with the composer of the tune "Naomi," Lowell Mason (1792–1872), the Presbyterian choir director of the Bowdoin Street Church in Massachusetts, whose minister, Lyman Beecher (1775–1863), was father of Harriet Beecher Stowe (1811–1896) and Henry Ward Beecher (1813–1887). In his intelligent and sober expositions of hymns, especially in the best-selling *Carmina Sacra*, Lowell Mason shines as a brilliant influence in the history of American choral singing.

John Mason's allusions to incense are metaphorical. He belonged to a school of churchmanship that tolerated it only in theory, considering its actual use regressive. However, the Caroline divines of the seventeenth century were not ill-disposed to it, and, although its common use in the Church of England was not revived until the ritualist movement of the nineteenth century, remnant use continued in Salisbury Cathedral, home of the Sarum Rite, into the eighteenth century. It stopped there only when a member of the Chapter, habituated to taking snuff in choir, objected that the incense offended his nostrils.

He who would valiant be

MONKS GATE

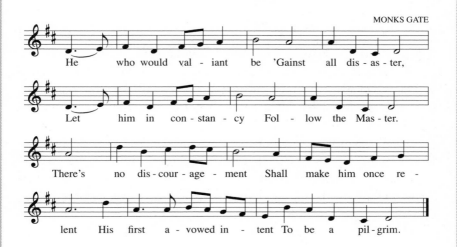

He who would val - iant be 'Gainst all dis - as - ter,

Let him in con - stan - cy Fol - low the Mas - ter.

There's no dis - cour - age - ment Shall make him once re -

lent His first a - vowed in - tent To be a pil - grim.

2. Who so beset him round
   With dismal stories,
   Do but themselves confound,
   His strength the more is.
   No foes shall stay his might,
   Though he with giants fight;
   He will make good his right
   To be a pilgrim.

3. Since, Lord, thou dost defend
   Us with thy Spirit,
   We know we at the end
   Shall life inherit.
   Then fancies flee away!
   I'll fear not what men say,
   I'll labor night and day
   To be a pilgrim.

HE WHO WOULD VALIANT BE

※

When this was sung at the state funeral of Winston Churchill in
1965, it was to the folk tune "Monks Gate," which Ralph Vaughan
Williams had adapted after hearing it in a place called by that name outside Horsham in Sussex. This deft archaeology surprised the provincial-
ism of my own youth, for when I heard it broadcast on that occasion, I was
a college student who had sung it only to the American "St. Dunstan's,"
which also serves the verses of "Master of Eager Youth," by Clement of
Alexandria. Williams had strong feelings against any tune other than
"Monks Gate" for the present hymn, and his wishes have been respected
by copyright, at least in his native land.

The words, of course, are not American either, although these quint-
essential phrases of old England helped complect New England and
much else besides. The excerpt is a theme for Mr. Valiant-for-Truth in
the second part of John Bunyan's *Pilgrim's Progress*, added in 1684 to the
1678 edition. The pilgrims sing it on their solemn way to the "Enchanted
Ground." The present text, from the *English Hymnal* of 1906, is altered
only in the opening lines, the original of which read:

> Who would true valour see,
> Let him come hither;
> One here will constant be,
> Come wind, come weather.

As a boy, I was taken by my father to catch a glimpse of Churchill
visiting Bernard Baruch at his Manhattan apartment, for Winston in
his great age was a heroic figure to me. Three years after the great man's
death, his generous daughter, Mary Soames, arranged for me to visit his
house; there at Chartwell I saw a large array of his paintings rather hap-
hazardly stacked on the walls of an outbuilding, tokens of his hope that
he might spend the first ten thousand years of eternity painting pictures

He who would valiant be

in the brightest colors. In New York in 1997, one of his pictures was auctioned for $183,000, but that is little less crass than pricing an early edition of Bunyan. His deliberate choice of this hymn for the funeral rites in St. Paul's Cathedral would indicate that, from the purview of natural virtue, he lived World War II as a spiritual battle, and in such combat nothing is more demeaning to human integrity than moral neutrality. It does not require a world war for that to be the case, of course. It threads the history of every soul. This hymn was sung at my ordination to the Catholic priesthood.

All praise to thee, my God

TALLIS' CANON

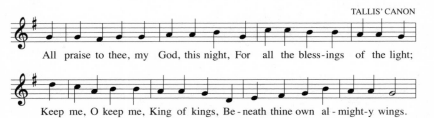

All praise to thee, my God, this night, For all the bless-ings of the light;

Keep me, O keep me, King of kings, Be - neath thine own al - might-y wings.

2. Forgive me, Lord, for thy dear Son.
   The ill that I this day have done;
   That with the world, myself, and thee,
   I, ere I sleep, at peace may be.

3. O may my soul on thee repose,
   And with sweet sleep mine eyelids close;
   Sleep that shall me more vigorous make
   To serve my God when I awake.

4. Praise God, from whom all blessings flow;
   Praise him, all creatures here below;
   Praise him above, ye heavenly host:
   Praise Father, Son, and Holy Ghost.

ALL PRAISE TO THEE, MY GOD

This is one of the best known of all spiritual songs, especially for its doxology and for the pleasure it gives when sung as a canon: that is, in counterpoint of two or more voices. Thus the tune is known as Tanis's Canon, the composer Thomas Tallis (ca. 1507–1585) being, like his pupil and confrere William Byrd (1542–1623), a bridge between the Catholic and early Anglican choral traditions. At the dissolution of the monasteries, Tallis lost his post at Waltham Abbey outside London but was compensated as a Gentleman of the Chapel Royal with royal patents for his music; as a lucrative and very practical gift from Queen Elizabeth, he shared with Byrd the monopoly on the paper used for printing music. Adapting the monastic texts to congregational use, he supplied harmonized settings for the 1567 Psalter of the Protestant archbishop of Canterbury, Matthew Parker (1504–1575). Parker was the first archbishop to present a wife at court, to the public discomfort of the queen.

In the complicated system of "modes" for sacred music, this canon from around 1567 is a form of the seventh mode. The modes represent a long history of trying to classify the different manners of using the scale as first developed by the Greek Pythagoras. In the fourth century, Saint Ambrose used four basic modes for the Liturgy in Milan, and Saint Gregory added another four in the sixth century. That great pope wanted greater variety for the Ambrosian modes, which consisted in D to D with a dominant A, E to E with a dominant B, F to F with a dominant C, and G to G with a dominant D. He added to these "Authentic Modes" four "Plagal [or Oblique] Modes," which were simply each Authentic Mode notched up to start with the former dominant. A humanist friend of Erasmus, the Swiss monk Henricus Glareanus (1488–1563), added four more modes and assigned to all twelve Greek names of his own invention. Tallis worked with only the eight modes to which he had access. He intended this tune for Psalm 62.

If this is somewhat obscure, it should be satisfying to any congregation to know that it is singing the plagal of the seventh, or Myxolydian, mode. The information may have given a sense of one-upmanship to the boys of Winchester College for whom the Bishop of Bath and Wells, Thomas Ken (1637–1711), wrote this hymn. Ken was a High Churchman of principle, meaning that he was habitually between a rock and a hard place. He spent a brief time in the Tower of London as one of the seven bishops who refused to proclaim James II's Declaration of Indulgence in 1687, allowing freedom of worship for Roman Catholics; but as a nonjuror, he also resigned his bishopric rather than take the Oath of Loyalty to William of Orange. In his colorful life he enjoyed the company of such literary giants as his brother-in-law Izaak Walton and Samuel Pepys, with whom he sailed to Tangiers. The man who gave final absolution to Charles II was a classical Laudian divine who remained celibate and professed on his own deathbed that he was dying "in the Holy Catholic and Apostolic Faith, professed by the whole Church, before the disunion of East and West: more particularly I die in the communion of the Church of England, as it stands distinguished from all Papal and Puritan Innovations."

The strife is o'er, the battle done

VICTORY

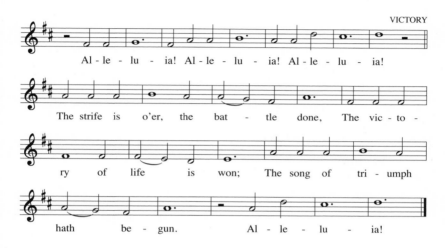

Al - le - lu - ia! Al - le - lu - ia! Al - le - lu - ia!

The strife is o'er, the bat - tle done, The vic - to -

ry of life is won; The song of tri - umph

hath be - gun. Al - le - lu - ia!

2. The powers of death have done their worst,
   But Christ their legions hath dispersed:
   Let shout of holy joy outburst. Alleluia!

3. The three sad days are quickly sped,
   He rises glorious from the dead:
   All glory to our risen Head! Alleluia!

4. He closed the yawning gates of hell,
   The bars from heaven's high portals fell;
   Let hymns of praise his triumphs tell! Alleluia!

5. Lord! by the stripes which wounded thee,
   From death's dread sting thy servants free,
   That we may live and sing to thee. Alleluia!

THE STRIFE IS O'ER,
THE BATTLE DONE

%

The combination of soaring alleluias and solemn tones in one of the more familiar Resurrection hymns conveys a sense of thrill all still mingled with myrrh from the tomb. The alleluias at the beginning and end actually are musical additions of William Henry Monk, who also wrote the Christmas music for "Hark! A thrilling voice is sounding." Monk coupled his work as an organist in many churches with teaching. Indeed, he seems to have loved spreading the joy of music as far as he could: from institutions for the blind to King's College, London, and the National Training School for Music. As the first editor of *Hymns Ancient and Modern*, in 1861, he produced one of the most influential hymnals of all time. It was something of a landmark in High Church expression, not to be outdone until the *English Hymnal* in 1906 dared even more Catholic sentiments. Until that time, hymn singing, as opposed to metrical psalmody and liturgical texts, was considered almost exclusively Evangelical. The heirs of the Oxford movement soon moved from the universities to city slums, where they often did heroic work, finding hymns particularly important in teaching unfamiliar devotions. Multiple revisions of the hymnal started by Monk sold a hundred million copies in less than a century.

Here Monk slightly alters a basic melody of Giovanni Pierluigi da Palestrina (ca. 1525–1594) written as part of his *Magnificat Tertii Toni*. Palestrina, the master of contrapuntal composition, appointed choir-master of the Julian Chapel in the Vatican, sought to serve the cause of the Counter-Reformation, just as Monk in his different clime would spend himself promoting Tractarianism in England. Palestrina was a friend of Saint Philip Neri, who founded the order represented by the great London Oratory Church, which stands very near Monk's Brompton birthplace.

The strife is o'er, the battle done

Monk's affinity for things Catholic is seen in his choice of this Jesuit hymn, traced to a songbook published in 1695 for the use of young scholars. According to venerable Jesuit practice, attenuated in the later history of the Society, the author is anonymous. The translator, Francis Pott (1832–1909), was a student of classical languages at Oxford when the Tractarian leader and professor of Hebrew Edward Bouverie Pusey (1800–1882) was at the height of his prestige. Increasing deafness led Pott to resign his active work as an Anglican parish priest in Ely in 1891. He continued to make important translations of Latin and Syriac liturgical texts. Men like Pott took their work seriously and were taken seriously. Even the pew edition of *The English Hymnal* lists the opening lines of hymns in its index in their original Greek, Latin, Syriac, German, Russian, Welsh, Irish, Italian, Danish, and Swahili. Pott died on October 26, 1909, the same day that General Oliver Otis Howard (b. 1830), founder of Howard University and promoter of the study of Negro spirituals, died in Vermont.

Lo! he comes, with clouds descending

HELMSLEY

Lo! he comes, with clouds de - scend - ing,

Once for our sal - va - tion slain;

Thou - sand thou - sand saints at - tend - ing

Swell the tri - umph of his train:

Al - le - lu - ia, al - le - lu - ia, al - le -

lu - ia! Christ the Lord re - turns to reign.

2. Every eye shall now behold him,
Robed in dreadful majesty;
Those who set at naught and
sold him,
Pierced, and nailed him to the
tree,
Deeply wailing, deeply wailing,
deeply wailing,
Shall the true Messiah see.

3. Those dear tokens of his passion
Still his dazzling body bears,
Cause of endless exultation

To his ransomed worshippers:
With what rapture, with what
rapture, with what rapture,
Gaze we on those glorious scars!

4. Yea, Amen! let all adore thee,
High on thine eternal throne;
Savior, take the power and glory;
Claim the kingdom for thine own:
Alleluia! Alleluia! Alleluia!
Thou shalt reign, and thou
alone.

LO! HE COMES, WITH CLOUDS DESCENDING

———————————— ❧ ————————————

As John Bacchus Dykes claimed to have thought up his music for "Lead, kindly Light" while walking along the Strand in London, so Thomas Olivers claimed that he heard this tune being whistled by someone passing by on some similar street. There is no earlier evidence of it, but Olivers is listed as its arranger rather than its composer. He may have heard something like it, which he rearranged in his mind, but the humility born of his newfound faith would not accept credit for it when it was contributed to John Wesley's *Sacred Hymns* in 1765. It was named "Olivers" for him, nonetheless. Four years later it was changed to its present form in the *Collection of Psalm and Hymn Tunes* of Martin Madan (1726–1790), where it was called "Helmsley."

Madan studied in Oxford at Christ Church, which had produced John and Charles Wesley, the latter being the author of this praise to the Second Coming of Christ. Like Charles, Madan also prepared at Westminster School. But his university years were well after the departure of the Wesleys, and he resisted any remnant influence of the "Bible Moths," as the proto-Methodist undergraduates had been known. As a young barrister, Madan belonged to a social group not quite as notorious as the "Hellfire" club, and, on a dare from its members, he went to hear and mock John Wesley. He was converted on the spot by the sermon: "Prepare to Meet Thy God." Once ordained in the Church of England, he became chaplain of an institution "for the restoration of unhappy females." The lot of these women seemed so hopeless that he decided the only possible solution for their unhappiness would be polygamy. The proposal as outlined in 1780 in his little volume *Thelyphthora* ("ruination of women") resulted in his transfer to a parish in Epsom, where he devoted himself to other subjects.

Another popular tune for this is "St. Thomas," composed by the Catholic exile John Francis Wade around the same time he wrote "Adeste

Fideles." It was intended as music for "Tantum Ergo." The Olivers tune lends itself better to choral embellishments and was the one sung on a memorable occasion in Oxford in the 1960s when the dean of Christ Church, Cuthbert Simpson, arriving by helicopter, was greeted by the cathedral choristers. The double entendre was not irreverent and not too inflated for the arrival of the dean and former Regius professor of Hebrew. Dean Simpson was a magnificent man, of whom many stories have been told, and I have recorded some of them myself, since he was frequently a gracious, if intimidating, host to me. I think of lunching with him in the deanery, which Charles I had occupied during the Civil War, as he advised me on a torrent of subjects, especially liturgical historicism. He was a man of violent speech. As I write, there is on my desk a copy of his portrait, by Graham Sutherland, in the Hall of Christ Church. He wears a mortarboard and holds a cigarette as he awaits Christ with clouds descending.

O Most Mighty! O Most Holy!

STEINER

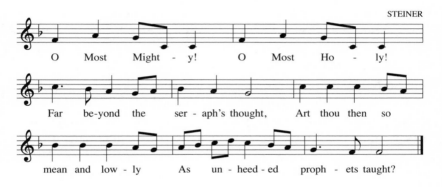

O Most Might - y! O Most Ho - ly!

Far be-yond the ser - aph's thought, Art thou then so

mean and low - ly As un - heed - ed proph - ets taught?

2. O the magnitude of meekness!
   Worth from worth immortal sprung;
   O the strength of infant weakness,
   If eternal is so young!

3. God all-bounteous, all-creative,
   Whom no ills from good dissuade,
   Is incarnate, and a native
   Of the very world he made.

O MOST MIGHTY!
O MOST HOLY!

—————— ❧ ——————

That so sturdy a hymn as this was the product of an unstable life is partly the work of grace and partly the fruit of good editorial pruning. Christopher Smart (1722–1771) was a Kentishman and scholar of Pembroke College, Cambridge, where a life considered riotous even by such convivial friends as the painter Hogarth and the actor Garrick lost him his fellowship. As a journalist in London, he had the resourcefulness to marry his boss's daughter and moonlighted by writing religious poems for university prizes. Dr. Johnson and Charles Burney enjoyed his friendship and esteemed his literary talent, but his gifts were quixotic, and soon his lack of discipline declined into outright madness. His life from 1756 was one of sporadic confinements to mental institutions and debtors' prisons. Dr. Johnson told Burney: "I did not think he ought to be shut up. His infirmities were not noxious to society. He insisted on people praying with him; and I'd as lief [sic] pray with Kit Smart as anyone else."

Through his distress, he composed numerous volumes, including his best-known poem, *A Song to David*, which he wrote as a lunatic in 1763, and the collection from which this hymn is taken: *Hymns and Spiritual Songs for the Fasts and Festivals of the Church of England*, in 1765. A volume written in the same year, *Hymns for the Amusement of Children*, finally found a publisher in Philadelphia twenty years after his death. Fortunately, editing by F. Bland Tucker cut from the hymn various evidences of its having been compromised by mental occlusion. Among the six stanzas of the original poem, "The Nativity of Our Lord," were spectacular lines, such as an anachronistic allusion to the Ottoman Empire: "Where is this stupendous stranger,/ Swains of Solyma, advise"; and some exotic ornithology: "Spinks and ousels sing sublimely."

Only in the twentieth century, in the *Hymnal 1940*, which was the *vade mecum* of my youth, were the distilled words set to music, and happily so, for the tune, "Steiner," is of the period and spirit of Smart in his healthier hours. It is named for the Swiss composer Johann Ludwig Steiner (1688–1761), who first published it in 1735 for his *Neues Gesang-Buch auserlesener geistreicher Liedern*. Steiner never left his native Zurich, where he led a life as halcyon as Smart's was beclouded and, as the city's official musician, rejoiced in the title "Stadttrompeter."

As pants the hart for cooling streams

MARTYRDOM

As pants the hart for cool - ing streams When heat - ed in the chase, So longs my soul, O God, for thee, And thy re - fresh - ing grace.

2. For thee, my God, the living God,
   My thirsty soul doth pine:
   O when shall I behold thy face,
   Thou Majesty divine?

3. Why restless, why cast down, my soul?
   Hope still, and thou shalt sing
   The praise of him who is thy God,
   Thy health's eternal spring.

4. To Father, Son, and Holy Ghost,
   The God whom we adore,
   Be glory, as it was, is now,
   And shall be evermore.

AS PANTS THE HART FOR COOLING STREAMS

---------------- ⸎ ----------------

Arid Erastian churchmanship in Hanoverian England had as a symbol
the double-decker pulpit, with the parish clerk below droning
psalm responses to the minister above. This vinegary distillation of
the antiphonal monastic choirs was one of the first things to go, along
with box pews, in the liturgical revival of the nineteenth century. The
eighteenth-century pulpit exchanges used prose psalmody, if we may use
that oxymoron, and the congregation would occasionally join in with
metrical versions of the psalms as a trope. Metrical psalms appeared in
English use with the collection of Thomas Sternhold (d. 1549) and John
Hopkins (d. 1570) in 1562. This attained almost canonical status, and
more than a few conservative congregations refused to replace them
with the updated settings by Tate and Brady, first published in 1696. As
these metrical translations were very broad and often showed haste in
preparation, Cranmer had disdained their employment, and Elizabeth I
tolerated them as a crumb tossed to the Calvinists. John Wesley deemed
the work of Sternhold and Hopkins "scandalous doggerel," as did the
Jewish-Anglican writer Isaac Disraeli (1766–1848), father of the Earl of
Beaconsfield. But the metrical texts paved the way for the hymns based
on nonliturgical texts that began to flower in the Established Church in
the nineteenth century.

This fine translation was published in Tate and Brady's 1696 *New
Version of the Psalms of David.* Its unadorned elegance is not characteristic of the formulaic neoclassicism of most of the *New Version.* Nahum
Tate (1652–1715) managed to become poet laureate, but his career as
a dramatist usually played second string to that of his Roman Catholic
colleague Dryden. He died impecunious, less because of talent neglected
than because of talent negligible. But he did ornament Christianity with
this paraphrase of part of Psalm 42, in diction preferable to Robert Lowth's

1783 translation as Englished by George Gregory in 1787: "As pants the wearied hart for cooling springs/ That sinks exhausted in the summer's chase." Lowth (1710–1787) was professor of poetry at Oxford and Bishop of London; his *De sacra poesi Hebraeorum: Praelectiones Academicae* was a seminal study of the poetic device of parallelism in Hebrew psalmody. Like Tate, Nicholas Brady (1659–1726) was born in Dublin and studied at Trinity College, but he also read at Christ Church, Oxford, where Sternhold had been educated when it was still "Cardinal College," named for Wolsey.

A hart, of course, is the archaism for a stag, derived from the Old English "heort," and sometimes "hert," as in Hertfordshire; the Greek Septuagint of Psalm 42 means "doe," but the translation of the Hebrew word as "stag" allows a nice English pun (hart / heart) that is not in the original. Graceful as a deer is the tune by the Scotsman Hugh Wilson (1764–1824), who, like the hymn writer Thomas Olivers, was a shoemaker. He also was a psalm leader in the strict manner of his branch of the Church of Scotland, the Original Secession Church, which was formed in 1733 and joined with the Relief sect in 1847 to form the United Presbyterians. The tune, which may be based on a Scottish ballad, was published the year after Wilson's death as "Martyrdom," perhaps in the erroneous belief that Wilson's native village was named Fenwick for a seventeenth-century Covenanter considered a martyr by the Presbyterians.

O come, all ye faithful

ADESTE FIDELES

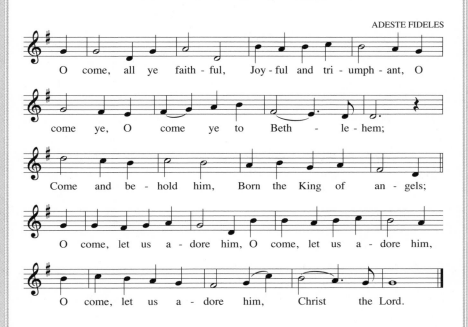

O come, all ye faith-ful, Joy-ful and tri-umph-ant, O
come ye, O come ye to Beth - le - hem;
Come and be-hold him, Born the King of an - gels;
O come, let us a - dore him, O come, let us a - dore him,
O come, let us a - dore him, Christ the Lord.

2. God of God,
   Light of light,
   Lo! he abhors not the Virgin's womb:
   Very God,
   Begotten, not created; *Refrain*

3. Sing, choirs of angels,
   Sing in exultation,
   Sing, all ye citizens of heaven above;
   Glory to God
   In the highest; *Refrain*

4. See how the shepherds,
   Summoned to his cradle,
   Leaving their flocks, draw nigh to
       gaze;

   We too will thither
   Bend our joyful footsteps; *Refrain*

5. Child, for us sinners
   Poor and in the manger,
   We would embrace thee, with love
       and awe;
   Who would not love thee,
   Loving us so dearly? *Refrain*

6. Yea, Lord, we greet thee,
   Born this happy morning;
   Jesus, to thee be glory given;
   Word of the Father,
   Now in flesh appearing; *Refrain*

O COME, ALL YE FAITHFUL

———————————— ✄ ————————————

Flushed with success at the Battle of Prestonpans in 1745, Charles Edward Louis Philip Casimir Stuart, "Bonnie Prince Charlie" (1720–1788), presided at a great ball in Holyrood Palace, Edinburgh, in 1746, awash in kilts and candlelight, before the Battle of Culloden Moor, where he was crushed by the forces of the Duke of Cumberland. When the bagpipes died, a coterie of Jacobites followed him into romantic and hapless exile, some joining the already substantial population of English-speaking Catholics in the town of Douai in Flanders. The valiant but not always politically astute William Cardinal Allen (1532–1594) had established colleges for the training of refugee English priests there in 1568, in Rome in 1575, and in Valladolid in 1589.

Authorship of one of our most clarion Christmas hymns can be traced to John Francis Wade (ca. 1711–1786), an English Catholic layman who reproduced and sold music for the expatriates in Douai, many of whom returned to England after 1794, when the French Revolution suppressed their college. Homeward-bound Benedictines would found Downside Abbey in 1814. Other priests repaired to St. Edmund's Old Hall in Ware, where a handsome manuscript of Wade dated 1760 was found and carefully studied, among others, by Dom John Stephan. Thus, while this grand processional is rightly represented in the Church's treasury as a Latin hymn, it is of modern Latinity; even the venerable invitatory antiphon it uses ("Venite adoremus") was evidently written in Wade's first draft as a double imperative ("Venite adorate").

Wade almost certainly wrote the music, too, and a manuscript of 1746 found in Clongowes College, Ireland, supports Stephan's suggestion of a date between 1740 and 1743. The tune may have been drawn in part from a song, "Pensa ad amare," in Handel's 1723 opera *Ottone*. Wade's version with its fugued refrain proved its singability by being paraphrased as an "English air" in Favart's vaudeville *Acajou*, staged in Paris in 1744. At times it was referred to as a Portuguese air, but only because of its

O come, all ye faithful

association with the chapel of the Portuguese embassy in London. There, as at the Spanish embassy chapel that gave rise to the glorious church of St. James, Spanish Place, whose music still flourishes, English Catholics could worship when public celebration of the Mass was still proscribed.

The Anglican translator of Wade's text, Frederick Oakeley (1802–1880), was assigned to a chapel on Margaret Street, London, in 1839 and made a point of adapting Latin hymns to dissuade his Tractarian congregation from what he considered the unworthy ditties of the Evangelicals. His 1841 copy received fourth and fifth stanzas from sources including another Anglican clergyman, William Mercer (1811–1873), who translated a version the Jesuits had reintroduced to France. *Murray's Hymnal* of 1852 altered Oakeley's opening line, "Ye faithful, approach ye," to the present one. Three weeks after Newman's reception into the Roman Catholic Church, Oakeley was received, on October 29, 1845, and died as a canon of Westminster Cathedral. The advanced ritualism of his Margaret Chapel is shown in a sketch, still hanging in Pusey House, Oxford, of the early use of surplices and lights at a Communion Service. In what is now All Saints', Margaret Street, I made my first confession as an Anglican. Its music attracted Edward VII and Alexandra when they were Prince and Princess of Wales, quite to the displeasure of Queen Victoria, whose taste for the exotic did not extend to divine worship.

O 'twas a joyful sound to hear

MOUNT SION

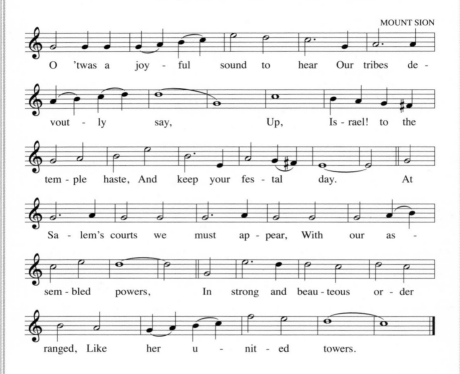

O 'twas a joy - ful sound to hear Our tribes de - vout - ly say, Up, Is - rael! to the tem - ple haste, And keep your fes - tal day. At Sa - lem's courts we must ap - pear, With our as - sem - bled powers, In strong and beau - teous or - der ranged, Like her u - nit - ed towers.

2. O ever pray for Salem's peace,
   For they shall prosperous be,
   Thou holy city of our God,
   Who bear true love to thee.
   May peace within thy sacred
       walls
   A constant guest be found;
   With plenty and prosperity
   Thy palaces be crowned.

3. For my dear brethren's sake, and
       friends
   No less than brethren dear,
   I'll pray: May peace in Salem's
       towers
   A constant guest appear.
   But most of all I'll seek thy good,
   And ever wish thee well,
   For Sion and the temple's sake,
   Where God vouchsafes to dwell.

O 'TWAS A JOYFUL
SOUND TO HEAR

———————————— ℅ ————————————

When the American *Book of Common Prayer* was ratified in October 1789, this paraphrase of Psalm 122 from Tate and Brady's *New Version* of 1698 was one of the metrical psalms and twenty-seven hymns published along with it. In England, no hymns were authorized as part of Prayer Book use except for the "Veni Creator" as part of the Ordinal, and that was without prescribed music. The Prayer Book, actually adapted from that of the Episcopal Church in Scotland rather than the Church of England, was revised free of royalist connections for the new republic. Its preface, one of the glories of eighteenth-century English prose, written by the Rev. Dr. William Smith (1727–1803), first provost of what is now the University of Pennsylvania, set forth the revisers' purpose: "seeking to keep the happy mean between too much stiffness in refusing, and too much easiness in admitting variations in things once advisedly established." More recent liturgical guidelines have not been so well expressed or happy in issue.

The 1886 tune by Horatio William Parker (1863–1919), later organist of Trinity Church, Copley Square, in Boston, cannot begin to match the psalm's incomparable setting by Charles Hubert Hastings Parry (1848–1918), nor should it, for it is not meant as an anthem and certainly not for grand orchestration and antiphonal choirs. But if it is not an anthem, it is almost more than a hymn, and that is a dangerous thing without disciplined direction. Properly sung, Parker's hymn would make his Sunday congregation in Boston sound like the heirs of the Jews climbing the Temple stairs in Jerusalem, but improved in their situation and relieved of the obligation to sacrifice bulls and goats inside the vestibule.

A native of Massachusetts, Parker was dean of the Yale School of Music from 1904 until his death. He began as organist in various small parishes before studying music in Germany and returned to teach music in the Episcopal Cathedral School in Garden City, Long Island, whose cathedral is a miniature Salisbury. The similarly connected girls' school, St. Mary's, once had a distinguished reputation and produced luminaries such as Clare Booth Luce. Garden City was, in fact, planned as a little cathedral town in the English style by the merchant Alexander Turney Stewart (1803–1876), who built the world's largest dry-goods store on lower Broadway in Manhattan in 1848 and an even larger department store in 1862. Leaving an estate of thirty million dollars, he was buried in the cathedral crypt like a medieval knight, and some wretch's attempt to steal the corpse for ransom was a Victorian sensation. I enjoyed working at the cathedral for one year as a seminarian, instructing a group of youths of the Beatles generation, whose ears were already distracted by Sirens inferior to Horatio Parker. In 1893 Parker wrote an oratorio, *Hora Novissima*, with words by Bernard of Cluny, a better librettist than Brian Hooker, who worked with him on the opera *Mona*, which won the ten-thousand-dollar Metropolitan Opera Prize in 1911. His waning powers were taxed in 1914 to produce one more opera, *The Fairyland*, in honor of a Los Angeles municipal celebration.

When I survey the wondrous Cross

ROCKINGHAM

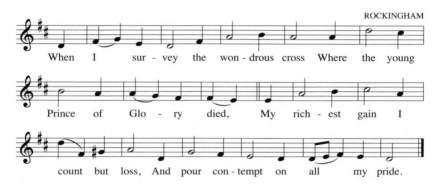

When I sur-vey the won-drous cross Where the young
Prince of Glo-ry died, My rich-est gain I
count but loss, And pour con-tempt on all my pride.

2. Forbid it, Lord, that I should boast,
   Save in the cross of Christ, my God:
   All the vain things that charm me most,
   I sacrifice them to his blood.

3. See, from his head, his hands, his feet,
   Sorrow and love flow mingled down!
   Did e'er such love and sorrow meet,
   Or thorns compose so rich a crown?

4. Were the whole realm of nature mine,
   That were an offering far too small;
   Love so amazing, so divine,
   Demands my soul, my life, my all.

WHEN I SURVEY THE WONDROUS CROSS

※

In closing his letter to the Christians of Galatia, Saint Paul wrote words that were seared into his flesh: "But far be it from me to glory except in the cross of our Lord Jesus Christ, by which the world has been crucified to me, and I to the world" (Gal. 6:14). One would expect the Apostle to be on the lips of the author, Isaac Watts (1674–1748), who was a fervent Nonconformist when he wrote this (as he aged, he seemed more drawn to Unitarianism, at least in sympathy). But it is somewhat surprising to encounter in the third stanza expressions that are almost verbatim from Saint Bernard of Clairvaux in the "Salve Mundi Salutaris": specifically, the seventh section, "Salve caput cruentatum," which we have as "O Sacred Head, sore wounded." The poet Robert Bridges (1844–1930), in compiling his own *Yattendon Hymnal*, was of the opinion that this was one of the few English hymns capable of matching classical Latin verse. But the imagery is logical to anyone meditating on the corporal suffering of the Lord; and Watts was a logical man, or at least he attended to the subject so well that his manual *Logic* (1725) was used for years as a basic text in Oxford. Watts wrote this hymn in 1707, when he had accomplished the mystical thirty-three years of Christ, so the Crucifixion must have been of particular moment to him.

He was the sort of chronic invalid who outlives all predictions; after ten years as pastor of independent Congregationalists in London, he quietly spent the rest of his life after 1712 at a friend's country estate. During that period he wrote much philosophy and theology and such hymns as "Joy to the world!" and "O God, our help in ages past," but some for which he is most famous were written in a space of two years before he turned twenty-two. And his mind was great enough to produce, in 1715, the first book of hymns for children, containing lines such as: "Let dogs delight to bark and bite,/ For God hath made them so." Altogether,

When I survey the wondrous Cross

there are about six hundred hymns extant from the pen of this prodigy, whose chief importance is in the impact he had on the development of the hymn-singing tradition. Especially his hymnals *Horae Lyricae* (1706) and *Hymns and Spiritual Songs* (1707) moved Protestant congregations to employ music in worship beyond the scope of the metrical psalms that had confined the churches to Old Testament expression and typology. In Westminster Abbey one will see a monument attesting to a nation's regard for his life and work.

The sound and sense of this hymn are inseparable from the memory of the long Good Friday services of my choirboy days. The tune "Rocking-ham" was adapted from an earlier one called "Tunbridge" by the Doncaster historian Edward Miller (1731–1807). In 1790 he published *The Psalms of David with Tunes*, which included this; King George III may have heard it, for at least he awarded Miller twenty-five pounds for having written the book. Miller studied under the great Charles Burney, having run away from home to do it. An accomplished harpsichordist as well as organist, he also played the German flute in Handel's orchestra. Robert Southey's (1774–1843) miscellany *The Doctor*, whose imaginary Dr. Daniel Dove is of Doncaster, refers obliquely to him.

There is a land of pure delight

CAPEL

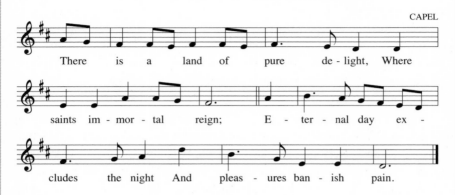

There is a land of pure de - light, Where saints im - mor - tal reign; E - ter - nal day ex - cludes the night And pleas - ures ban - ish pain.

2. There everlasting spring abides,
   And never-fading flowers;
   Death, like a narrow sea, divides
   This heavenly land from ours.

3. Bright fields beyond the swelling flood
   Stand dressed in living green;
   So to the Jews fair Canaan stood,
   While Jordan rolled between.

4. But timorous mortals start and shrink
   To cross the narrow sea;
   And linger, trembling on the brink,
   And fear to launch away.

5. O could we make our doubts remove,
   Those gloomy doubts that rise,
   And see the Canaan that we love,
   With faith's illumined eyes:

6. Could we but climb where Moses stood,
   And view the landscape o'er,
   Not Jordan's stream, nor death's cold flood,
   Should fright us from the shore!

THERE IS A LAND OF
PURE DELIGHT

———————— ✄ ————————

Recent hymn writing has been plagued by the affectation of pseudo folk music, a perverse genre that flourished among the "flower children" of the 1960s. Their pathological music had a near-fatal effect on the Church in her most vulnerable moment of liturgical revision, and the dolorous effects are still with us. In the late nineteenth century, many folk-music societies sprang up, interested in preserving the real thing. One of the most fertile regions for collecting such music was the southern Appalachians of the United States, where so many Scottish, English, and Irish settlers had preserved tunes and dances from their old countries. In Scotland, George Thomson (1757–1850) set a standard for preserving music on the verge of distinction, and Robert Burns (1759–1796) obliged him by writing words that gave the music a new lease on life. The lyricist Thomas Moore (1779–1852), a friend of Lord Byron, did something similar in Ireland. Among the luminaries in this anthropology was Lucy Broadwood (1858–1929), the niece of an Anglican clergyman, John Broadwood, who encouraged her researches into English tunes. What is known as "Capel" is a song of indeterminable date, but unmistakably English, which she heard sung in Surrey by a group of Gypsies who had learned it somewhere in the course of their peripatetic lives. Equally charming is the circumstance of the lines, written by Isaac Watts suppos- edly at the age of twenty-one, while he was gazing toward the New Forest from a promontory on the Southampton estuary. Local inhabitants were confident enough of this oral tradition to commemorate it with a statue of Watts on the site. In decadent theology, which is little more than theosophy, a reverse kind of Platonism makes heaven a symbol for earth; one prime example is the contemporary tendency to replace theology altogether with nature mysticism, looking for gods inside trees instead of adoring God's own Son hanging on a tree. But Watts reached back to a mystical tradition enigmatic to his own Nonconformist upbringing, interpreting earthly splendors as a foretaste of higher and deeper realities beyond time and space. The fourth stanza bespeaks commonsensical psychology, which knows how mortal reflexes in full face of heavenly glory "fear to launch away." Words so practical set to music so beguiling help to ease the passage; and in this enterprise Watts, who was decidedly not a Thomist, echoes the Angelic Doctor writing on heaven in the twelfth article of the Apostles' Creed: "It consists in the pleasant companionship of all the blessed, a companionship that is replete with delight: since each one will possess all good things together with the blessed, for they will all love one another as themselves and, therefore, will rejoice in the happiness of others' goods as their own, and consequently the joy and gladness of one will be as great as the joy of all."

The spacious firmament on high

CREATION

The spa-cious fir-ma-ment on high, With all the
blue e-the-real sky, And span-gled heav'ns, a
shin-ing frame, Their great O-rig-i-nal proclaim. The un-wea-ried sun from day to day Does his Cre-
a-tor's pow'r dis-play; And pub-lish-es to
ev-'ry land The work of an al-might-y hand.

2. Soon as the evening shades prevail,
   The moon takes up the wondrous
      tale,
   And nightly to the listening earth
   Repeats the story of her birth:
   Whilst all the stars that round
      her burn,
   And all the planets in their turn,
   Confirm the tidings, as they roll
   And spread the truth from pole
      to pole.

3. What though in solemn silence all
   Move round the dark terrestrial
      ball?
   What though no real voice nor
      sound
   Amid their radiant orbs be found?
   In reason's ear they all rejoice,
   And utter forth a glorious voice;
   For ever singing as they shine,
   "The hand that made us is
      divine."

THE SPACIOUS
FIRMAMENT ON HIGH

———————————— ✄ ————————————

"P apa" Franz Joseph Haydn was no less kindly to the English than to his own people. His famous visit to England in 1791 permitted him to indulge his anglophilism, and the populace obliged by fawning over him as the darling of many days. Although he was eager to visit an old violinist friend, Mr. Jung, who was living in Oxford, he tarried in London and missed his first concert in the university. There was a loud Hanoverian uproar in the Sheldonian Theatre, with cursing and ticket waving, but the same Haydn was given an honorary degree a few months later in the same theater and responded with a week of concerts that made him a handsome sum. At least he paid for his doctoral gown and the customary ringing of the bell, unlike Handel, who refused to pay his half-a-guinea. Seven years later, in Vienna, Haydn first performed his oratorio *The Creation* and wrote that he had knelt daily in prayer during the days of its composition. As for its premiere: "One moment I was as cold as ice, the next I was on fire. More than once I was afraid I should have a stroke." It was a stroke, but of genius, that in the nineteenth century coupled the music of the oratorio's chorus "The heavens are telling" with the words of this ode by Joseph Addison (1672–1719). Addison wrote it for the *Spectator* (no. 465) in 1712, a year before staging his tragedy *Cato* and three years before his appointment as secretary for Ireland. The inspiration is the opening of Psalm 19, but soon the planets take, as it were, their own course. More than once in schooldays I was warned that this was a pompous Deism at full throttle. But the throttle is thrilling, and while it does not make it all the way through the cycle of Redemption, it is very good about the Creation and Creation's Creator, which is all it intended to be good about. When it was published in 1712, a year before Anthony Collins (1676–1729) published his Deist apology, *A Discourse of Free-Thinking*, "reason" was capitalized, but that does not make Addison a Deist ideologue; printers were extravagant capitalizers in those days, and "voice," "hand," and "divine" had capitals, too.

The infallible Dr. Johnson laureled Addison as the epitome of "an English style, familiar but not coarse, and elegant but not ostentatious," vindicating what Dryden had predicted years before upon reading the youth's Latin verse. The thought of the ode being set to Haydn would certainly have pleased Addison himself, who wrote in the *Song for St. Cecilia's Day*: "Music, the greatest good that mortals know,/ And all of heaven we have below." But it would have little fazed Charles Lamb (1775–1834), who in unexplained pique wrote to Mrs. William Hazlitt in 1830: "Some cry up Haydn, some Mozart,/ Just as the whim bites. For my part,/ I do not care a farthing candle/ For either them, or for Handel."

How bright these glorious spirits shine!

BALLERMA

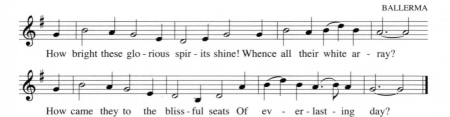

How bright these glo - rious spir - its shine! Whence all their white ar - ray?

How came they to the bliss - ful seats Of ev - er - last - ing day?

2. Lo, these are they from sufferings
   great
   Who came to realms of light,
   And by the grace of Christ have won
   Those robes that shine so bright.

3. Now with triumphal palms they
   stand
   Before the throne on high,
   And serve the God they love amidst
   The glories of the sky.

4. Hunger and thirst are felt no more,
   Nor sun with scorching ray;
   God is their sun, whose cheering
   beams
   Diffuse eternal day.

5. The Lamb, which dwells amid the
   throne,
   Shall o'er them still preside,
   Feed them with nourishment
   divine,
   And all their footsteps guide.

6. In pastures green he'll lead his
   flock
   Where living streams appear;
   And God the Lord from every eye
   Shall wipe off every tear.

How bright these glorious spirits shine!

On July 26, 1808, as Napoleon was seizing American ships arriving in French ports, the son of a French soldier and himself a former officer of the Irish Brigade (his mother was Irish) died in London, with his gun packed away and a violin by his side. Although born in Bordeaux in 1741, François Hippolyte Barthélémon spent most of his life in Britain as a violinist and composer, which career he embarked upon at the advice of his own commanding officer. As conductor of the Vauxhall Gardens orchestra during Haydn's visit to London in 1771, he received friendship and encouragement from the grand man and went on to write some operas and anthems. In 1921, Thomas Hardy wrote a poem in tribute to him and to the years he spent, from 1770 to 1776, providing music in the park, and one stanza reads almost like a descant to this hymn:

> [The sun] lit his face — the weary face of one
> Who in the adjacent gardens charged his string,
> Nightly, with many a tuneful tender thing,
> Till stars were weak, and dancing hours outrun.

His tune, sometimes called "Spanish Air" and more often "Ballerma," is so called because he wrote it as the setting for an old Spanish poem, "Belerma [sic] and Durandarte." It was altered by a Scottish weaver, Robert Simpson (1790–1832), who sang in a Congregationalist church. He wanted it to serve a 1781 Scottish metrical paraphrase of Isaac Watts' own 1707 paraphrase of portions of Revelation 7. Among those "from suff'rings great" mentioned in that chapter is, by divine assurance and canonical guarantee, Saint Hippolytus, one of Barthélémon's patrons and a patron of my French grandfather, Hippolyte Adolphe, too. I should have enjoyed either of those names, but when I was born neither was in vogue, for different reasons. Aurelius Clemens Prudentius (348–ca. 410) wrote a hymn in thanksgiving for cures received through the intercession of Hippolytus, who died as a martyr with Saint Pontian in Sardinia in the third century. If the story of this hymn is colorful, much more colorful, like all colors condensed, are those saints whose robes are white.

Come, gracious Spirit, heavenly Dove

GOOD SHEPHERD, ROSEMONT

Come, gra-cious Spir-it, heav'n-ly Dove, With light and com-fort from a-bove; Be thou our guard-ian, thou our guide; O'er ev-'ry thought and step pre-side.

2. The light of truth to us display,
   And make us know and choose they way;
   Plant holy fear in every heart,
   That we from thee may ne'er depart.

3. Lead us to Christ, the living Way,
   Nor let us from his precepts stray;
   Lead us to holiness, the road
   That we must take to dwell with God.

4. Lead us to heaven, that we may share
   Fulness of joy for ever there;
   Lead us to God, our final rest,
   To be with him forever blest.

COME, GRACIOUS SPIRIT, HEAVENLY DOVE

※

Hymns sung by the people gathered as the Church are stronger and more consistent with their purpose when they are plural in voice. The "we" encompasses the "I." This is not an absolute rule, and some of the finest evangelical verse flies in the face of it. The chief exception is the Creed, which is a confession of the individual's allegiance to the corporate Faith of the whole ecclesiastical body. So it is pedantic and wrong to translate the Latin *credo* as "We believe" on the basis of the Greek plural *pisteuomen*. The Nicaean formulary uses this plural as a conciliar manifesto, but it was customarily used liturgically in the first person singular. Curiously, then, the mistaken pluralization of the Creed has been accompanied by an overuse of subjective personalization in much hymnody of the current liturgical revisionism. This is true of the extended use of "Amazing Grace," which is a flawed but dignified example of Evangelical piety, wholly out of keeping with Catholic worship; it is more glaringly the case with such notorious inventions as the "You who …" hymn ("On Eagles' Wings"), which pastiches Exodus 19:4 as evidence that even angels, at least the Angel of Good Taste, can become comatose.

The 1859 edition of the *Church Psalter and Hymn Book*, edited by William Mercer (1811–1873), rector of St. George's, Sheffield, and Sir John Goss (1800–1880), professor of harmony in the Royal Academy of Music, changed the text from personal to plural pronouns. Thus they made more suitable for liturgical use a hymn with distinctly Evangelical inspiration. Its author was Simon Browne (1680–1732), a minister of the Independent Church, Old Jewry, in London, where he was a neighbor of Isaac Watts; this hymn of 1720 is actually more a revision of than a sequel to Watts' "Come, Holy Spirit, heavenly Dove," of 1707. The Reverend Mister Browne was a classicist and lexicographer, as well as a storyteller for children. But the poor man never recovered from the shock of accidentally killing a highwayman in legitimate self-defense. His verses are especially poignant in view of his subsequent depressions and near-suicidal despair.

Robert B. Miller, born in England in 1915, came to the United States after taking his music degree at Oxford in 1938 and became organist at the Church of the Good Shepherd in Rosemont, Pennsylvania. He wrote the melody, which is named "Good Shepherd, Rosemont," in 1940. Two years later he returned to fight in the Battle of Britain as an officer in the Royal Air Force, and he subsequently became conductor of the Tunbridge Wells Choral Society. The Church of the Good Shepherd is some nine miles west of Philadelphia, in a beautiful situation, and had a tradition of fine music. The people knew their hymns and sang them well, and the choir of boys was affiliated with the Royal School of Church Music, drawing many of its members from the Montgomery Country Day School. I was curate there for two years and rector for seven. During that time, a new organ was installed, replacing the one Mr. Miller had used. Countless times did I hear this hymn sung in its original home. If it is not the most beguiling musical line, it is excellent nonetheless and reminds many of Rosemont, which was not without its own enchantments. The seven gifts of the Holy Spirit invoked here were symbolized by the seven lamps hung in the sanctuary within the sturdy rood screen, and I trust they hang there still.

O God, our help in ages past

ST. ANNE

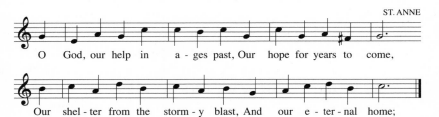

O God, our help in a-ges past, Our hope for years to come,

Our shel-ter from the storm-y blast, And our e-ter-nal home;

2. Under the shadow of thy throne
   Thy saints have dwelt secure;
   Sufficient is thine arm alone,
   And our defense is sure.

3. Before the hills in order stood,
   Or earth received her frame,
   From everlasting thou art God,
   To endless years the same.

4. A thousand ages in thy sight
   Are like an evening gone,
   Short as the watch that ends the night
   Before the rising sun.

5. Time, like an ever-rolling stream,
   Bears all its sons away;
   They fly, forgotten, as a dream
   Dies at the opening day.

6. O God, our help in ages past,
   Our hope for years to come,
   Be thou our guide while life shall last,
   And our eternal home.

O GOD, OUR HELP
IN AGES PAST

—————————— ✄ ——————————

Among the musicians commemorated in Westminster Abbey, George Frederic Handel shares a space near William Croft (1678–1727), and, as Handel adorned the vaults of the world with his "Hallelujah Chorus," Croft's memorial inscription does not fail to remind: "Having resided among mortals for fifty years, behaving with the utmost candor ... he departed to the heavenly choir ... that being near, he might add to the concert of angels his own Hallelujah." Croft also added to our lesser and lower choir the resounding tune "St. Anne," which has ornamented numberless solemn occasions these generations since. Handel made use of a breath of it to introduce his Chandos anthem "O praise the Lord." As Bach also adapted it for his Fugue in E-flat, it may have been around in some form before Croft arranged it as we have it; but to Croft is credited the authorship.

The name honors St. Anne's, Soho, which London parish Croft served as organist from 1700 to 1711. Croft was a colleague of Jeremiah Clark and a protégé of the court musician and composer John Blow (1649–1708), who may also have been a mentor of Purcell. He succeeded Blow as organist of Westminster Abbey and remained as the organist at the Chapel Royal after the suicide of Clark, who had shared that position; thus he played for both Queen Anne and King George I. Croft first used "St. Anne" as a setting for "As pants the hart" in his *Supplement to the New Version of Psalms*, which was published in the year he took over at the abbey.

Isaac Watts rephrased and rhymed Psalm 90:1–5, which read as follows in the *Great Bible* (not the King James) translation of the Psalter attached to the *Book of Common Prayer*:

> Lord, thou hast been our refuge from one generation to
> another.

Before the mountains were brought forth, or ever the earth
and the world were made, thou art from everlasting, and
world without end.
Thou turnest man to destruction; again thou sayest, Come
again, ye children of men.
For a thousand years in thy sight are but as yesterday when
it is past, and as a watch in the night.
As soon as thou scatterest them they are even as a sleep;
and fade away suddenly like the grass.

In Watts' *Psalms of David, Imitated in the Language of the New Testament*, as edited in 1741 from the 1719 original text, there are several stanzas that do not appear in the common version of today. There is one particularly admirable one, intended to follow the present fourth stanza: "The busy tribes of flesh and blood/ With all their lives and cares/ Are carried downwards by the flood/ And lost in following years."

One has long found this hymn a solid evidence of the theological virtue of hope by its stolid realism. This neither despairs nor presumes but takes the voice of Abraham "who against hope believed in hope" (Rom. 4:18). The tone is immeasurably preferable to the depressing affection of cheer in more than a few latter-day hymns trotted out at funerals, bubbling as they do halfway between amateur Stoicism and quiet hysteria. Imagine how the effigies of Handel and Croft and Watts must have trembled in the abbey in supernal agitation as Elton John banged his lachrymose lament on a piano during the funeral of the Princess of Wales in 1997.

Conquering kings their titles take

ORIENTIS PARTIBUS

Con-qu'ring kings their ti-tles take From the foes they cap-tive make;

Je-sus, by a no-bler deed, From the thou-sands he hath freed.

2. Yea, none other Name is given
   Unto any under heaven
   Whereby souls in mortal strife
   Rise to gain eternal life.

3. Let us gladly for that Name
   Bear the cross, endure the shame,
   Suffer with him joyfully,
   Death, through him, is victory.

4. Jesus, who dost condescend
   To be called the sinner's Friend,
   Hear us, as to thee we pray,
   Glorying in thy Name today.

CONQUERING KINGS
THEIR TITLES TAKE

⅍

John Chandler (1806–1870), the translator of these words by an un
known medieval hand, was a major figure in the preservation of much
early material that might well have been lost in the tumultuous and iconoclastic generations that followed him. He saved more than a hundred
significant texts, including this, of which the first modern transcription
is found in the Nevers Breviary of 1727. Chandler's fidelity to sources
is evident throughout his basic work *The Hymns of the Primitive Church,
Now First Collected, Translated, Arranged* (1837). In that same year, 1837,
he also succeeded his father as vicar of Witley in Surrey, where he published many more translations and sermons. The hymn itself recollects a
medieval custom that perdured well into the seventeenth century in Sens
and is known to have been kept in Rouen as early as the tenth: the Feast
of the Ass. It reenacted the Flight into Egypt and was observed during
Christmastide, usually coincident with the Feast of the Circumcision on
January 1. In the paraliturgy, a song such as this accompanied a woman
and child as they rode an ass up the aisle to the high altar. Romanti-
cally uninformed historicists in our own time have occasionally tried to
revive the ceremony, almost invariably turning past whimsy into present
ridiculousness. In a parish in the Wall Street area of New York, where I
later served as curate, an ass had been led through the church with such
ill effect that the pseudo-tradition was promptly discontinued.

The music is also from the Sens Breviary, a folk song well known by
the early thirteenth century, indicating that the text is at least that old.
There is a fetching symmetry in the literature of Chandler: with a large-
ness of spirit, considering that his Oxford college was Corpus Christi, he
wrote a biography of William of Wykeham (1324–1404), who secured a
papal charter for New College in 1379. Today its choir of boys is one of
the finest in the university. The Reverend William Archibald Spooner

Conquering kings their titles take

(1844–1930) was warden of New College from 1903 to 1924, by which time he had so splendidly accustomed himself to the affliction of metathesis that it became named for him. As dean from 1876 to 1889, he regularly led services in the magnificent chapel (where the founder's crosier is displayed) and uttered one of the best-attested spoonerisms when he announced the hymn, "Kinquering congs their titles take."

On Jordan's bank the Baptist's cry

WINCHESTER NEW

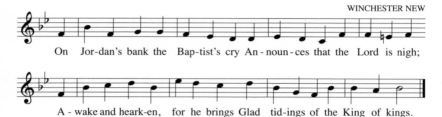

On Jor-dan's bank the Bap-tist's cry An-noun-ces that the Lord is nigh;

A-wake and heark-en, for he brings Glad tid-ings of the King of kings.

2. Then cleansed be every breast from sin;
   Make straight the way of God within;
   Prepare we in our hearts a home,
   Where such a mighty guest may come.

3. For thou art our salvation, Lord,
   Our refuge, and our great reward;
   Without thy grace we waste away,
   Like flowers that wither and decay.

4. To heal the sick stretch out thine hand,
   And bid the fallen sinner stand;
   Shine forth, and let thy light restore
   Earth's own true loveliness once more.

5. All praise, eternal Son, to thee,
   Whose advent doth thy people free,
   Whom with the Father we adore
   And Holy Ghost for evermore.

ON JORDAN'S BANK
THE BAPTIST'S CRY

In 1838, as vicar of the University Church of St. Mary the Virgin in Oxford, John Henry Newman published his *Lectures on Justification*, motivated by the confidence that the Church of England maintained the theology of the early Fathers in a *via media* between Protestant and Roman distortions, staking its claim to be authentically Catholic. But the restlessness of his argument can be detected the same year in his edition of the *Hymnes du nouveau bréviaire de Paris*, a compilation from 1736, which included some hymns by Charles Coffin (1676–1749). There the present hymn, first published in Coffin's *Hymni Sacri*, also of 1736, was placed as an Advent ferial hymn to be sung at Lauds. Newman's access to the work of France's premiere Latinist and rector of the University of Paris suggests a widening of his interest in the Church on the continent.

There is a slight parallel here with the conversations of the archbishop of Canterbury, William Wake (1657–1737), concerning the French Catholics. In February 1718, as William Croft was providing sacred music for the Court of St. James and Isaac Watts was completing his *Psalms of David* and two years after becoming Primate of All England, Wake began a correspondence with the theologian Louis Ellies Dupin (1657–1719) on the possibilities of union between the Church of England and the French Church. But Wake's principles were Liberal, and the association he sought was with Gallicanism, a theological sentiment distanced from papal authority and for which Dupin was a leading apologist. There was a time when Newman might have thought that ecclesiastical model plausible; but, starting around 1839, his mind increasingly turned toward the legitimacy of the papal claims, and his views sharpened in the preparation of the *Essay on the Development of Christian Doctrine*. Newman concluded that the Church of England was as Arian as what he had described in 1833 in his *Arians of the Fourth Century*, and he submitted to Rome in 1845.

John Chandler (1806–1870) supplied this translation, slightly altered since, in his *Hymns of the Primitive Church, Now First Collected, Translated, Arranged.* Published in 1837, it may have stimulated Newman's interest. The German melody, now widely known as "Winchester New," was found in the 1690 collection *Musicalisch Hand-buch der geistlichen Melodien* and has been used in English worship since 1742. The solemn cadences are well suited to the sonorously rolling days of Advent, and so too the translation. One must give thanks that it was not altered more recently to read "On Jordan's bank the Baptizer's cry."

Hail the day that sees him rise

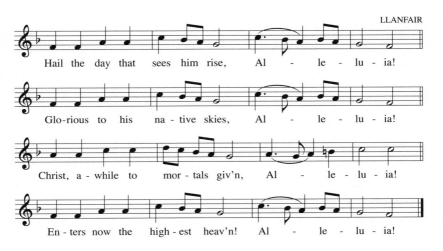

LLANFAIR

Hail the day that sees him rise, Al - le - lu - ia!
Glo-rious to his na - tive skies, Al - le - lu - ia!
Christ, a - while to mor - tals giv'n, Al - le - lu - ia!
En - ters now the high - est heav'n! Al - le - lu - ia!

2. There the glorious triumph waits; Alleluia!
   Lift your heads, eternal gates! Alleluia!
   Wide unfold the radiant scene; Alleluia!
   Take the King of glory in! Alleluia!

3. See! he lifts his hands above; Alleluia!
   See! he shows the prints of love: Alleluia!
   Hark! his gracious lips bestow, Alleluia!
   Blessings on his Church below. Alleluia!

4. Lord beyond our mortal sight, Alleluia!
   Raise our hearts to reach thy height, Alleluia!
   There thy face unclouded see, Alleluia!
   Find our heaven of heavens in thee. Alleluia!

Hail the Day That
Sees Him Rise

———————— ❦ ————————

Had the parents of Charles Wesley (1707–1788) been less generous and prolific, the world of sacred hymnody would be immeasurably impoverished. Or almost immeasurably so. For Charles was their eighteenth child and produced what are variously estimated to be somewhere close to sixty-five hundred hymns: fifty-five hundred or so if you combine some of the sequences, but sixty-one hundred seems a reliable figure. In them we find a significant transition from the stereotypical formality of the metrical psalm paraphrases to more personalized evangelistic hymns. As a hymn writer, he was to revivalism what John Mason Neale was to restorationism.

He also produced two singularly gifted sons. Charles Jr. (1757–1834) began his career at the keyboard at the age of three; and Samuel (1766–1837) was the leading organist of his day, having composed his first oratorio at the age of eight and reaching great heights with his motet for eight parts, "In exitu Israel." His temporary conversion to Catholicism at the age of eighteen was chalked up to a nervous temperament; a fall into a large street hole when he was twenty-one affected his nerves permanently, but he lived a successful life in the world of music, which the bewildered usually find sufficiently spacious for their purposes. He befriended Mendelssohn and promoted the cause of Bach. Charles Wesley himself was a man of congenial ways and a mind more predictable than his brother's; John's decision to ordain his own clergymen deeply grieved the old-fashioned High Churchmanship of Charles, who was Caroline in theology as well as name. Although he was one of the group of Oxford undergraduates first called Methodists because of their regular rule of life, he eschewed denominationalism and separatism and remained an Anglican. But Charles was always faithful to their fraternity. This Ascension hymn appeared in 1739 in their *Hymns and Sacred Poems*, and while Charles characteristically named his brother a coauthor, it is certainly his own work.

An air of domestic attractiveness drew many notables to the subscription concerts in Charles Wesley's house in Marylebone. Humbler were the circumstances of the Welshman Robert Williams (ca. 1781–1821), who is the probable author of "Llanfair." His diary dates it July 14, 1817. Williams was born blind and supported himself by weaving baskets. Typical of his race, he had a fine voice and an instinct for harmony, which he practiced until his death in Mynydd Ithel. Williams was born on the island of Anglesey. The first Marquis of Anglesey, Henry William Paget (1768–1854), lost a leg at Waterloo in a famous scene standing next to the Duke of Wellington; his son George (1818–1880) commanded the third line in the Charge of the Light Brigade at Balaclava. During a holiday in Massachusetts in 1969 with one of their descendants and heirs, I watched the television broadcast of Neil Armstrong's moon landing. Many worlds transected in those hours on a quiet New England village commons, but the Ascended Christ sees them all, all the Georgian drawing rooms and drenched battlefields and Yankee villages and planets; and I suppose that blind Mr. Williams saw them all, too, in his very small and wonderful portion of earth, when he sang.

O for a thousand tongues to sing

ARLINGTON

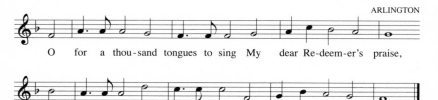

O for a thou-sand tongues to sing My dear Re-deem-er's praise,

The glo-ries of my God and king, The tri-umphs of his grace!

2. Jesus, the Name that charms our fears,
   That bids our sorrows cease;
   'Tis music in the sinner's ears,
   'Tis life and health and peace.

3. He speaks; and, listening to his voice,
   New life the dead receive,
   The mournful broken hearts rejoice,
   The humble poor believe.

4. Hear him, ye deaf; his praise, ye dumb,
   Your loosened tongues employ;
   Ye blind, behold your Savior come;
   And leap, ye lame, for joy!

5. My gracious Master and my God,
   Assist me to proclaim
   And spread through all the earth abroad
   The honors of thy Name.

O FOR A THOUSAND
TONGUES TO SING

%

The year 1738 was a relatively quiet one, although the War of the Austrian Succession was brewing and Robert Walpole went against his better judgment in preparing for war with Spain. But the year meant one thing of determinative moment to Charles Wesley, for on Pentecost, May 21, he experienced a spiritual conversion that became the fulcrum of his life. Such a vivid instant, like November 23, 1654, for Pascal, was bound to be conspicuous in an age weighted with spiritual lethargy; and Wesley advertised himself so as not to hide his light under a bushel. On the first anniversary of his interior awakening, he wrote this hymn, alluding to words spoken by the Moravian leader Peter Böhler. Both he and his brother John had frequent encounters with the Moravians, most decisively so on their trip to Georgia in 1735 (the year Charles received Anglican orders). He spent a year there as secretary to Governor Oglethorpe. To Charles's request for advice on right worship of Jesus Christ, Bailer replied, "Had I a thousand tongues, I would praise him with them all." The Methodist movement owed its music as much as anything else to these disciples of Jan Hus, for whom hymnody had been both creed and propaganda. Their collection of approximately four hundred songs of praise, which appeared in 1504, is the earliest known vernacular hymnal. This hymn of Charles Wesley had eighteen stanzas and was abbreviated variously; the present form is the way John edited it for the *Wesleyan Hymn Book* of 1780. Charles spent eighteen years after his spiritual renewal engaged in strenuous itinerant preaching before settling down to a cure of souls in London, in solid testimony to the influence of 1738. But his old Laudian roots would not be uprooted by a force as ephemeral as mere emotionalism. Thus, while he spoke about tongues, he did not mean speaking in tongues; he meant the highest praise that reason enlightened by faith can attain in the form of congruent poetry and harmony.

The melody to which my early years were accustomed was a lyrical and meditative one, but rather thin and difficult: "Stracathro," written in 1832 by a Glasgow merchant and amateur musician, Charles Hutcheson (1792–1860). "Arlington" is preferable, not least because it was known by 1762 and thus accessible to Wesley. Both, of course, are in Common Meter (8 6. 8 6.), a standard of the age and a favorite of the Wesley brothers. Its composer, Thomas Augustine Arne (1710–1778), was the leading native English composer of his century (Handel being a naturalized subject). Arne wrote the music for "Rule, Britannia!" as part of the masque *Alfred*, with libretto by the Scottish poet James Thomson (1700–1748). The gorgeously breathless tune was first performed on August 1, 1740, in the gardens of Cliveden House in Maidenhead, where rain forced the latter part of the performance indoors. At the time, Cliveden was a residence of Frederic, Prince of Wales. Later it passed into the hands of the Astor family. In October 1995, in the library, I celebrated what I am told was the first Mass ever to be said in that venerable house. When the public celebration of the Mass was still proscribed, Arne, a devout Catholic, had written music for use in the Sardinian embassy chapel in London. Thus the composer of "Rule, Britannia!" also gave us, among other liturgical music, a very fine setting for "O Salutaris Hostia." Arne, incidentally, may have been the first to provide annotated programs for concerts: the flyer for a performance of catches and glees he gave at the Drury Lane Theatre in 1768 includes explanations of the selections with historical and critical notes.

Guide me, O thou great Jehovah

CWM RHONDDA

Guide me, O thou great Je - ho - vah, Pil - grim through this bar - ren land; I am weak, but thou art might - y; Hold me with thy pow'r - ful hand; Bread of heav - en, Bread of heav - en, Feed me till I want no more, Feed me till I want no more.

2. Open now the crystal fountain,
Whence the healing spring doth flow;
Let the fire and cloudy pillar
Lead me all my journey through;
Strong Deliverer, Strong Deliverer,
Be Thou still my strength and shield,
Be Though still my strength and shield.

3. When I tread the verge of Jordan,
Bid my anxious fears subside;
Bear me thro' the swelling current,
Land me safe on Canaan's side;
Songs of praises, songs of praises
I will ever give to Thee,
I will ever give to Thee.

GUIDE ME, O THOU
GREAT JEHOVAH

─────────────── ✗ ───────────────

William Williams (1717–1791) was the Charles Wesley of Wales, having composed about a thousand hymns, 80 percent of which were in Welsh. To claim the laurels of the greatest hymn writer of what have probably been the greatest hymn-singing people is a very great boast indeed. Born in Cefn-y-coed, he studied medicine at Llwynll-wyd and served as an Anglican deacon in Llanwrtyd, showing that the Welsh make up in erudition what they may lack in vowels. The Church of Wales, known as the Anglican Church in Wales since its disestab-lishment in 1920, was in Williams' time increasingly fraught with ab-senteeism and pluralism, notwithstanding the efforts of the Society for Promoting Christian Knowledge, and especially those of the Anglican divine Griffith Jones (1683–1761), to promote education and the Welsh language. Dissent quickly spread, and, by the nineteenth century, Wales was mostly Methodist. Williams himself was denied priestly ordination in his church because of his Calvinist tendencies and became a preacher of the Methodist Connection.

Peter Williams (1722–1796), author of the first Bible commentary in Welsh, in 1771 translated this singularly majestic hymn, which had first appeared in 1745 with the opening verse that is still thrilling when sung at a Cymanfa Ganu, or hymn-sing: "Argylwydd arwain trwy'r anialwch." The received version is based on another translation by William Wil-liams himself, perhaps assisted by his son John, somewhat abbreviated and retaining part of Peter's version for the third stanza.

Evangelicals had a liking for the divine name Jehovah, which is curious, since it derives from a medieval Catholic misreading of the unuttered Hebrew name for God, "Yahweh." As a wrong rendering, it is better than the pedantic use of "Yahweh" in modern hymnody, which may scandalize Jews and reverent Christians. Better to use Jehovah as a pious euphemism like Adonai or Lord, in the double name of humility and good taste.

While many English tunes have been used for this hymn, unsurpassed is "Cwm Rhondda," credited to the Welsh poet John Hughes (1832–1887), who wrote the pastoral poem "Owain Wyn" and many other poems and songs under his pen name (taken from his middle name) Ceiriog. It is unfortunate that it is neglected in most of the older English hymnals, because it lends itself so well to the multiple-part singing characteristic of its homeland, as anyone can attest who has attended an Eisteddfod, or heard five thousand Welshman singing in spontaneous four-part-harmony in the Royal Albert Hall. The only people I have heard match the talent are the Samoans, whose hymns taken from tribal rites would have been the envy of Palestrina. The Welsh talent goes back, of course, to the Druids. More than a century before the birth of Christ, Poseidonius of Apomea wrote of their bards that, "even among the most savage non-Greeks, frenzy yields to wisdom, and Mars respects the Muses." In 1882, Giraldus Cambrensis recorded: "In their musical concerns they do not sing in unison, like the inhabitants of their countries, but in many different parts, so that in a company of singers, which one very frequently meets with in Wales, you will hear as many different parts and voices as there are performers." The same may also be said, less encouragingly, of Welsh theology. However, the invocation of the Hebrew wanderings as a type of salvation for the Welsh soul gives the hymn a scope that Moses could not have imagined from his side of the Jordan.

Soldiers of Christ, arise

ST. ETHELWALD

Sol - diers of Christ, a - rise, And put your ar - mor on, Strong in the strength which God sup - plies Thro' his e - ter - nal Son.

2. Strong in the Lord of hosts,
   And in his might power:
   Who in the strength of Jesus trusts
   Is more than conqueror.

3. Stand then in his great might,
   With all his strength endued,
   And take, to arm you for the fight,
   The panoply of God.

4. From strength to strength go on,
   Wrestle, and fight, and pray:
   Tread all the powers of darkness down,
   And win the well-fought day.

5. That, having all things done,
   And all your conflicts past,
   Ye may o'ercome, through Christ alone,
   And stand complete at last.

SOLDIERS OF CHRIST, ARISE

In spiritual combat, a dyspeptic and slothful soul will try to make a virtue of pacifism. None of that is in the apostolic literature, and it certainly finds no corner in this hymn. "Wherefore take unto you the whole armor of God, that you may be able to withstand in the evil day, and having done all, to stand. Stand, therefore, having your loins girt about with truth, and having on the breastplate of righteousness; And your feet shod with the preparation of the gospel of peace; Above all, take on the shield of faith, where you shall be able to quench all the fiery darts of the wicked. And take the helmet of salvation, and the sword of the Spirit, which is the word of God" (Eph. 6:13–17). The imagery obtains in the prayer of the priest vesting for Mass in the amice, which is likened to the helmet. Loss of heart for war "against the rulers of the darkness of this world" underlies the shoddiness that may characterize preparation for the Holy Sacrifice in sullen times. The amice, we are told, is now optional, and, in a morose climate, anything optional is abandoned; so it is with the amice, indeed, with care for vesture and vesting in general.

These lines are as if they were written for vesting at ordinations. I vividly remember a tutor of mine being clothed to them during his consecration as an Anglican bishop in Texas. He was a worthy man and, I hope, is gathered all above now, but it would be far more impressive to sing this as a man is clothed in the vesture of valid Orders. Charles Wesley published this with his brother in their *Hymns and Sacred Songs* in 1749. Charles was sufficiently persuaded of the legitimacy of his ordination that he blanched when John set out to ordain his own clergy without license. His words certainly are valid, for they harken to Saint Paul in Romans 13:2 and 2 Corinthians 6:7 and, most literally, in the aforementioned counsel to the Ephesians to which Saint Patrick alluded in his "Breastplate" hymn. Originally, Charles had some sixteen stanzas of exegetical text in the hymn.

The stirring music was written by a Methodist of London, Isaac Smith (1725–1800), who was a linen draper. The tune appeared in 1770 in a hymnal he wrote under a title that indicates that his gifts were more musical than literary: *A Collection of Psalm Tunes in Three Parts, Adapted to Each Measure as Sung in Several Churches, Chapels and Meeting-Houses in and about London*. All will sympathize with Smith's own little battle in a war that will last to the end of the earthly history of the Church Militant: he wanted very much for congregations to meet for a couple of hours weekly for musical rehearsals so that "the mistakes of those who sing out of tune or out of time will easily be corrected." It takes a hymn as vibrant as this to lift the spirit from the lugubriousness of those oft-quoted words.

God moves in a mysterious way

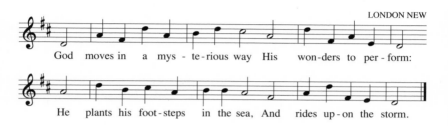

LONDON NEW

God moves in a mys-te-rious way His won-ders to per-form:

He plants his foot-steps in the sea, And rides up-on the storm.

2. Deep in unfathomable mines,
   With never-failing skill,
   He treasures up his bright designs,
   And works his sovereign will.

3. Ye fearful saints, fresh courage take;
   The clouds ye so much dread
   Are big with mercy, and shall break
   In blessings on your head.

4. Judge not the Lord by feeble sense,
   But trust him for his grace;
   Behind a frowning providence
   He hides a smiling face.

5. His purposes will ripen fast,
   Unfolding every hour:
   The bud may have a bitter taste,
   But sweet will be the flower.

6. Blind unbelief is sure to err,
   And scan his work in vain;
   God is his own interpreter,
   And he will make it plain.

GOD MOVES IN A
MYSTERIOUS WAY

⸻ ℁ ⸻

Practically all that exists of Purcell's music was first published by Henry Playford (1657–ca. 1706), who inherited the business of his father, John (1623–ca. 1686). As governments came and went, they provided whatever music was in vogue, becoming the leading music publishers in London. Assisted by John's nephew and namesake (1655–1685), they sold music for domestic use when most theatrical and church music was proscribed during the Commonwealth and Protectorate. Henry's *Banquet of Musick* (1691) is a helpful guide to the ways music survived in those dark days, and he provides a detailed list of music tutors for organ and virginal, voice and viol. At the Restoration in 1660, the Playford firm was quick to supply the needs of the court, even dedicating music to the Catholic queen dowager, Henrietta Maria, widow of Charles I.

The books on psalmody that he edited and published in the 1670s had an important influence in the development of harmonized plainchant into what is now known as "Anglican Chant." The Playford shop was also a social center for musicologists; much of what Samuel Pepys (1633–1703) writes about music in his *Diary* is informed by what he learned there, and a large part of the music and literary collection he left to Magdalen College, Oxford (including two thousand ballads), he obtained there. John Playford arranged "London New" for his *Psalms and Hymns in Solemn Musick* in 1671. It was called "Newton," for a Scottish village, when it first appeared in 1635 in *The Psalmes of David*. That Scottish Psalter, like the 1564 Psalter of John Knox, drew many tunes, and possibly this, from the Genevan Psalters and began a generation or so that is called the golden age of metrical psalmody.

The poet William Cowper (1731–1800) was grandnephew of the first Earl Cowper (1665–1723), the first Lord Chancellor of Great Britain after the union with Scotland, the negotiation for which involved his diplomacy. William was also a cousin of Martin Madan, whose book in favor of polygamy, *Thelyphthora*, provoked his sober reply, *Anti-Thelyphthora*. Cowper never recovered from mourning the death of his mother when he was six years old and suffered deep depressions throughout his life. Trained as a lawyer, he trembled at the prospect of a civil examination to qualify as a clerk of the House of Lords in 1763 and attempted suicide. Shortly afterward, he wrote this hymn under the title "Light shining out of darkness." For all his burdens and melancholia, he was not without a sense of the droll. He records, for example, that a parish clerk asked him, instead of a local poet, to write some mortuary verse, because the other fellow "is a gentleman of so much reading that the people of our town cannot understand him." Hard circumstance may have chiseled the simple and emotive style that made him the age's leading figure in the transition from neoclassicism in letters. His hymn is to be sung *cum dignitate*, as he struggled, successfully, to live despite "frowning providence."

Rock of ages, cleft for me

TOPLADY

Rock of a - ges, cleft for me, Let me hide my-self in thee;

Let the wa - ter and the blood From thy side, a heal-ing flood,

Be of sin the dou - ble cure, Cleanse me from its guilt and pow'r.

2. Should my tears forever flow,
   Should my zeal no languor know,
   All for sin could not atone:
   Thou must save, and thou alone;
   In my hand no price I bring,
   Simply to thy cross I cling.

3. While I draw this fleeting breath,
   When mine eyelids close in death,
   When I rise to worlds unknown
   And behold thee on thy throne,
   Rock of ages, cleft for me,
   Let me hide myself in thee.

ROCK OF AGES,
CLEFT FOR ME

O ne of the great hymns of the standard repertoire is hackneyed only in the minds of hacks. In three verses are summed up the content of mystical devotion to the Side of Christ, which the Catholic understands to be also a prophecy of the birth of the Church. The fact that the composition is by an Evangelical, actually an angular Calvinist, only serves to show how in its own day the Evangelical movement was a *protoevangelion* of the Catholicism that had been taken away from the land but would return, praying the Anima Christi:

> Sanguis Christi, inebria me.
> Aqua lateris Christi, lava me.

> Blood of Christ, inebriate me.
> Water from the side of Christ, wash me.

The Anglican priest Augustus Montague Toplady (1740–1778) was educated at Westminster School and Trinity College, Dublin. After 1758, when he embraced a radical brand of Calvinism, he turned against John Wesley as decidedly as he had once turned to him under the influence of a Wesleyan lay preacher in Ireland. What the Tractarians would try to do for their Church from a Catholic point of view, Toplady undertook from his own side of the fence in 1774, writing *The Historic Proof of the Doctrinal Calvinism of the Church of England*. Its brittle tone made a weak foil in any duel with weapons tempered by irenicism.

A year later, one stanza of his celebrated lines appeared in the *Gospel Magazine*; and the full text, several stanzas of which have since been conflated or dropped, was published in an essay about four months before the declaration of American independence. The portent of Toplady's article was the burden of his nation's moral debt incurred by sin. By this time, he had given up his parish in Devonshire to become minister of the French Calvinist Church in Leicester Fields, London. I was one of many who grew up with the story that he wrote his hymn during a thunderstorm, sheltering in a cave in the Mendips, but that is only a legend. The only thundering when he wrote it was from his own pulpit.

"Toplady" is a tune inseparable from the hymn, although purists have thought it inadequate to the sturdiness of the Rock it sings. I found it very fine, except for periods when High Church snobbery held sway. Thomas Hastings (1787–1872) wrote it specifically for Toplady's text in 1830 and published it the following year. As a colleague of Lowell Mason, he was his friend's peer as an influence on early American sacred song. The story of his family moving by oxcart from his native Connecticut to Oneida County, New York, when he was twelve, is well known; his musical services to the state of New York during the rest of his life are even better known and merited honors. For a glimpse of American life in one of the nation's most seminal and energetic periods from an unusual and revealing perspective, one could hardly surpass (excepting, of course, Frances Trollope) his memoirs of congregations, choristers, and clergymen published in 1854: A *History of Forty Choirs*.

Glorious things of Thee are spoken

AUSTRIA

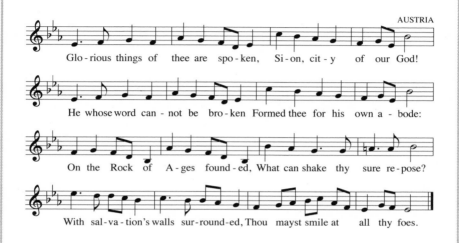

Glo-rious things of thee are spo-ken, Si-on, cit-y of our God!

He whose word can-not be bro-ken Formed thee for his own a-bode:

On the Rock of A-ges found-ed, What can shake thy sure re-pose?

With sal-va-tion's walls sur-round-ed, Thou mayst smile at all thy foes.

2. See the streams of living water,
 Springing from eternal love,
 Well supply thy sons and daughters,
 And all fear of want remove:
 Who can faint while such a river
 Ever flows their thirst to assuage?
 Grace, which like the Lord the Giver,
 Never fails from age to age.

3. Round each habitation hovering,
 See the cloud and fire appear
 For a glory and a covering
 Showing that the Lord is near.
 Thus deriving from their banner,
 Light by night, and shade by day,
 Safe they feed upon the manna
 Which he gives them when they
 pray.

4. Blest inhabitants of Sion,
 Washed in the Redeemer's blood!
 Jesus, Whom their souls rely on,
 Makes them kings and priests to
 God.
 'Tis his love his people raises
 Over self to reign as kings:
 And as priests, his solemn praises
 Each for a thank-offering brings.

5. Savior, if of Sion's city
 I, through grace, and member am,
 Let the world deride or pity,
 I will glory in thy name:
 Fading is the worldling's pleasure,
 All his boasted pomp and show;
 Solid joys and lasting treasure
 None by Sion's children know.

Glorious things of Thee are spoken

—————————— ⅗ ——————————

As Franz Joseph Haydn was dying in 1809, he managed on the keyboard a few last notes: these, which he had written as the Austrian national anthem. In the reign of the last Holy Roman Emperor, the Imperial High Chancellor decided that Franz II deserved an anthem equivalent to "God Save the King" and one that would be an encouraging volley to the "Marseillaise" of the French revolutionaries. First he commissioned the poet Lorenz Leopold Haschka (1749–1827) to write the words for "Gott erhalte Franz den Kaiser!" Then Haydn produced the music, expanded from a Croatian folk tune he had known since childhood, "Vjutro rano se ja vstanem." Its first public performance was as a birthday present for the Kaiser on February 12, 1797. The words for which it was composed inspired the popular name for the string quartet in C, op. 76, no. 76: the "Emperor Quartet," which contains variations on the melody, lengthened in tempo.

Graceful and good Haydn played it as the French were shelling Vienna at the orders of the Kaiser's future son-in-law, Napoleon. This is to be remembered when the hymn is freighted with the unhappy associations of later years. The evil man who died in a German bunker in 1945 did not play it. His death was a *Götterdämmerung*; and he sullied Haydn's music with the cacophony of his miserable life. Man is a miscreant if he lets immediate memories ruin something so noble.

The *Olney Hymns* of John Newton (1725–1807) contain this text of his, written by 1779 at the latest. Newton's spectacular conversion from life as an impressed seaman who became a slave-trader and then an Anglican clergyman has made him a fixture in the specialized kind of romance enjoyed by the Evangelicals, to whose party he adhered. Newton also wrote "Amazing Grace," whose overwrought Calvinist expression is belabored in today's Catholic parishes, which have long been capable of producing works even more bathetic.

Glorious things of Thee are spoken

"A servant of slaves in Africa," as he wrote in his own epitaph, he was "preserved, restored, pardoned and appointed to preach the Faith he had long labored to destroy." He learned Hebrew and Greek while working as surveyor of tides in Liverpool from 1755 to 1760. The bishop of Lincoln ordained him after the archbishop of York rejected his views as extreme. While vicar of Olney, he gave William Cowper a place to recover mentally. Cowper wrote 67 of the hymns in the *Olney Hymns*, and Newton wrote the other 280. While Cowper was much helped by the attentions paid him in the country parish, he seems to have relaxed more after 1779, when he was not so closely tied to Newton, whose "born-again" heartiness was as oppressive as it was edifying. When Mr. Lunardi rose in a hot-air balloon in 1784, humorless Newton complained to the Earl of Dartmouth: "A person is talked of and admired by thousands for venturing up with a balloon ... while he who came down from Heaven to dwell for a time with men, and to die for them, is slighted and disregarded." The College of New Jersey, then more of a Calvinist stronghold than it now is as Princeton University, made Newton an honorary Doctor of Divinity in 1792.

As the minister of St. Mary's Church, Woolnoth, London, he became totally blind, and when he died, the people sang his words, "I once was blind, but now I see." The integrity of his life supplied whatever may be wanting in parts of that hymn. But nothing is wanting in this hymn to Sion's God, a meditation on Isaiah 33:20–21. This should be Newton's most popular achievement, and if it is not, that is commentary, not on the hymn, but on us.

There is a fountain filled with blood

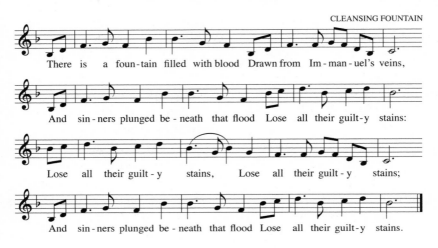

There is a foun-tain filled with blood Drawn from Im-man-uel's veins,

And sin-ners plunged be-neath that flood Lose all their guilt-y stains:

Lose all their guilt-y stains, Lose all their guilt-y stains;

And sin-ners plunged be-neath that flood Lose all their guilt-y stains.

2. The dying thief rejoiced to see That fountain in his day,
   And there may I, though vile as he, Wash all my sins away:
   Wash all my sins away, Wash all my sins away;
   And there may I, though vile as he, Wash all my sins away.

3. Dear dying Lamb, Thy precious blood Shall never lose its pow'r,
   Till all the ransomed Church of God Be saved to sin no more:
   Be saved to sin no more, Be saved to sin no more;
   Till all the ransomed Church of God Be saved to sin no more.

4. E'er since by faith I saw the stream Thy flowing wounds supply,
   Redeeming love has been my theme And shall be till I die:
   And shall be till I die, And shall be till I die;
   Redeeming love has been my theme And shall be till I die.

5. When this poor lisping, stamm'ring tongue Lies silent in the grave,
   Then in a nobler, sweeter song I'll sing Thy pow'r to save:
   I'll sing Thy pow'r to save, I'll sing Thy pow'r to save;
   Then in a nobler, sweeter song I'll sing Thy pow'r to save.

THERE IS A FOUNTAIN
FILLED WITH BLOOD

⸹

There were certain extravagantly potent hymns that I was not formally taught in youth, for they were victims of the "ghastly good taste" in which the Anglican choral tradition found repose. But I sought them out in a spirit of aesthetical prurience. I looked forward to the annual arrival of an Evangelical tent mission, which would come punctually in midsummer near my house with the intention of converting New Jersey and its contiguous regions. So I watched the tent go up and the spreading of sawdust—it was authentic sawdust, just as I had been told the Baptists spread on the ground. And then an electric organ was installed and tested. I did not attend the actual worship, for I abjured the mixing of cults, but from outside the canvas one could hear this hymn, and I have ever since enjoyed it for its excellence and its power to shock squeamish piety. For it does speak of blood in a deliberate way, with all the blatancy that the frankness of William Cowper could muster and with all the nearly expressionist drama of Grünewald's Isenheim *Small Crucifixion*.

The text appeared as the fifteenth of the *Olney Hymns* in 1779. Another of Cowper's hymns in that collection, "Hark my soul!" was first published in 1768 and was later translated into Italian by Prime Minister Gladstone, and he was no slouch when it came to judging the worth of letters. Cowper himself was in the process of translating some of Milton's Italian poems when he died in 1800, having already used his Greek to translate Homer in 1791. The Italian affinity is no coincidence, for there is nothing in this sawdust hymn that does not translate spiritually into—or, more accurately, from—Latin piety, in the same way we have remarked of "Rock of Ages" by Augustus Montague Toplady. The thumpingly bold tune "Cleansing Fountain" was arranged by Lowell Mason from a traditional American frontier melody, which means that its roots are most likely Scots-Irish. The lively fuguing is typical of the period. The whole effect makes this hymn a congenial cousin of those patriotic songs that do not shy from saying what they mean. The paramount example, of course, is the stunning couplet of Henry Carey (ca. 1687–1743) in the British national anthem: "Confound their politics,/ Frustrate their knavish tricks." Slightly less adroit are the words James Ryder Randall (1839–1908) wrote effervescently for the Maryland state song: "Avenge the patriotic gore/ That flecked the streets of Baltimore."

A far older anthem and a more venerable city were the meditation of Cowper in this hymn's writing: "In that day there shall be a fountain opened to the house of David and to the inhabitants of Jerusalem for sin and for uncleanness" (Zech. 13:1). Cowper had the sense to celebrate the fulfillment of this prophecy on Calvary by giving us a hymn about blood that stirs the blood.

I love thy kingdom, Lord

ST. THOMAS

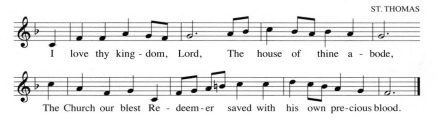

I love thy king-dom, Lord, The house of thine a-bode,

The Church our blest Re-deem-er saved with his own pre-cious blood.

2. For her my tears shall fall;
   For her my prayers ascend;
   To her my cares and toils be given,
   Till toils and cares shall end.

3. Beyond my highest joy
   I prize her heavenly ways,
   Her sweet communion, solemn vows,
   Her hymns of love and praise.

4. Jesus, thou friend divine,
   Our Savior and our King,
   Thy hand from every snare and foe
   Shall great deliverance bring.

5. Sure as thy truth shall last,
   To Sion shall be given
   The brightest glories earth can yield,
   And brighter bliss of heaven.

I LOVE THY KINGDOM, LORD

───────────── ❧ ─────────────

Because *The Psalms of David* as paraphrased by Isaac Watts were in-
complete, a Congregational society in Connecticut commissioned
the president of Yale College, Timothy Dwight (1752–1817), to produce
what was called, fairly enough, *Dwight's Watts*. He published it in 1800,
the year of the death of Cowper, with thirty-three of his own hymns, to
complete the Psalter. It could not have been easy work for him, especially
because of his chronically bad eyesight. The condition may have been
the result of the hard study forced upon him in childhood by an exacting
mother, Mary, the daughter of the redoubtable Puritan preacher Jonathan
Edwards (1703–1757), who defined himself for posterity with his sermon
"Sinners in the Hands of an Angry God." His treatise of 1754, *A Careful
and Strict Enquiry into the Modern Prevailing Notions of the Freedom of Will
Which Is Supposed to Be Essential to Moral Agency, Virtue and Vice*, was
unrelieved in its radical Calvinism, so that Boswell told Johnson that
"the only relief I had was to forget it."

Mary's home tutelage paid off: Dwight entered Yale at the age of thirteen, having already accomplished the first two years of college. Somewhat
more adaptable than his ancestor, Timothy was a successful pastor, farmer,
and chaplain at West Point during the American Revolution, winning
the esteem of George Washington before joining the faculty of Yale. He
cannot be held accountable for his brother Theodore, who promoted the
farcical anti-Catholic screed *Awful Disclosures*, by Maria Monk. Dwight
was, however, evidently grateful for his theological heritage, and his
son Sereno Edwards Dwight (1786–1850) edited his great-grandfather's
works. One of his grandsons, also Timothy Dwight, was president of Yale
from 1886 to 1898.

Handel has been thought by some to have written the tune "St.
Thomas," which fits the architecture of the stanzas brilliantly, but the
composer is more likely Aaron Williams (1731–1776), a Presbyterian
of London who taught music and also did engraving while compiling

hymnbooks for the promotion of song among dissenting congregations. "St. Thomas," which sometimes goes by Williams' own name, was first recorded in 1770, in the fifth edition of his *American Harmony, or Universal Psalmodist*. There he used it for Psalm 48, while here it serves Dwight's allusions to Psalm 137. Absent is the wistfulness of the Babylonian captives, for the New England divines thought they had come out of exile. Also overlooked is the concluding, ninth, verse of the psalm, which choirboys traditionally have sung to great effect when using the silvery settings of Anglican chant.

Brightest and best of the sons of the morning

MORNING STAR

Bright - est and best of the sons of the morn - ing,
Dawn on our dark - ness, and lend us thine aid;
Star of the east, the ho - ri - zon a - dorn - ing,
Guide where our in - fant Re - deem - er is laid.

2. Cold on his cradle the dew-drops are shining,
   Low lies his head with the beasts of the stall;
   Angels adore him in slumber reclining,
   Maker and Monarch and Savior of all.

3. Shall we then yield him, in costly devotion,
   Odors of Edom, and offerings divine,
   Gems of the mountain, and pearls of the ocean;
   Myrrh from the forest, and gold from the mine?

4. Vainly we offer each ample oblation,
   Vainly with gifts would his favor secure;
   Richer by far is the heart's adoration,
   Dearer to God are the prayers of the poor.

5. Brightest and best of the sons of the morning,
   Dawn on our darkness, and lend us thine aid;
   Star of the east, the horizon adoring,
   Guide where our infant Redeemer is laid.

BRIGHTEST AND BEST OF THE SONS OF THE MORNING

———————— ❧ ————————

The brightest and best hymn writer of recent centuries was Reginald Heber (1783–1826). If he has been overlooked as a significant poet in an age of heroic poets, his words suffice as a remarkably generous endowment of pious letters. Of all his matchless poems, this one of happy inspiration is the best. All Epiphany is summed here: haunting, majestic, poignant, and ethereal and domestic.

Heber was elected a Fellow of All Souls upon his Anglican ordination in 1807. At the age of forty, he became second bishop of Calcutta and died three years later. As a bishop of the Established Church, he had canonical oversight of millions of souls, mostly Hindu and Muslim. Only a fraction did he convert, so he may have seemed to have been a shooting star when he died in Trichinopoly of sudden apoplexy. But we have these prayers of his "heart's adoration," and rare is the man who has left such a continuing sermon.

Heber, of Evangelical impetus and dead before ritualism ever scented the breeze, had nonetheless a liturgical sensibility and wrote this specifically for the Feast of the Epiphany. It was included in his posthumous *Hymns, Written and Adapted to the Weekly Church Service of the Year* in 1827. One imagines him singing it as he traversed his vast domain in his long caravan with its large retinue — for which he was occasionally criticized, although such was obligatory to his estate and circumstances. If his domestic arrangements were different from those of Saint Francis Xavier, his selfless ventures were a golden vignette of the best imperial benefactions. He would have sung "Brightest and best" to an old Scottish tune for which he wrote it and which enjoyed a name appropriate for the caravans of Persian Magi or English missionaries: "Wandering Willie." Of the tunes to which it is ordinarily sung today, "Morning Star" conspicuously fits the feel of the season and the text. It was composed in 1892 by James B. Harding (ca. 1859–1911), organist and choirmaster of St. Andrew's, Islington, in London; and although it was first part of a longer anthem, it stands mightily on its own as a hymn, provided it is not sung too slowly.

The opening line, repeated at the end, is probably a conscious conceit alluding to the "morning stars" and "sons of God" in Job 38:7. Literalist detractors from time to time have sniffed some sort of Zoroastrianism in it. Rather, it sings a piety of shimmering beauty, and a man of Heber's churchmanship would have been the first to mock any imputation of idolatry, especially as he wrote in another poem about the heathen who "bows down to wood and stone" and, collaterally then, things in the sky. The present danger in this hymn is its tendency to provoke envy in any poet — that is, most of the literary world — incapable of the imagery, especially in the second and third stanzas.

From Greenland's icy mountains

MISSIONARY HYMN

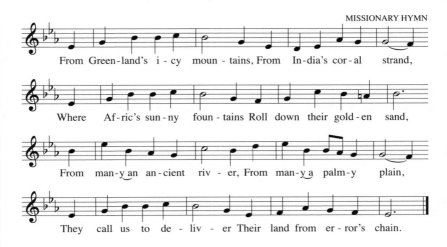

From Green-land's i - cy moun - tains, From In-dia's cor - al strand,

Where Af - ric's sun - ny foun - tains Roll down their gold - en sand,

From man-y an an-cient riv - er, From man-y a palm-y plain,

They call us to de - liv - er Their land from er - ror's chain.

2. Can we, whose souls are lighted
   With wisdom from on high,
   Can we to men benighted
   The lamp of life deny?
   Salvation, O salvation!
   The joyful sound proclaim,
   Till each remotest nation
   Has learnt Messiah's name.

3. Waft, waft, ye winds, his story,
   And you, ye waters, roll,
   Till, like a sea of glory,
   It spreads from poll to poll;
   Till o'er our ransomed nature
   The Lamb for sinners slain,
   Redeemer, King, Creator,
   In bliss returns to reign.

From Greenland's
icy mountains

⚛

In every fifth or sixth breath, Saint Paul seems to make appeals like the one in Romans 15:26: "For it hath pleased them of Macedonia and Achaia to make a certain contribution for the poor saints, which are at Jerusalem." Those who object to mission appeals are mostly those who have failed to give to mission appeals. On the vigil of Pentecost 1819, four years before setting out for Calcutta, Reginald Heber wrote this to be sung the next morning in the parish church of Wrexham, when there was to be read the King's national letter for a missionary collection on behalf of the Society for the Propagation of the Gospel. The idea of a hymn was his father-in-law's. Dean Shipley's daughter would publish a two-volume *Life of Reginald Heber* four years after the death of her husband, whom she accompanied as a missionary.

In the sixteenth century, the Jesuits went to India, where a small Christian presence had existed for eleven hundred years, claiming foundation by the Apostle Thomas. King Frederick IV of Denmark had sent the first Lutheran missionaries to Tranquebar in South India in 1706. Since 1614, Anglican missionaries had traveled there, and in 1701 a royal charter had been granted the Society for the Propagation of the Gospel, to minister to British subjects in foreign parts and to evangelize non-Christian peoples. But the East India Company discouraged them from proselytizing, out of political and commercial interests. In the eighteenth century this became a heated question, especially as Evangelical Anglicans pressed for conversions. Indifferentism was not in their blood. Nonconformist clergymen had freer rein. William Carey (1761–1834), a self-educated shoemaker of Northamptonshire, managed to get to India on a Dutch ship; preached in hundreds of villages; promoted social reforms, including the prohibition of *suttee*; translated the Bible into Bengali and twenty-four other local languages and dialects; and published dictionaries in Sanskrit, Punjabi, Marathi, and Telugu.

From Greenland's icy mountains

Now that the whole world is pagan and ripe for harvest, notably the industrialized West, the valiant accomplishments of these early peripatetics are a goad. There was a time—and it has not passed among the Solons of pluralism—when hymns like Heber's were mocked. Some of its lines had already been dropped when I learned the hymn, for their exasperation cried in a diction remote to armchair evangelists:

What though the spicy breezes/ Blow soft o'er Ceylon's isle;
Though every prospect pleases,/ And only man is vile.

Heber's grave is a monument to the price he paid to ransom souls from a vileness peculiar to no race or place but universal to ignorance. He could have stayed in his leafy parish back home or in his gracefully vaulted chapel at All Souls, but he made a treeless place his parish and died for all the souls there. For him the Gospel was not a rhetorical exercise.

According to a popular account, "Missionary Hymn" was music written in half an hour in 1823 by Lowell Mason while working in a bank in Savannah, Georgia. A young woman, Mary W. Howard, had liked Heber's words printed in the *Evangelical Magazine* in 1821. Not so bold to approach Mason herself, she sent a boy with a request for something to sing it to. The parish in Rosemont, Pennsylvania, sent a team of volunteer surgeons to Kerala in the 1970s when I was rector. The hymn was sung at a service when they were about to leave, and it seemed as vibrant then as it must have seemed in 1819.

Sun of my soul, thou Savior dear

HURSLEY

Sun of my soul, thou Sav - ior dear, It is not night if thou be near; O may no earth - born cloud a - rise To hide thee from thy ser - vant's eyes.

2. When the soft dews of kindly sleep
   My weary eyelids gently steep,
   Be my last thought, how sweet to rest
   For ever on my Savior's breast.

3. Abide with me from morn till eve,
   For without thee I cannot live;
   Abide with me when night is nigh,
   For without thee I dare not die.

4. If some poor wandering child of thine
   Have spurned today the voice divine,
   Now, Lord, the gracious work begin;
   Let him no more lie down in sin.

5. Watch by the sick; enrich the poor
   With blessings from thy boundless store;
   Be every mourner's sleep tonight,
   Like infant's slumbers, pure and light.

6. Come near and bless us when we wake,
   Ere through the world our way we take,
   Till in the ocean of thy love
   We lose ourselves in heaven above.

Sun of my soul,
thou Savior dear

꧋

Long before I had any interest in Newman, John Keble was the saintly
model I revered. It was to me a profound moment when, as an Anglican seminarian, I climbed up into the pulpit in the University Church
of St. Mary the Virgin in Oxford, for it was Keble's pulpit to me, not
Newman's or any of their venerable predecessors. I still have Richmond's
drawing of Keble in my room. And when a friend wanted to give me a
specially cherishable gift, he gave me a first edition of Keble's *Christian
Year*, a collection of poems on the liturgical cycle first published anonymously in 1827, from which this hymn is taken.

Keble contributed to nine of the *Tracts for the Times*, which set up
the standard for the High Churchmen in the Church of England. Tract
89, "On the Mysticism Attributed to the Early Fathers of the Church,"
made him especially suspect among Protestants. While he never became
a Catholic, he promoted Catholic principles in the Established Church
and wrote a defense of the doctrine of the Real Presence in the Eucharist
nine years before he died.

Keble's name would be whispered by undergraduates when he was
spotted on the High Street in the university, which now has a Keble College. As a Catholic Oratorian, Newman would compare him with Saint
Philip Neri: "I can fancy what Keble would have been, if God's will had
been he should be born in another place and age; he was formed on the
same type of extreme hatred of humbug, playfulness, nay, oddity, tender
love for others, and severity, which are the lineaments of Keble." He was
elected Professor of Poetry in Oxford in 1831 and did indeed publish
much verse of varying quality, besides such scholarly undertakings as a
translation of Saint Irenaeus. *The Christian Year* was welcomed with rapture hard to understand apart from what the author himself meant to so
many. Thomas Arnold (1795–1842) said the parts he saw in manuscript

in 1823 were unmatched by anything in the English language. Typical of Keble, who devoted his life to the parish priesthood from 1836 on, he spent the royalties on refurbishing—according to received gothic revival canons—his country parish of Hursley, near Winchester.

It was to Hursley that Newman, as a Catholic, came in September 1865 as Mrs. Keble was dying, and there he had a moving and awkward reunion with his old friend from the Oriel Common Room and Dr. Pusey. At first Keble did not recognize Newman at the gate. It is one of the tragic and compelling scenes of the Victorian age. Keble's hymn is based on Luke 24:29, when the two on the Emmaus Road finally recognize their Lord and would have him stay. All is amber and evening light, and Keble translates it into the tranquil idiom of English evensong. The tune is named for Keble's parish, although it is based on one found in the Empress Maria Theresa's *Katholisches Gesangbuch* in Vienna in 1774.

In 1866, Richard Meux Benson (1824–1915), a former student of Christ Church, founded in Oxford the first Anglican religious order for men, the Society of Saint John the Evangelist, after being inspired by a sermon preached by Keble. When old and infirm, he liked to sit in the garden in his wheelchair singing "Sun of my soul, thou Savior dear." When asked why he did not choose to stay inside by the fire, he replied, "The sun needs no poking."

Holy, Holy, Holy

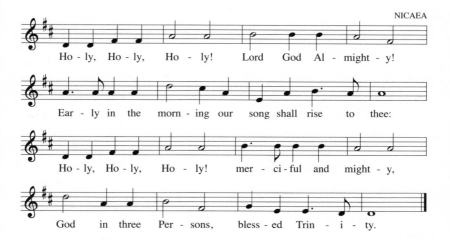

NICAEA

Ho - ly, Ho - ly, Ho - ly! Lord God Al - might - y!

Ear - ly in the morn - ing our song shall rise to thee:

Ho - ly, Ho - ly, Ho - ly! mer - ci - ful and might - y,

God in three Per - sons, bless - ed Trin - i - ty.

2. Holy, Holy, Holy! all the saints adore thee,
   Casting down their golden crowns around the glass sea;
   Cherubim and seraphim falling down before thee,
   Which wert, and art, and everymore shalt be.

3. Holy, Holy, Holy! though the darkness hid thee,
   Though the eye of sinful man thy glory may not see,
   Only thou art holy; there is none beside thee,
   Perfect in power, in love, and purity.

4. Holy, Holy Holy! Lord God Almighty!
   All thy works shall praise thy Name, in earth, and
       sky, and sea;
   Holy, Holy, Holy! Merciful and mighty,
   God in three Persons blessèd Trinity.

HOLY, HOLY, HOLY

W hen I was a boy, there were certain hymns sung so frequently by
my choir that the choirmaster had only to call out their number,
and we were at the ready. Mention of "266," according to the order of
our hymnal, still reminds me of Mr. Vogel at the old upright in the base-
ment of the parish house, calling on us to start up "Holy, Holy, Holy,"
by Reginald Heber. There seemed to me no incongruity in singing that
hymn of angels, rhymed by a missionary to India, next to a billiards room
that boasted a large painting luridly depicting Custer's Last Stand.

The first public record of Heber's trope on the *Sanctus* of the Eucharist
comes in the third edition of the *Selection of Psalms and Hymns for the
Parish Church of Banbury* in 1826, the year of his death in a faraway land.
The singing of the *Sanctus* in the Eucharist is alluded to by both Saint
Clement of Rome in the first century and Origen early in the third. The
hymn is as old as the seraphim (see Isa. 6:3), who are ageless, though
after 1552 the Book of Common Prayer did not include the "*Benedictus
qui vent*" of the Catholic Liturgy.

In 325, the Ecumenical Council of Nicaea affirmed the triumph of
Trinitarianism over Arianism. Its creed, a precursor of what is somewhat
anachronistically called the Nicaean, was a version of the baptismal
creed of the Church in Jerusalem, to which were added four anti-Arian
anathemas. The only two dissenting bishops, Secundus of Ptolemais and
Theonas of Marmarica, were excommunicated and banished. Thus was
achieved a unity of the Church reflective of the unity of the three Divine
Persons. So it was seemly that John Bacchus Dykes should have named
this music of his "Nicaea," especially as Heber had intended the hymn for
Trinity Sunday. The words and music appeared in 1861 in *Hymns Ancient
and Modern*. I used to think it was sung too much, but that is not so in
our days of unsteady courtship between song and theology.

Dykes was a child prodigy at the organ and helped to establish the
University Musical Society at Cambridge. Much of his composing was

Holy, Holy, Holy

done while a precentor at Durham Cathedral, which post he assumed in 1849, the year he was made an honorary doctor of music in the University of Durham; later he was a vicar in the city. Tension between prelates and choral directors in matters of musical taste is not unprecedented; the flagrant animosity between the bishop of Durham, Charles Baring (1807–1879), and Dykes was heightened by the former's distaste for the Catholic sympathies of the latter. The frustrated Dykes found release in setting hymns by Newman and others like him to fine song and playing them within earshot of his bishop. He died on January 22, 1876, in the asylum at Ticehurst in Sussex.

In the instance of "Nicaea," Bishop Baring could hardly object to honoring the Holy Trinity without offending Saint Bede and Saint Cuthbert, near whose bones in his cathedral he would have to lie himself. The bishop's great-grandnephew converted and became the Catholic literary apologist Maurice Baring (1874–1945), pictured with G. K. Chesterton (1874–1936) and Hilaire Belloc (1870–1953) in 1932 in the painting by Sir James Gunn in the National Portrait Gallery.

God that madest earth and heaven

AR HYD Y NOS

God that mad - est earth and heav - en, Dark - ness and light;

Who the day for toil has giv - en, For rest the night,

May thine an - gel - guards de - fend us, Slum - ber sweet thy mer - cy send us,

Ho - ly dreams and hopes at - tend us, This live - long night.

2. Guard us waking, guard us sleeping,
   And when we die,
   May we in thy mighty keeping,
   All peaceful lie:
   And when death to life shall wake us,
   Thou wilt in thy likeness make us;
   Then to reign in glory take us
   With thee on high.

GOD THAT MADEST
EARTH AND HEAVEN

---·❧·---

O n August, 25, 1829, President Andrew Jackson instructed Martin Van Buren, then secretary of state, to begin negotiations for the purchase of Texas. On that same day, Felix Mendelssohn wrote a letter from Llangollen in Wales in which he described the music provided by his host's personal harpist. Going back to Druid roots, the Welsh harp and its sister instrument, the plucked and bowed "crwth," provided accompaniment for the bards. The princes had their court bards, who were both singers and harpists, and well into the nineteenth century did the grander houses have their domestic bards, just as great English and American houses had their resident organists. A year or two before going to Calcutta, Reginald Heber visited a Welsh house where the resident harpist played this tune, "Ar hyd y nos," which goes back long before notice of it in 1794 in *Musical and Poetical Relicks of the Welsh Bards*. The author of that anthology, Edward Jones (1752–1824), born in Merionethshire, became court bard to the prince of Wales. Immediately, Heber wrote what is now the first stanza. It appeared in 1827, the year after his death, as a vespers hymn in his *Hymns, Written and Adapted to the Weekly Church Service of the Year*.

The second stanza is the work of Richard Whately (1787–1863), a polymath at Oxford, whose *Elements of Logic* and *Elements of Rhetoric* had enormous influence. Newman said, "He knew me better than I knew myself," and cited him in his *Apologia* as the singular influence in his own rational development. Of conservative disposition in religious matters, he satirized the early German biblical critics in *Historic Doubts Relative to Napoleon Bonaparte*; it is a nineteenth-century version of Ronald Knox's spoof on skeptical Bible scholars in his essay "proving" that the author of *In Memoriam* was not Tennyson but Queen Victoria. As a strong defender of the doctrine of apostolic succession, Whately's writing on episcopal government of the Church paved the way for the Tractarian movement.

Whately was a most affable and lively character in the Oriel Common Room, although Newman's tutor, Thomas Short, objected to his habit of spitting into the fire. He supported Peel's bill for Catholic Emancipation in Ireland in 1829, and the younger Newman, then fervently anti-Catholic, opposed it. This started a chill between the two, but Newman still thought he might be invited along when Whately was appointed Anglican archbishop of Dublin in 1831. The new prelate worked closely with Peel and others to develop a system of elementary schools for all Ireland. In 1838 he prepared his addition to Heber's hymn and placed it in *Sacred Poetry Adapted to the Understanding of Children and Youth: For the Use of Schools*. The first four lines, of course, rhyme the antiphon for Compline: "Salva nos, Domine, vigilantes, custodi nos dormientes; ut vigilemus cum Christo, et requiescamus in pace."

When Newman became a Catholic, Whately's conservatism ironically put him at odds with his friend again. At Oriel, Newman had written that Whately was "a great talker who endured very readily the silence of his company." His line took on new meaning after his conversion. In the early 1850s, when Newman lived in Dublin as Rector of the Catholic University of Ireland, Whately ignored him as he walked his dogs on St. Stephen's Green.

I praised the earth, in beauty seen

CAREY

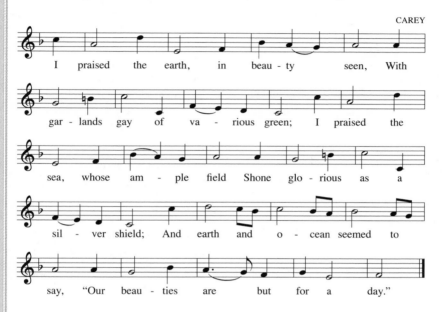

I praised the earth, in beau - ty seen, With gar - lands gay of va - rious green; I praised the sea, whose am - ple field Shone glo - rious as a sil - ver shield; And earth and o - cean seemed to say, "Our beau - ties are but for a day."

2. I praised the sun, whose chariot rolled
   On wheels of amber and of gold;
   I praised the moon, whose softer eye
   Gleamed sweetly through the summer sky;
   And moon and sun in answer said,
   "Our days of light are numberèd."

3. O God, O Good beyond compare
   If thus thy meaner works are fair,
   If thus thy beauties gild the span
   Of transient earth and sinful man,
   How glorious must the mansion be
   Where thy redeemed shall dwell with thee!

I PRAISED THE EARTH,
IN BEAUTY SEEN

Here is an instance of words and music not supporting each other—for they stand sufficiently by themselves—but positively enjoying each other. The transporting music, sublime if things lilting are subliminal, would elevate a lesser text. As for the imagery, it is as transitional from neoclassicism to romanticism as Fra Angelico's Cortona painting of the Annunciation is from Gothicism to the Renaissance. I do not think that is an extravagant comparison. Reginald Heber and Henry Carey (ca. 1687–1743) are figures unfairly neglected by the clichés of the critical canons.

Carey's music first was used for a poem of Joseph Addison on the Twenty-Third Psalm, printed in 1723 in the *Introduction to Psalmody* by John Church (1675–1741), who was choirmaster of Westminster Abbey from 1704 until his death. Carey was probably the illegitimate son of the Marquess of Halifax, George Savile (1633–1695), who was sent by King Charles II to treat with William of Orange and who subsequently provided Dryden's prototype of Jotham in his turgid *Absalom and Achitophel*. Carey was a talented but tormented figure who wrote stage music, poems, and a compilation of his own songs in 1740. This collection, *The Musical Century: In One Hundred English Ballads on Various Subjects and Occasions*, does not include "God Save the King," which his son, George Saville (1743–1807), attributed to him. George was a popular singer who was out to get a pension by trafficking in a claim to the national anthem, but his argument was weak. Not only did his father not mention it among his own songs, but George alleged that his father had written it in response to the Stuart rebellion of 1745, two years after his father's death. It is truer that his father was the author and composer of "Sally in Our Alley."

Heber's hymn sounds more like Addison than Addison does himself in his psalm paraphrases. Heber was even less guilty of the imputation of

I praised the earth, in beauty seen

Deism than was Addison, as the last line of each stanza indicates. The modern version is a very slight alteration of the original as it appeared in 1827 in Heber's *Hymns, Written and Adapted to the Weekly Church Service of the Year*. Heber, in the manner of his time, had a thoroughly classical education and lagged not far behind his half-brother Richard (1773–1833), a classical scholar and editor of classical Latin texts. Reginald's second stanza alludes more naturally than Alexander Pope might to the sun god Apollo with lighted tiara, who fed ambrosia to his horses and then rolled through the heavens in a chariot of gold with chrysolite wheels.

This is a hymn of bright dappled days, to be sung in the mornings of country parishes. Anyone from Dame Julian of Norwich to Miss Marple would fit in. But as the last line of each stanza reminds, in the meadows is the sound of a scythe reaping, and Heber's sun is not so dazzling that it hides the reaper or the sound of his mortal sweep.

Heber's family had some gene that passes on poetry. He was the great-uncle of the exotic Sitwells: Edith, Osbert, and Sacheverell. Dame Edith undid what was classical in Heber by her affectation of the Gothic. Her book of 1933, *The English Eccentrics*, was not exhaustive; at least it did not include her father, Sir George Reresby Sitwell, who spent much of his life pursuing the history of the spoon.

Praise my soul, the King of Heaven

LAUDA ANIMA

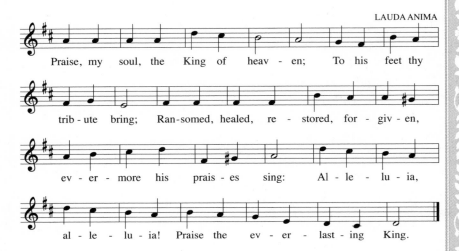

Praise, my soul, the King of heav - en; To his feet thy trib - ute bring; Ran-somed, healed, re - stored, for - giv - en, ev - er - more his prais - es sing: Al - le - lu - ia, al - le - lu - ia! Praise the ev - er - last - ing King.

2. Praise him for his grace and favor
   To our fathers in distress;
   Praise him still, the same as ever,
   Slow to chide, and swift to bless:
   Alleluia, alleluia!
   Glorious in his faithfulness.

3. Father-like he tends and spares us;
   Well our feeble frame he knows;
   In his hand he gently bears us,
   Rescues us from all our foes.
   Alleluia, alleluia!
   Widely yet his mercy flows.

4. Angels, help us to adore him;
   Ye behold him face to face;
   Sun and moon, bow down before him,
   Dwellers all in time and space.
   Alleluia, alleluia!
   Praise with us the God of grace.

PRAISE MY SOUL, THE KING OF HEAVEN

✄

This variation on Psalm 103 by Henry Francis Lyte (1793–1847) has much in spirit, but little in actual transcription, of the praise that begins, in the Psalter of the *Great Bible*: "Bless the Lord, O my soul: and all that is within me, bless his holy name." Lyte was a thorough Celt, born in Scotland and educated in Ireland at the Royal School of Enniskillen and Trinity College, Dublin. In the hints of neurasthenia about his temperament, he resembled Gerard Manley Hopkins (1844–1889), who spent unhappy days in Dublin and few of his days anyplace else for very long. As the Society of Jesus showed remarkable patience with Hopkins, so did the Church of England regularly try to find some suitable sinecure for Lyte, who was ordained in 1815 and who settled, after various unsuccessful pastoral adventures, as perpetual curate of a fishing village of Devonshire. The fisherfolk of Lower Brixham failed to hide their lack of interest in Lyte's enthusiasm for ancient etymology and classical metrics. Having the financial resources to remove to the sort of fishing village he preferred, Lyte went to France and died in Nice.

Psalm 103 is introduced as "A Psalm of David" or, in the Douai-Rheims Bible, "For David himself," setting a royal stamp on the original text, which has not been lost. Lyte's paraphrase from the House of David, itself altered modestly by various editors since its first use in the *Spirit of the Psalms* in 1826, has become a standard of ceremonies in the House of Windsor. Its brilliant opening burst accompanied the entrance procession of the Princess Elizabeth at her wedding in Westminster Abbey in 1947, elevating the gray mood of postwar England, rationed and socialized.

The music, published in 1869, was written specifically for Lyte's verses by John Goss (1800–1880), professor of harmony in the Royal Academy of Music for forty-seven years. Knighted by Queen Victoria and made an honorary doctor of music by the University of Cambridge, he died covered with laurels, all of this commemorated by a cenotaph in the crypt of St. Paul's Cathedral, where he was organist. He was taught to play the organ by his father, a parish organist of Portsmouth. In 1811, his father's brother was able to get his nephew a placement as chorister in the Chapel Royal. This uncle was celebrated in London as a countertenor, or male alto. The falsetto voice, still sought after in the Regency period, requires special training and is not to be confused with the artificial male soprano or alto, the castrato, perhaps the most famous of whom was the Spanish court singer for Philip V, Carlo Broschi Farinelli (1705–1782). Early in the seventeenth century, castrati even replaced falsettists in the Sistine Chapel. As late as 1829 the eunuch Giovanni Battista Velluti sang in concert in London.

Young Goss came under the tutelage of Thomas Attwood (1765–1838), who would himself serve as a professor in the Royal Academy when it was founded in 1823, and thus Goss continued a musical apostolic succession from Mozart, who had taught Attwood. When George IV was an unfettered prince of Wales, he had had enough sense and philanthropy to send Attwood to study in Vienna under the Master. Attwood became an adept courtier and played for the king in the new exotic Royal Pavilion in Brighton. But he was no dilettante. It was largely through his influence that Mendelssohn attained public attention. Attwood is buried directly under the organ in St. Paul's Cathedral.

Abide with me

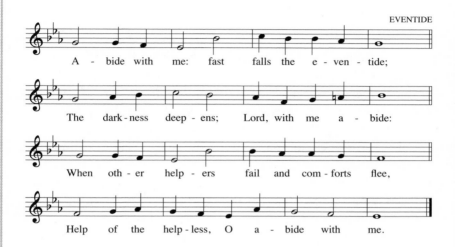

EVENTIDE

A - bide with me: fast falls the e - ven - tide;

The dark - ness deep - ens; Lord, with me a - bide:

When oth - er help - ers fail and com - forts flee,

Help of the help - less, O a - bide with me.

2. Swift to its close ebbs out life's little day,
   Earth's joys grow dim, its glories pass away,
   Change and decay in all around I see;
   O thou who changest not, abide with me.

3. I need thy presence every passing hour;
   What but thy grace can foil the tempter's power?
   Who, like thyself, my guide and stay can be?
   Through cloud and sunshine, Lord, abide with me.

4. I fear no foe, with thee at hand to bless;
   Ills have no weight, and tears no bitterness.
   Where is death's sting? where, grave, thy victory?
   I triumph still, if thou abide with me.

5. Hold thou thy cross before my closing eyes;
   Shine through the gloom, and point me to the skies;
   Heaven's morning breaks, and earth's vain shadows flee:
   In life, in death, O Lord, abide with me.

ABIDE WITH ME

Inconsistencies in oral tradition tend to certify the essential whole. Very clearly, for example, disputed accounts of when Henry Francis Lyte wrote "Abide with me" make certain that he did write it, and that he wrote it in some nostalgic valediction. In a letter of August 25, 1847, he refers to it as his "latest effusion"; and as he died three months later, it would have been an intimation of his own death. The common belief that it originated as such is probably incorrect. A family tradition of Sir Francis LeHunte, corroborated by a manuscript of the text, maintains that Lyte wrote it after leaving the deathbed of Sir Francis's invalid brother, William Augustus LeHunte, who pleaded "abide with me" at their parting. That would place the composition in 1820, and Lyte most likely recalled the hymn as his own death approached. Three stanzas have long been omitted, and one of them anticipates a little of the third stanza of Henry William Baker's paraphrase of Psalm 23:

> Thou on my head in early youth didst smile;
> And, though rebellious and perverse meanwhile,
> Thou has not left me, oft as I left thee;
> On to the close, O Lord, abide with me!

Lyte's own music for the hymn, which was published in September 1847, seems to have been approved by few. The universally beloved "Eventide" was written by William Henry Monk in 1861, although this involves another contested tradition: Mrs. Monk claimed after his death that her husband had written it while they watched a sunset, while others remembered that his poetry came to him in the more prosaic circumstance of a committee meeting during the editing of *Hymns Ancient and Modern*. There are worse ways to dawdle during such meetings.

Mahatma Gandhi's favorite hymn was Newman's "Lead, kindly Light," and in the fiftieth year of Indian independence, Mother Teresa's favorite hymn, "Abide with me," was sung at her funeral in Calcutta during the liturgical absolution of the body. It happened to be the 150th anniversary of its first printing. Although Newman held that "to be alive is to change and to be perfect is to have changed often," his Christian Platonism would have admired the "change and decay" in counterpoint to "thou who changest not" as addressed by Lyte *sub specie aeternitatis*. Like the canticles in Bernard of Cluny's *De Contemptu Mundi*, this could easily form a chain with Keble's "Sun of my soul" and Ellerton's "The day thou gavest."

Lead, kindly Light

LUX BENIGNA

Lead, kind-ly Light, a - mid the en - circ - ling gloom, Lead thou me
on; The night is dark, and I am far from home; Lead thou me
on; Keep thou my feet; I do not ask to see
The dis - tant scene; one step e - nough for me.

2. I was not ever thus, nor prayed that thou
Shouldst lead me on;
I loved to choose and see my path; but now
Lead thou me on.
I loved the garish day, and, spite of fears,
Pride ruled my will: remember not past years.

3. So long thy power hath blest me, sure it still
Will lead me on
O'er moor and fen, o'er crag and torrent, till
The night is gone;
And with the morn those angel faces smile
Which I have loved long since, and lost awhile.

LEAD, KINDLY LIGHT

After a lecture I had given in Tennessee, I met a woman whose father as a boy, along with his classmates at the Birmingham Oratory School in England, had called their founder, John Henry Cardinal Newman, "Jack" behind his back. Hilaire Belloc records somewhere that he did the same. Newman was very human, and, among his other human acts, he contracted fever while on a Mediterranean holiday in 1833. It happened after he had left the company of his friend Hurrell Froude and Froude's father and was alone in the Sicilian village of Castro Giovanni. The fever lasted three weeks. Then he boarded an orange boat for Marseilles and was becalmed in the Straits of Bonifacio. "When I was most qualmish I solaced myself with verse-making." Among the more than eighty verses that issued was "The Pillar of the Cloud," widely known as "Lead, kindly Light." Light to the feverish is garish. Newman's whole life seemed that way in such a moment, particularly so since he had been morally rattled by his introduction to Latin culture lived alive, and not as his neoclassical mind had met its mellow moons and mute thunder in the iambics of Virgil and Cicero. Florid Rome of his fervid tour was "corrupt and under a curse." Yet it stayed in his mind even when his mind came to rights. A dozen years before his conversion to the Catholicism of Rome, his words were burdened with prophecy: the garish day would yield to a kindlier light once one step yielded to another in trust of finding the way.

In a letter of 1874, Newman declines to explain what he had written long before, for no author should be held accountable for what he said "when home-sick, or seasick, or in any other way sensitive or excited." Coleridge never said that of his poetry written under the influence of opium, but then he attained only to Xanadu and not heaven. So Newman's "angel faces" still challenge interpretation. They are, I think, poetic diction, instead of theology, for the "angelic" human friends, whose pictures stayed on his mantels and even surrounded his altar.

Poetry was not Newman's chief claim to laurels. In the 1920s Professor Joseph Reilly sniffingly faulted the poem for contradictory images and found it distinguished for the uniquely popular success of its technical unsuccess. Newman humbly, if extravagantly, attributed his hymn's popularity to the tune written thirty-two years later by the Anglican clergyman of High Church sympathies John Bacchus Dykes (1823–1876). Dean Church and J. E. T. Street made a gift of a "fiddle" in 1865, which brought Newman's stiff fingers back to his beloved form of relaxation. Heaven performed in the Oratory School orchestra. The very probable thought of him playing Dykes' tune is one of the most palpably Victorian scenes imaginable. The hymn's appeal remains, and I recall talking about it in the longest conversation I ever had with Cardinal Cooke, two days before he ordained me.

In the crisis of his Sicilian fever, Newman kept muttering, "I have not sinned against the light." The line is freighted with common psychology, Platonism, and mystical religion, but most certain is his life itself as a hymn of grace, and all the accomplishments of his long life are variations on that theme. Back in Oxford, one month after he wrote "Lead, kindly Light," he heard John Keble (1792–1866), Professor of Poetry, preach the Assize Sermon on "National Apostasy" and called that the start of the Oxford movement.

Round the Lord in glory seated

MOULTRIE

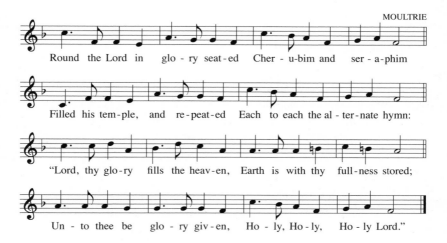

Round the Lord in glo-ry seat-ed Cher-u-bim and ser-a-phim

Filled his tem-ple, and re-peat-ed Each to each the al-ter-nate hymn:

"Lord, thy glo-ry fills the heav-en, Earth is with thy full-ness stored;

Un-to thee be glo-ry giv-en, Ho-ly, Ho-ly, Ho-ly Lord."

2. Heaven is still with glory ringing,
Earth takes up the angels' cry,
"Holy, Holy, Holy," singing,
"Lord of hosts, the Lord Most High."
With his seraph train before him,
With his holy Church below,
Thus unite we to adore him,
Bid we thus our anthem flow:

3. "Lord, thy glory fills the heaven,
Earth is with thy fullness stored;
Unto thee be glory given,
Holy, Holy, Holy Lord."
Thus thy glorious Name confessing,
With thine angel hosts we cry,
"Holy, Holy, Holy," blessing
Thee, the Lord of hosts Most High.

ROUND THE LORD
IN GLORY SEATED

⁒

Cambridge and Oxford conspire to produce this florid praise of the
Thrice-Holy. The composer, Gerard Francis Cobb (1838–1904), was
presented for the M.A. by Trinity College in Cambridge, and the author,
Richard Mant (1776–1848), belonged to Trinity College in Oxford. He
actually anticipated by a generation Newman's career from Trinity to a
fellowship in Oriel College.

All Byzantine rites include the "Trisagion" chant: "Holy God, Holy
and Mighty, Holy and immortal, have mercy on us." It passed through
the Gallican Rite of the tenth century to the Roman rite by the twelfth
century and is retained in the Solemn Reproaches of Good Friday. Omis-
sion of the venerable Reproaches constitutes one of the most depraved
vandalizations of the Church's Liturgy. Serving an office of preservation
not unlike John Mason Neale, Richard Mant went to the sources of
chants like this and thus revived in his own denomination many liturgical treasures that have become lost by profligacy within the Catholic
Church herself. This hymn, in fact a trope on the "Trisagion," is typical
of Mant's scholarship, which usually surpassed his poetry, though this
hymn is creditable by any measure. Mant coauthored a commentary on
the Bible in 1814, an annotation of the *Book of Common Prayer* in 1820,
and a *History of the Church of Ireland* in 1840. He was consecrated Anglican
bishop of Killaloe and Kilfenoragh in 1820 and three years later became
bishop of Down and Connor. This Protestant prelate in 1837 published
*Ancient Hymns from the Roman Breviary . . . to Which Are Added Original
Hymns*, and it is in this volume that "Round the Lord in glory seated" first
appears. Bishop Mant preceded by only a few years the hymnography of
Cecil Frances Alexander, whose interests were similar if less specialized.

Although the hymn was published a year before the birth of Cobb,
its author would probably have approved of its use, with perhaps slight

Round the Lord in glory seated

reservations about its lushness. Cobb's affinity for choral anthems tending toward the romantic is evident in this specimen of high Victoriana. It can indeed be deformed by organists overdoing the swells, but its grandeur is a vivid memory to this writer, and it can have similar effect if sung at a stately pace but not too slowly. Bishop Mant may have had graver reservations about Cobb's two principal interests outside music: the promotion of unity between the Roman Catholic and Anglican Churches and the promotion of bicycling. While Cobb failed in the former, he became president of the National Cyclists' Union in 1878.

Jesus, tender Shepherd, hear me

BROCKLESBURY

Je-sus, ten-der Shep-herd, hear me; Bless thy lit-tle lamb to-night:

Through the dark-ness be thou near me, Keep me safe till morn-ing light.

2. All this day thy hand has led me,
   And I thank thee for thy care;
   Thou hast warmed me, clothed, and fed me;
   Listen to my evening prayer.

3. Let my sins be all forgiven;
   Bless the friends I love so well:
   Take us all at last to heaven,
   Happy there with thee to dwell.

Jesus, tender
Shepherd, hear me

—————————— ❧ ——————————

There is everything childlike and nothing childish about this piece, and that has to be credited in part at least to the gentle goodness of the two women who died so young after bequeathing it to the literature of hymnody. Mary Lundie Duncan, a Scotswoman born in 1814 in Kelso, near the birthplace of Henry Francis Lyte, died of a fever at the age of thirty-six. She wrote these words, and many like them, for her two children. Born in 1830, Charlotte Alington Barnard was an Englishwoman who wrote both music, including more than a hundred ballads, and two volumes of poetry, before dying in her thirty-ninth year. Her tune bears the name of Brocklesbury, her village near Dover.

"Evening Prayer" is another tune used with this hymn. Although it has a distinguished lineage, being an arrangement by the great Victorian John Stainer of opening bars from Beethoven's Andante in F, Barnard's tune is the one I and so many others grew up with in America, and in this instance the claims of the nursery take precedence over mature critics. The assertion that she wrote more than a hundred ballads is not exaggerated, given the popularity of ballads in their nineteenth-century revival. The ballad as a mannered form has various definitions and a very long and ambiguous history extending to well before the eleventh century. Dr. Johnson scorned many of them as unworthy doggerel, but their narratives could be politically potent, especially when set to catchy music. In the seventeenth century, Puritan and Cavalier governments alike regulated them and required licensing for ballad singers.

In the nineteenth century, a more erudite and less discursive *ballade* in France revived the troubadour tradition; but in England that century was conspicuous for the sentimentality of "drawing room ballads." Charlotte Barnard's best-known ballad continues to be the pleasantly lachrymose "Come Back to Erin," which joins the company of so many beloved song tributes to Ireland not by Irishmen. What is called the "Common Meter" in hymnody has sources in the typical ballad structure, which, as in this hymn, consists in stanzas of four alternately rhyming lines, the first and third having four measures, the second and fourth having three, with each measure containing a doubled rhythm.

Duncan's text, like Barnard's music, is just the right sentiment for young children: tender but neither condescending nor trivial. They should not be beneath anyone who wants to be fit for the Kingdom of heaven. The author said these words to her children in the Manse in Cleish in Kinross-shire, where she lived as the wife of the local minister, William Wallace Duncan, whom she married in 1836. As she wrote most of her poetry by the year before her death, they were meant for those three years old and younger. We have them today only because Mary's mother collected them in a memoir in 1841. The image of the Good Shepherd is, on the other hand, among the oldest we have of the Lord in the art of the catacombs. Before I was old enough to be a choirboy, my favorite spot in Sunday School was seated beneath an engraving of the Good Shepherd, and I very much liked singing this pastoral hymn in a not very bucolic voice.

Nearer, my God, to thee

BETHANY

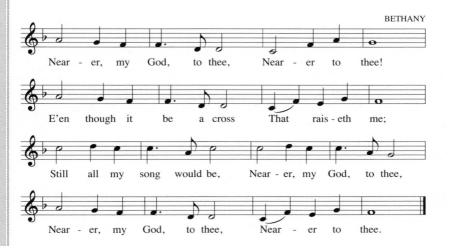

Near - er, my God, to thee, Near - er to thee!

E'en though it be a cross That rais - eth me;

Still all my song would be, Near - er, my God, to thee,

Near - er, my God, to thee, Near - er to thee.

2. Though like the wanderer,
   The sun gone down,
   Darkness be over me,
   My rest a stone;
   Yet in my dreams I'd be
   Nearer, my God, to thee,
   Nearer, my God, to thee,
   Nearer to thee.

3. There let the way appear
   Steps unto heaven;
   All that thou sendest me
   In mercy given;
   Angels to beckon me
   Nearer, my God, to thee,
   Nearer, my God, to thee,
   Nearer to thee.

4. Then, with my waking thoughts
   Bright with thy praise,
   Out of my stony griefs,
   Bethel I'll raise;
   So by my woes to be
   Nearer, my God, to thee,
   Nearer, my God, to thee,
   Nearer to thee.

5. Or if on joyful wing,
   Cleaving the sky,
   Sun, moon, and stars forgot,
   Upwards I fly,
   Still all my song shall be,
   Nearer, my God, to thee,
   Nearer, my God, to thee,
   Nearer to thee.

NEARER, MY GOD, TO THEE

---- ❧ ----

Eliza Flower (1803–1846) wrote the music to which this poem by her sister Sarah Flower Adams (1805–1848) first was sung. It has accompanied countless solemn ceremonies, civic and parochial, perhaps more than almost any other hymn in the English-speaking world. As a popular hymn for special commemorations and memorial rites, it forms a trio with "O God, our help in ages past" (1719) and "Rock of ages" (1776). The sisters were born in Harlow, Essex, their father being a respected political writer, Benjamin Flower, editor of the *Cambridge Intelligencer* and respected for his literary talent at least as much as for his political acumen. Both daughters seem to have inherited the artistic touch and shared as well the principles of Unitarianism.

As a noncredal heresy that subscribes simply to the unipersonality of God, Unitarianism goes back to figures like Martin Cellarius (1499–1564). It did not become a discernible sect in England until an Anglican clergyman, Theophilus Lindsey (1723–1808), a friend of the discoverer of oxygen, the radical theologian Joseph Priestley (1733–1804), broke from the Church of England in 1773, wrote an *Apology on Resigning the Vicarage of Catterick*, and established in London the Essex Chapel in 1774. A later congregation, that of the South Place Chapel, was the object of Eliza's musical attentions.

Sarah, who married the inventor William Bridges Adams in 1834, revised and wrote numerous hymns to meet the reduced theological needs of the Unitarians; these were published (1840–1841) by the Southgate Religious Society. Since Unitarianism rejects doctrines of the Fall of man, the divinity of Christ, atonement, and eternal punishment, it has not been a fountainhead of mystical verse. It has not failed, of course, to produce literary figures of the stature of William Ellery Channing (1780–1842) and Ralph Waldo Emerson (1803–1882). Sarah's religious epic poem *Vivia Perpetua* and her shaky catechism *The Flock at the Fountain* did not gain her a place in their pantheon—if Unitarians permit that term. But her hymn has etched her a place in the annals. It has undergone many revisions to give it a more Christian expression, but it maintains its original allusion to Jacob's Ladder (Gen. 28). Sarah died in London on the day President Polk signed a bill prohibiting slavery in the Oregon Territory, an act that would have met with her approval.

The durability of the hymn owes much to Lowell Mason, who wrote its splendid tune "Bethany," giving it special impetus in the United States. He claimed to have received the melody for the irregular meter while going to sleep and remembered it in the morning. A plausible theory holds that he had a subconscious recollection of a very similar melody, a Scottish air popularized by the Baroness Nairne (1766–1845). Lady Carolina was a sort of female Robert Burns, writing poetry for old Scottish folk tunes. These include "Lass o' Gowrie," "Charlie Is My Darling," "Laird o' Cockpen," and the undying "Will Ye No Come Back Again?," which still has an emotive effect on those who attend the Stuart cause.

The King of love my shepherd is

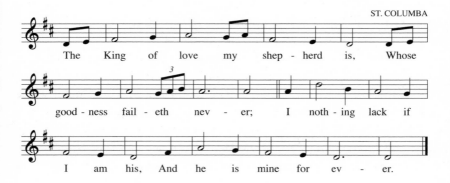

ST. COLUMBA

The King of love my shep - herd is, Whose good - ness fail - eth nev - er; I noth - ing lack if I am his, And he is mine for ev - er.

2. Where streams of living water flow,
   My ransomed soul he leadeth,
   And where the verdant pastures grow,
   With food celestial feedeth.

3. Perverse and foolish oft I strayed,
   But yet in love he sought me,
   And on his shoulder gently laid,
   And home, rejoicing, brought me.

4. In death's dark vale I fear no ill
   With thee, dear Lord, beside me;
   Thy rod and staff my comfort still,
   Thy cross before to guide me.

5. Thou spread'st a table in my sight;
   Thy unction grace bestoweth;
   And O what transport of delight
   From thy pure chalice floweth!

6. And so through all the length of days
   Thy goodness faileth never:
   Good Shepherd, may I sing thy praise
   Within thy house for ever.

THE KING OF LOVE
MY SHEPHERD IS

---- ❧ ----

Although John Bacchus Dykes wrote a sturdy tune to this ethereal paraphrase of Psalm 23, the old Irish air now called "St. Columba" has attained new popularity with it. Its opening notes are similar to another old air, "Soggarth Seamus O'Fin." Of unknown date, it was saved for posterity by the Anglo-Irish painter and violinist of Dublin George Petrie (1789–1866). Petrie was an Anglican who, like John Pentland Mahaffy (1838–1919), provost of Trinity College in Dublin, pioneered Celtic antiquarianism. It is to Petrie that we owe our information about the round towers of the Irish landscape. Petrie also preserved for us the gorgeous "Londonderry Air," based on another ancient tune of anonymous authorship. He received it from a woman of Limavady, Jane Ross, who wrote down folk tunes of Ireland the way Lady Nairne did for Scotland. The first text written for it was by an Anglo-Irish inspector of schools, Arthur Percival Graves (1846–1931). The immortal words of "Danny Boy" were written by the English lawyer Frederic Edward Weatherly (1848–1929), who also wrote "Roses of Picardy."

In 1902 Charles Villiers Stanford included "St. Columba" in his important *Complete Collection of Irish Music as Noted by George Petrie*. Like Stanford, a giant both in the revival of Irish folk music and in the extension of Anglican choral music, the author of the words was a product of Cambridge University. In 1844 Henry William Baker graduated from Trinity College, where Stanford was appointed organist in 1873. An Anglican vicar of Herefordshire, he also was a baronet, inheriting the title from his father, Admiral Sir Henry Loraine Baker. The organist of Baker's parish in Monkland, John Bernard Wilkes was the arranger of the Moravian tune for Milton's hymn "Let us with a gladsome mind." Baker was also a distinguished Latinist, translating many old Catholic hymns and writing many of his own. He was a principal influence behind the book that was of central importance in promoting High Anglicanism: *Hymns Ancient and Modern*. His paraphrase of Psalm 23, which was printed in 1874, is based on an equally beautiful version by that beautiful soul George Herbert that begins:

> The God of love my shepherd is
> And he that doth me feed;
> While he is mine, and I am his,
> What can I want or need?

As paraphrases go, it marks a wide step forward from the frequent clumsiness of the earlier metrical psalms. Its widespread use now among Roman Catholics would have pleased both Herbert and Baker, as well as, we may safely assume, King David.

Saint Peter wrote: "For you were straying like sheep, but have now returned to the shepherd and guardian of your souls" (1 Pet. 2:25). The voice is redolent with Christ's command: "Feed my sheep" (see John 21:15–17). As that Resurrection dialogue atoned for Peter's threefold denial, it has to strike a tender chord in all pastors: "Perverse and foolish oft I strayed, But yet in love he sought me."

I think when I read that sweet story of old

SALAMIS

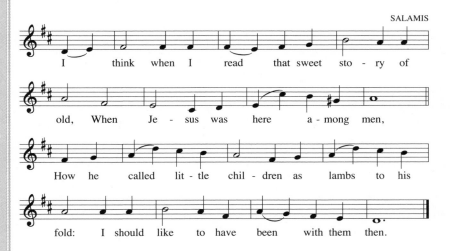

I think when I read that sweet sto - ry of old, When Je - sus was here a - mong men, How he called lit - tle chil - dren as lambs to his fold: I should like to have been with them then.

2. I wish that his hands had been placed on my head,
   That his arms had been thrown around me,
   And that I might have seen his kind look when he said
   "Let the little ones come unto me."

3. Yet still to his presence in prayer I may go,
   And know that I share in his love;
   And if I thus earnestly serve him below,
   I shall see him and serve him above.

I THINK WHEN I READ THAT
SWEET STORY OF OLD

※

Two signal endeavors of the Evangelical revival in the Church of England were the British and Foreign Bible Society and the Sunday School Union. The first was established in 1794 as a pan-Protestant effort, when ecumenism was rare. Although half of the Society's directors were Anglican, attempts to include the *Book of Common Prayer* with the Bible were resisted, as were the Baptist influences of the missionary William Carey. The Society eventually translated the Bible into every known tongue. Sunday Schools were begun in 1780 by the Gloucester philanthropist Robert Raikes (1735–1810) to help remedy ravages of the Industrial Revolution: widespread illiteracy and ignorance of religion. The movement was not without opposition from strict Evangelicals, who suspected a violation of the Sabbath, and from mill owners and others who profited from child labor. In the 1790s the latter sniffed in the prospect of universal education the scent of Girondist revolution. Demagogues cited what was happening in France, as though Raikes's progressive use of phonetics and other advanced educational methods would lead to a Reign of Terror.

Ironically, like the Methodist movement, the Sunday Schools helped to smother the sparks of social anarchy. One friend of Raikes's ideals was Hannah More (1745–1833), who, like the amateur musicologist Charles Burney, enjoyed an eclectic circle of friends, including Joshua Reynolds, David Garrick, and Samuel Johnson. Methodist in tendency, she remained an Anglican and received the support of some of the episcopate. She insisted that the parish schools provide instruction in useful trades, such as spinning. In this, Hannah More was an Anglo-Saxon version of the magnificent Saint John Bosco and his Salesians, whose labors did much to undercut the exploitation of misery by the Garibaldini. Her contemporary in the new United States was Saint Elizabeth Ann Seton.

I think when I read that sweet story of old

The father of Jemima Thompson Luke (1813–1906) was a patron of the Bible Society and the Sunday School Union. His scheme for "floating chapels" for seamen was so picturesquely popular that it spread to New York, where a "floating chapel" in the harbor launched, as it were, the famous Seamen's Church Institute. Jemima was a serious pedagogue herself and was increasingly so after her marriage to a Congregationalist minister, Samuel Luke, in 1843. Two years earlier, on a visit to a Sunday School on Gray's Inn Road, London, she was enchanted by a "Greek air" of unknown origin that the children were singing. A short while later, while alone in a stagecoach, she wrote two of these stanzas in the space of an hour on the back of an envelope. The third was added later as an evangelistic touch. The "Greek" tune, since called "Salamis" and sometimes "Athens," for which Miss Thompson wrote the words was printed with the text in the same year, 1841, in the *Sunday School Teacher's Magazine*. It was a favorite in the Sunday School of my youth and was frequently illustrated in the children's songbooks with pictures of Christ surrounded by all races and clans, usually with a representative of my own denomination on His knee. The hymn, like all solid hymns for children, is really for adults serious about the interior life. The Catholic child will want to be taught that the prayer of access to our Lord's presence, referred to in the third stanza, is most perfectly realized in the Holy Eucharist.

All things bright and beautiful

ROYAL OAK

All things bright and beau-ti-ful, All crea-tures great and small,

All things wise and won-der-ful, The Lord God made them all.

Each lit-tle flow'r that o-pens, Each lit-tle bird that sings,

He made their glow-ing co-lors, He made their ti-ny wings.

2. The purple-headed mountain,
   The river running by,
   The sunset, and the morning
   That brightens up the sky. *Refrain*

3. The cold wind in the winter,
   The pleasant summer sun,
   The ripe fruits in the garden,
   God made them every one. *Refrain*

4. He gave us eyes to see them,
   And lips that we might tell
   How great is God Almighty,
   Who has made all things well. *Refrain*

ALL THINGS BRIGHT
AND BEAUTIFUL

Cecil Frances Alexander, wife of the Anglican archbishop of Armagh, William Alexander (1824–1911), wrote, in addition to the paraphrase of the words to "St. Patrick's Breastplate," well over four hundred of her own hymns. This, one of her many children's songs, was a favorite of my early years when I was obliged to copy it out in the still unfinished project of learning decent handwriting. These classes in the Palmer method of penmanship were in a public grammar school, when reference to God's handiwork was not yet considered subversive of constitutional principles.

Mrs. Alexander is unfortunately notorious for her confidence in vassalage expressed in the original third stanza, now absent from most versions:

> The rich man in his castle,
> The poor man at his gate,
> God made them high and lowly
> And ordered their estate.

But if there was a bit of dottiness in her obliviousness to circumstances less halcyon than her own, she seems to have had a widely generous heart, and part of her point, after all, was not so much how God made men but that He did make them. Her husband, as Protestant Primate of All Ireland, was in fact a good friend of Michael Cardinal Logue of Armagh and Catholic Primate of All Ireland (1840–1924), and the two shared an interest in Saint Augustine and the Latin classics. On one occasion, the Marchioness of Aberdeen, wife of the viceroy of Ireland, thought it discreet not to tell Dr. Alexander that she was going to pay a protocol visit to the popish claimant to his See. When she called on the cardinal, she found Mrs. Alexander playing his hostess and pouring tea. The improbability of the scene is uniquely Irish; the creaturely delight of the song should be a gift to children everywhere. And not only children: everyone may join in the refrain repeated after each stanza, if they intend to be childlike enough to inherit the Kingdom of heaven, where God is King and needs no lord lieutenants and has no rivals.

In 1915 the words were matched to a supposedly seventeenth-century English tune by Martin Shaw (1875–1958). Martin and his brother Geoffrey (1879–1943) promoted the revival of interest in Purcell and sought to prune English church music of the excesses of lesser romantic exercises. There is an element of greatness in bending down to hand this tune to young voices without condescension.

Once in royal David's city

IRBY

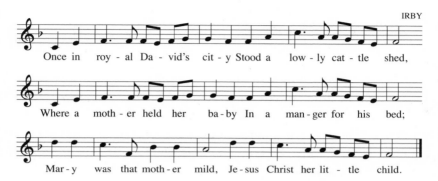

Once in roy - al Da - vid's cit - y Stood a low - ly cat - tle shed,

Where a moth - er held her ba - by In a man - ger for his bed;

Mar - y was that moth - er mild, Je - sus Christ her lit - tle child.

2. He came down to earth from
   heaven,
   Who is God and Lord of all,
   And His shelter was a stable,
   And His cradle was a stall;
   With the poor, and mean, and
   lowly,
   Lived on earth our Savior holy.

3. And through all His wondrous
   childhood
   He would honor and obey,
   Love and watch the lowly maiden,
   In whose gentle arms He lay:
   Christian children all must be
   Mild, obedient, good as He.

4. For he is our childhood's pattern;
   Day by day, like us He grew;
   He was little, weak and helpless,
   Tears and smiles like us He knew;
   And He feeleth for our sadness,
   And He shareth in our gladness.

5. And our eyes at last shall see Him,
   Through His own redeeming love;
   For that Child so dear and gentle
   Is our Lord in heaven above,
   And He leads His children on
   To the place where He is gone.

6. Not in that poor lowly stable,
   With the oxen standing by,
   We shall see Him; but in heaven,
   Set at God's right hand on high;
   Where like stars His children
   crowned
   All in white shall wait around.

ONCE IN ROYAL
DAVID'S CITY

It is a Catholic liturgical custom to genuflect at the *Incarnatus est* when the Creed is recited on the feast of the Nativity of Our Lord. Such was not a practice in the Church of Ireland when the husband of Cecil Frances Alexander was Protestant archbishop of Armagh. Her personal votive to the Incarnation was this fine poem, which was included in her *Hymns for Little Children* in 1848, two years before she married the future Protestant Primate of All Ireland. Indeed, she specifically intended it as a catechesis on the third article of the Apostles' Creed: "who was conceived by the Holy Ghost, born of the Virgin Mary," just as her hymn "All things bright and beautiful" was on the second article, "Maker of heaven and earth."

One would have difficulty finding verse for children more respectful of them and so congenial without being maudlin. Here sentiment proves itself without lapsing into manipulative sentimentalism. The hymn sung today, with increasing affection, is exactly as Mrs. Alexander wrote it. Many have first encountered it through recordings of the Festival of Lessons and Carols sung in King's College Chapel in Cambridge. That service is in fact a modern invention, largely the inspiration of the Reverend Wilfred Knox, when he was dean of the chapel. He was a brother of Monsignor Ronald Knox and shared many of his literary gifts. Wilfred remained an Anglican and founded the Oratory of the Good Shepherd, an Anglican adaptation of the Oratory of St. Philip Neri, as it had been instituted in France by Pierre de Berulle (1575–1629). As an Episcopalian, I was one of the few American members of the Oratory, and it was a rare privilege to spend retreats in England enjoying the company of such diverse personalities as Eric Mascal, the Thomist and nonpareil limericist, and the modernist Alec Vidler, dean of St. George's Windsor and mentor of Malcolm Muggeridge.

Once in royal David's city

The tune "Irby" has been universally associated with the hymn since its first publication the year after Mrs. Alexander's book appeared. Whether or not the composer, Henry John Gauntlett (1805–1876), really wrote ten thousand melodies, as is claimed, his influence on organ music and construction was exceptional and lasting. Four years before Gauntlett wrote "Irby," Mendelssohn called him one of the most "masterly" organists of the age. Born a few weeks after the Lewis and Clark expedition reached the Great Falls of the Missouri, Gauntlett lived a life of quiet adventure himself. Obliged by his family to pursue a career in law, he found various ways to pursue his chief love, music, which had enthralled him from his childhood in Shropshire. He played the organ regularly in several London parishes, including St. Bartholomew's, Smithfield, near the site of the executions of some three hundred heretics under Queen Mary. It would have pleased him to know that his music resounds on the great organ of King's Chapel today. Like his contemporary Thomas Helmore, Gauntlett was a proponent of Gregorian chant and would have grieved at its wanton neglect in our time.

Faith of our fathers!

ST. CATHERINE

Faith of our fa - thers! liv - ing still In spite of dun - geon,
fire, and sword: O how our hearts beat high with joy
When-e'er we hear that glo - rious word: Faith of our fa - thers,
ho - ly faith! We will be true to thee till death.

2. Our fathers, chained in prisons dark,
   Were still in heart and conscience free:
   And truly blest would be our fate
   If we, like them, should die for thee.
   Faith of our fathers, holy faith!
   We will be true to thee till death.

3. Faith of our fathers! Mary's prayers
   Shall win all nations unto thee:
   And through the truth that comes from God
   Mankind shall then indeed be free.
   Faith of our fathers, holy faith!
   We will be true to thee till death.

4. Faith of our fathers! We will love
   Both friend and foe in all our strife:
   And preach thee, too, as love knows how,
   By kindly deeds and virtuous life.
   Faith of our fathers, holy faith!
   We will be true to thee till death.

FAITH OF OUR FATHERS!

❦

Frederick William Faber (1814–1863) may have helped sanctify Newman by the various ways he mortified him. His influence for the good in a difficult period for Catholics in England exacts admiration even from those conscious of his atrabilious temperament. No less insightful a man than Blessed Dominic Barbieri, the Passionist missionary to England, said that the community established shortly after his reception into the Catholic Church on November 17, 1845, the Brothers of the Will of God, would more accurately have been named the Brothers of the Will of Faber. Faber did go on to head, from 1849, the London Oratory, now in the Brompton Road, where he is buried and worthily revered.

His pious writings, such as *All for Jesus* and *Growth in Holiness*, were an admixture of brilliant simplicity, enchanting style, and occasionally pious slush; and the topography of his spiritual verse had higher peaks and deeper valleys perhaps than that of anyone of the period, save a few, including William Wordsworth, to whom he dedicated his "Sights and Thoughts in Foreign Churches and among Foreign Peoples" in 1842. Faber's voluminous output is more remarkable for his constant struggle with ill health, although the attention he called to his infirmities was not less constant; and his relatively early death was a relief from both his suffering and his frequent rhetorical anticipations of it.

"Faith of our fathers!" could have a better tune, and in fact it has several. But "St. Catherine" is sacrosanct by habit. Also known variously as "St. Finbar" and "Tynemouth," it is an alteration in 1874 by James George Walton (1821–1905) of music credited ten years earlier to Henri Frederick Hemy (1818–1888), the English-born Roman Catholic son of German immigrants. Hemy was organist in the Catholic church in his native Newcastle and also taught music at the seminary at Ushaw, Durham. It was founded in 1794 and removed to Ushaw in 1808 as a continuation of the English college in Douai, and it was there that the historian John Lingard taught; it has produced the cardinals Wiseman, Bourne, De la

Puente, and Merry del Val. In my upbringing, "St. Catherine" was the standard tune, although, in singing it, I was unaware that it was for a Catholic hymn—a doubly Catholic hymn, actually, inasmuch as Faber wrote two versions for his 1849 collection *Jesus and Mary*: one for the conversion of Protestant England and one for the prosperity of Catholic Ireland. Given the causalities of secularization, all nations now might qualify for his stanza, which did not go unremarked in his own day:

> Faith of our fathers! Mary's prayers
> Shall win our country back to thee;
> And through the truth that comes from God,
> England shall then indeed be free.

Just substitute "our land" for "England." If I could have mistaken this for an Anglican hymn in my youth, that indicates the sanguinous route of Christianity to our day. More repulsive than the various tyrannies and impositions that menaced those saints—and heretics—who were willing to die for their beliefs is the opinion (which I have heard expressed more than once) that talk of dying for the Faith is bravado. Those who think that advertise the spiritual sadness known as sloth. Not so soulless, but more mindless, is the complaint that references to our fathers exclude our mothers.

O little town of Bethlehem

ST. LOUIS

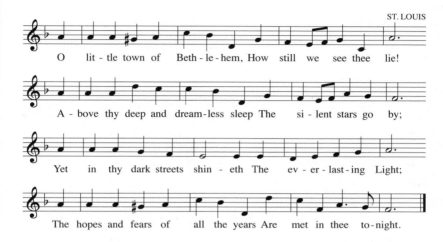

O lit - tle town of Beth - le - hem, How still we see thee lie!

A - bove thy deep and dream-less sleep The si - lent stars go by;

Yet in thy dark streets shin - eth The ev - er - last - ing Light;

The hopes and fears of all the years Are met in thee to-night.

2. For Christ is born of Mary,
   And gathered all above,
   While mortals sleep, the angels keep
   Their watch of wondering love.
   O morning stars, together
   Proclaim the holy birth!
   And praises sing to God the King,
   And peace to men on earth.

3. How silently, how silently,
   The wondrous gift is given!
   So God imparts to human hearts
   The blessings of his heaven.
   No ear may hear his coming,
   But in this world of sin,
   Where meek souls will receive
      him, still
   The dear Christ enters in.

4. Where children pure and happy
   Pray to the blessed Child,
   Where misery cries out to thee,
   Son of the mother mild;
   Where charity stands watching
   And faith holds wide the door,
   The dark night wakes, the glory
      breaks,
   And Christmas comes once more.

5. O holy Child of Bethlehem!
   Descend to us, we pray;
   Cast out our sin and enter in,
   Be born in us today.
   We hear the Christmas angels
   The great glad tidings tell;
   O come to us, abide with us,
   Our Lord Emmanuel!

O LITTLE TOWN OF
BETHLEHEM

———————— ❧ ————————

In 1903, Ralph Vaughan Williams made one of his finest discoveries, a folk tune from Surrey named for the village of Forest Green, where he heard it. Sentiment and lineage, however, explain the wider use of "St. Louis" with the poem by Phillips Brooks (1835–1893). It was specifically written for it in 1868 by Brooks's organist, Lewis H. Redner (1831–1908), who was also a rich real-estate developer and superintendent of the Sunday School.

Phillips Brooks was a dominant figure in a golden — and even garish — age of pulpit oratory. It has been said that his epitaph, "Born in Boston. Died in Boston," is the finest any corpse can have. But that would be disputed in Philadelphia, where he served as rector of Holy Trinity, Rittenhouse Square, from 1862 to 1869, when he went on to Trinity Church, Copley Square, in Boston and became bishop of Massachusetts in 1891.

I used to find Brooks an unpalatable figure, not only because of his theological opinions, but also because of his brooding aspect, which seemed quietly tormented by an interior struggle between mystical piety and Yankee assurance. There is no doubt that he had an enormous appeal. His death caused a wide sensation of grief, and he was raised to iconic heights on the reredos of the National Cathedral in Washington, D.C., and in stained glass in many Anglican churches, including St. Margaret's, Westminster. While he was alive, his photograph was a fixture in many American homes, and his "Phillips Brooks Calendar," which was a European-style monthly diary, still is published as such. His cult was all the more remarkable when clergymen of his denomination were not often cut from the cloth that made romantic heroes.

His were the times when the House of Bishops would attend their General Convention in J. P. Morgan's private train, with Louis Sherry as caterer. But he was suspect for his liberal theological views, influenced by Frederick Denison Maurice (1805–1872) of King's College, London, who attacked Newman's theory of the development of doctrine. He even more resembled the gifted but depressive Frederick William Robertson (1816–1853), the "Broad Church" preacher of Brighton, whose panegyric on the death of Queen Adelaide this author remembers reciting in homiletics class. The statue by Augustus Saint-Gaudens outside his Boston church, showing him in necktie and academic pulpit robes rather than customary vesture, bespeaks the theistic confidence of his lectures on preaching given at Yale in 1877, with their strictures on the influence of personality.

Brooks made a long trip to the Holy Land in 1865, when rectors of his grandeur could absent themselves from their flocks for leisurely stretches. Upon his return to Philadelphia from the sheep of Bethlehem, he wrote this hymn for the children of his Sunday School. Brooks never married and had an honest, if avuncular, solicitude for the little ones. The church on Rittenhouse Square, where I preached a couple of times, is a more modest version of the Richardsonian Romanesque pile that is Trinity Church on Copley Square: an elephantiasis in stone, which, like my old college chapel, flaunts all that was wrong about religion gone the way of romantic vagueness. One of Mr. Brooks's successors there took to reading the Communion Service facing the people from behind the altar, in what was considered aggressively Broad Church style. In the days before liturgical alterations, it was remarked with some irony that the only clergyman other than the Rector of Holy Trinity who used that posture was the pope.

Hark, hark my soul!

PILGRIMS

Hark, hark my soul! an - gel - ic songs are swell - ing

O'er earth's green fields and o - cean's wave - beat shore;

How sweet the truth those bless - ed strains are tell - ing

Of that new life when sin shall be no more!

Refrain

An - gels of Je - sus, an - gels of light,

Sing - ing to wel - come the pil - grims of the night.

2. Onward we go, for still we hear them singing,
   "Come, weary souls, for Jesus bids you come";
   And through the dark, its echoes sweetly ringing,
   The music of the Gospel leads us home. *Refrain*

3. Far, far away, like bells at evening pealing,
   The voice of Jesus sounds o'er land and sea,
   And laden souls, by thousands meekly stealing,
   Kind Shepherd, turn their weary steps to thee. *Refrain*

4. Rest comes at length, though life be long and dreary,
   The day must dawn, and darksome night be past;
   Faith's journeys end in welcome to the weary,
   And heaven, the heart's true home, will come at last. *Refrain*

5. Angels, sing on! your faithful watches keeping;
   Sing us sweet fragments of the songs above;
   Till morning's joy shall end the night of weeping,
   And life's long shadows break in cloudless love. *Refrain*

HARK, HARK MY SOUL!

———— ✄ ————

These markedly beautiful expressions from the *Oratory Hymns* of Frederick William Faber have been the consolation of many, and not only the bereaved, since they first entered the general literature in 1854. In that same year, the London Oratory, which Newman had sent Faber to establish in 1849, was removed from King William Street to its present location in South Kensington. When it appeared under the title "The Pilgrims of the Night," the hymn contained some of Faber's indelicacies with shaky metaphors. Instance the next-to-the-last stanza of the original edition:

> Cheer up, my soul! faith's moonbeams softly glisten
> Upon the breast of life's most troubled sea;
> And it will cheer thy drooping heart to listen
> To those brave songs which angels mean for thee.

Even more challenging to the Muse was a line, in what had been the second stanza, warning that "death finds out his victim in the dark." Faber's poetry, like the man, is a flagrant chiaroscuro of brilliance and occlusions of it, but what has been edited down to us is better than we deserve, with the word pictures of bells at evening pealing, and so forth. My first fond recollection of this particular hymn is of it sung in Mount Kisco, New York, at a requiem for a beloved clergyman who had long championed the Oxford movement principles. In the bright little jewel box of a church designed by Ralph Adams Cram, the body was carried out as these words were sung, and incense accompanied it, clouds whose fragrance was unfamiliar in those surroundings.

There could hardly be a finer musical accompaniment than the one the organ builder Henry Thomas Smart composed especially for it, as he made clear by calling it "Pilgrims." It was first used in 1868 in *Hymns Ancient and Modern*. The inclusion of a hymn by a convert Catholic priest attests to the respect its author engendered as much as to the quality of words and music.

For all the saints

SINE NOMINE

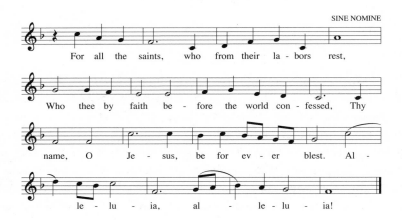

For all the saints, who from their la - bors rest,

Who thee by faith be - fore the world con - fessed, Thy

name, O Je - sus, be for ev - er blest. Al -

le - lu - ia, al - le - lu - ia!

2. Thou wast their rock, their fortress, and their might:
   Thou, Lord, their Captain in the well-fought fight;
   Thou, in the darkness drear, their one true light. Alleluia, alleluia!

3. O may thy soldiers, faithful, true, and bold,
   Fight as the saints who nobly fought of old,
   And win, with them, the victor's crown of gold. Alleluia, alleluia!

4. O blest communion, fellowship divine!
   We feebly struggle, they in glory shine;
   Yet all are one in thee, for all are thine. Alleluia, alleluia!

5. And when the strife is fierce, the warfare long,
   Steals on the ear the distant triumph song,
   And hearts are brave again, and arms are strong. Alleluia, alleluia!

6. The golden evening brightens in the west;
   Soon, soon to faithful warriors cometh rest;
   Sweet is the calm of paradise the blest. Alleluia, alleluia!

7. But lo! there breaks a yet more glorious day;
   The saints triumphant rise in bright array;
   The King of glory passes on his way. Alleluia, alleluia!

8. From earth's wide bounds, from ocean's farthest coast,
   Through gates of pearl streams in the countless host,
   Singing to Father, Son, and Holy Ghost. Alleluia, alleluia!

FOR ALL THE SAINTS

⸭

Processions should go somewhere, and solemn processions should stop here and there along the way: inside a church they may pause at shrines for a prayer before continuing. These "stations" symbolize the progress of the Church Militant toward heaven and require hymns long enough for the walk and noble enough for the dignity of the occasion. One such is here in grand form by William Walsham How (1823–1897). At Oxford he was at Wadham College, and in 1851 became rector of Whittington. In 1865 he had been appointed chaplain of the English Church in Rome. (Pope Pius IX gave permission for the church's construction on the Via del Babuino, with the proviso that its entrance not face the street.) This Church of England bishop—in 1879 a suffragan bishop in the East End of London and then appointed in 1888 first bishop of Wakefield—was conspicuous for his work among the poor of the urban slums and for his instruction of children. Many of his fifty-four published hymns were for the children, and the artful simplicity of all his hymns makes them easily understood by them. During a brief period in the late 1960s, I worked in two parishes in the East End where his name was still revered. Thus his alliterative career: William Walsham of Wadham, Whittington, and Wakefield.

His song of praise for All Saints' Day was published first in *Hymns for Saints' Days and Other Hymns* in 1864. This book he did not edit, but he did edit *Psalms and Hymns* in 1854, the year he became rural dean of Oswestry and, from Rome, was a principal force behind *Church Hymns*, which came out in 1871. Although an alternate melody, "Sarum," by Sir Joseph Barnby (1838–1896), a precentor at Eton and fellow of the Royal Academy of Music, is more easily sung, "Sine Nomine," by Ralph Vaughan Williams, best fits the requirements for a processional hymn. If it challenges the capacities of a parish congregation, it can be helped by antiphonal singing with a schola. Williams spent a brief time in Paris studying with Ravel, but the influences on him are a truly catholic compendium of periods: medieval tonalities (as in his Mass in G Minor), English Tudor harmonics, and, more than anything else, regional folk music.

Williams wrote the music to grace How's text in the *English Hymnal* of 1906. That volume is outstanding for its cultivation of liturgical processions as a unique form, listing appropriate hymns in an appendix. In so doing, it followed the tradition of medieval "Processionals," which are conflations of litanies, stated prayers, and hymns culled from the Ritual, Missal, and Pontifical. Barnby may have had this in mind when he named his tune "Sarum" for the Sarum Processional, which was first compiled by Bishop Richard Poore (d. 1237), who moved his see from Old Sarum to the present Salisbury in 1219. It has roots in the literature of Saint Osmund (d. 1099), a Norman who became bishop of Sarum in 1078 and helped write the Domesday Book. The affective use of How's hymn did much to dispel the prejudice in his own Church cast by the twenty-second of the Anglican Thirty-Nine Articles, which typed the "Romish doctrine" of venerating the saints as a "fond thing vainly invented."

Now the day is over

MERRIAL

Now the day is o - ver, Night is draw - ing nigh,

Shad - ows of the eve - ning Steal a - cross the sky.

2. Jesus, give the weary
   Calm and sweet repose;
   With thy tenderest blessing
   May our eyelids close.

3. Grant to little children
   Visions bright of thee;
   Guard the sailors tossing
   On the deep, blue sea.

4. Comfort every sufferer
   Watching late in pain;
   Those who plan some evil
   From their sin restrain.

5. Through the long night watches
   May thine angels spread
   Their white wings above me,
   Watching round my bed.

6. When the morning wakens,
   Then may I arise
   Pure, and fresh, and sinless
   In thy holy eyes.

NOW THE DAY IS OVER

———————— ✄ ————————

Each evening hymn is a meditation on the mystery of death, and, as Sir Thomas Browne intended in his *Religio Medici* in the sixteenth century, the Christian knows the difference between a mystery and a question mark:

> Sleep is a death, O make me try,
> By sleeping what it is to die.
> And as gently lay my head
> On my grave, as now my bed.

So the repertoire of evening hymns has the sunset for metaphor, as morning hymns have the rising sun for a sign of the resurrection. The best hymns of the evening are quite simple, for the time of day is itself a text and tune. That is true of this composition by Sabine Baring-Gould (1834–1924), a perfect type of the industrious country vicar whose vicarage was also a study and font of all kinds of scholarship: historical and even esoteric, and perhaps not even a little eccentric. Few writers of his age were as prolific, and it is typical that much of his outpouring was written for children. Among the novels written from his parish of Lew Trenchard in Devon were *Mehalah*, *John Herring*, and *Richard Cable*. They are quite forgotten now, but not so his sixteen-volume *Lives of the Saints*, of which it was once said, and is still said by some, that no library is complete without a set. His *Curious Myths of the Middle Ages* is still consulted, as is his *Book of Werewolves*.

But his hymns have a greater immediacy, and everyone knows his "Onward Christian soldiers," although, even with its thumping music by Sir Arthur Sullivan, or perhaps because of that, it irritates some purists. Cardinal Farley of New York loathed it and banished it from his hearing. After Baring-Gould took his degree from Cambridge in 1854, he pursued his love of music as an assistant master of a choir school in Pimlico and then at Hurstpierpoint College. Heir to a considerable estate, he was able to indulge his musical interests beyond the normal confines of a clergyman, publishing two anthologies of folk songs that rank in historical importance with the collections of another English clergyman, John Broadwood; and, in 1898, he presented his own opera, *The Red Spider*. He wrote his own tune for this hymn, which he had composed for children in 1865, the year of his ordination to the Anglican priesthood, and it was included in an appendix to *Hymns Ancient and Modern* in 1868.

He named his tune "Eudoxia," and, as it is not likely that he referred to the wicked empress who banished Saint John Chrysostom, we may assume he meant the word's meaning as goodwill and praise. It has enjoyed a share of popularity, but the tune I long knew as almost synonymous with Evensong was "Merrial," composed as an alternative for this hymn by Joseph Barnby and included in 1869 in his *Original Tunes to Popular Hymns*. Knighted in 1892, he died in Pimlico, where Baring-Gould had begun his musical career. If Barnby's oratorio *Rebekah* has gone the way of *The Red Spider*, his name lives through many of the 246 hymns he wrote and gathered together in 1897 and through some of his part songs, the best known of which is "Sweet and Low."

I know not what the future hath

WILTSHIRE

I know not what the fu - ture hath Of
mar - vel or sur - prise, As - sured a - lone that
life and death God's mer - cy un - der - lies.

2. And if my heart and flesh are weak
   To bear an untried pain,
   The bruised reed he will not break,
   But strengthen and sustain.

3. No offering of my own I have,
   Nor works my faith to prove;
   I can but give the gifts he gave,
   And plead his love for love.

4. And so beside the silent sea
   I wait the muffled oar;
   No harm from him can come to me
   On ocean or on shore.

5. I know not where his islands lift
   Their fronded palms in air;
   I only know I cannot drift
   Beyond his love and care.

I KNOW NOT WHAT
THE FUTURE HATH

⚒

The antislavery movement in the United States was not without those self-righteous crusaders of fanatical excess who haunt and sometimes usurp worthy causes. No abundance of such types, especially among the fervid abolitionists of New England, can detract from those edifying and truly virtuous abolitionists at whose apex stands the Quaker poet John Greenleaf Whittier (1807–1892). The house in which he was born, in Haverhill, Massachusetts, built by his Puritan ancestor Thomas Whittier, is described in enchanting detail in *Snow-Bound* in 1866, one year after he wrote the poem "Eternal Goodness," whose sixteenth through twentieth stanzas comprise this hymn. At the time of its writing, Whittier had already spent nearly fifteen years in seclusion in Amesbury, Massachusetts, where he remained for the rest of his life.

Like the hymn writers Thomas Olivers of Wales, Hugh Wilson of Scotland, and William Carey of England, Whittier was a largely self-educated shoemaker as well as a farmer. And, like Wilson in particular, he was deeply imbued with the ballads of Robert Burns. Girding his pen as a sword, he became a fiery editorialist and secretary of the American Anti-Slavery Society. When the Philadelphia office of his newspaper, the *Pennsylvania Freeman*, was torched by a riotous mob in 1838, he entered upon a quieter, and even more productive, life of letters and became one of what is perhaps a minority of leading poets whose best works were written after their fiftieth year. Whittier's verse is profoundly Christian, even though the Society of Friends abjure—if Quakers can be said to abjure anything—the sacraments. He wrote poems entitled "The Crucifixion" and "The Call of the Christian" and hymns no less distinguished or simply elegant, such as "Immortal love for ever full" and "Dear Lord and Father of mankind" and these moving lines of "I know not what the future hath," especially its fourth and fifth stanzas. It would be difficult to find in any literature a pithier amalgamation of the doctrines of justification by faith and works than the third stanza.

Originally, the fine tune "Wiltshire" was composed for Psalm 48 and appeared in 1795 in a collection by George Thomas Smart: *Divine Amusement, Being a Selection of the Most Admired Psalms.* Sir George (1776–1867), not to be confused with Henry Thomas Smart, was one of that vast company of musical authors, including Jeremiah Clark, Thomas Tanis, Thomas Helmore, and John Goss, who began in the choir of the Chapel Royal. Smart was by far the most celebrated conductor of his day, multiplying the festival concerts he began in Dublin, and later was musical director of Covent Garden and the official organist of the Grand Lodge of the Freemasons. By this time Freemasonry had mixed connotations in the religious life of the English-speaking world. Even the first Catholic bishop of the United States, John Carroll (1735–1815), did not publish the papal condemnation of Freemasonry, because his own brother Daniel and so many Catholic friends belonged to the Lodge, as, for a while, did the Irish leader Daniel O'Connell. More important, Smart represents a virtual apostolic tradition of musical masters: his father had seen Handel in performance; he himself had visited Beethoven; and, in 1826, Carl Maria von Weber, at the age of forty, died in his house in London. A man of generous appreciation, Smart promoted the works of Mendelssohn and helped to establish the Mendelssohn Scholarship, the first recipient of which, in 1856, was Arthur Sullivan.

Praise to the Holiest in the height

NEWMAN

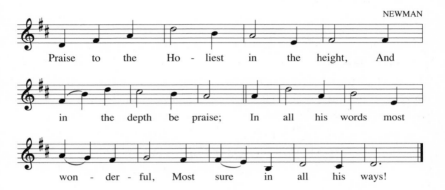

Praise to the Ho - liest in the height, And
in the depth be praise; In all his words most
won - der - ful, Most sure in all his ways!

2. O loving wisdom of our God!
   When all was sin and shame,
   A second Adam to the fight
   And to the rescue came.

3. O wisest love! that flesh and
      blood,
   Which did in Adam fail,
   Should strive afresh against the
      foe,
   Should strive, and should prevail;

4. And that a higher gift than grace
   Should flesh and blood refine:
   God's presence and his very self,
   And essence all-divine.

5. O generous love! that he who
      smote
   In Man for man the foe,
   The double agony in Man
   For man should undergo;

6. And in the garden secretly,
   And on the cross on high,
   Should teach his brethren, and
      inspire
   To suffer and to die.

7. Praise to the Holiest in the height,
   And in the depth be praise;
   In all his words most wonderful,
   Most sure in all his ways!

PRAISE TO THE HOLIEST IN THE HEIGHT

In the same year (1865) that John Bacchus Dykes wrote the tune for "Lead, kindly Light," John Henry Newman wrote his narrative "The Dream of Gerontius," describing the passage of a soul into eternity: not a gauzy shadowland, for eternal life is more real than the temporary earth of shaded light, and its guarding angels are more solid in their fleshlessness than man in his flesh. The previous year, Newman had thought he might die from nervous exhaustion after writing his autobiographical *Apologia pro Vita Sua*, standing all the while, in the length of days it took Handel to compose his *Messiah*. He quieted himself by writing what would become his own oratorio, but only after having set down, on Passion Sunday in 1864, a commendation of his soul to God the Holy Spirit, his favorite saints, and his guardian angel. Then, unlike most of his prose, which he painstakingly revised and revised again, the "Dream" flowed from his pen in the space of three weeks with practically no corrections. He meant the work as a personal meditation and offered it for publication only a couple of months later when asked to come up with something for the *Month*, a Jesuit review.

On his deathbed, the dying Gerontius becomes more conscious as he hears the Litany of the Dying and makes a solemn profession of faith. A higher consciousness in death realizes the support of his guardian angel ushering him past demons salivating to devour his soul. Five "Angelical Choirs" begin celestial antiphons in counterpoint to the "sour and uncouth dissonance" of the evil spirits. Having been brought to the "feet of Emmanuel" for particular judgment, Gerontius is lovingly lowered into the "penal waters" of purgatory by his angel, who promises, "Swiftly shall pass thy night of trial here,/ And I will come and wake thee on the morrow."

The hymn we have is the part sung by the "Fifth Choir of Angelicals." The entire work was set as an oratorio by Sir Edward Elgar (1857–1934)

Praise to the Holiest in the height

a year after the appearance of his *Enigma Variations*. Fittingly, Newman's patron, Saint Philip Neri, invented the prototype of the oratorio as a catechetical device in the sixteenth century, the first of its fully developed kind being performed in Rome at Santa Maria in Vallicella in 1600. The form was named for the Oratory of Saint Philip Neri, which Newman introduced to England. Elgar was no less Roman Catholic than British. The composer of "Land of Hope and Glory," unable to attend alien worship, could not hear his offertory anthem "O hearken Thou" performed at the coronation of George V. "Newman," a tune by Dykes, first published in 1868, promoted the hymn among Protestants and Catholics alike. Even more vigorous, if less well known in the United States, is "Gerontius," by the English Catholic Sir Richard Runciman Terry (1865–1938), whose career took him to the British West Indies, the Benedictine school at Downside, and Westminster Cathedral, where he promoted a choral tradition that remains one of the finest in the world.

On Newman's desk at the Birmingham Oratory is a lamp given him by Prime Minister Gladstone, who had this hymn sung at his own funeral. Newman and the English-speaking world were wonderfully struck when a carefully annotated copy of the whole poem was found on the body of General Gordon at Khartoum, slain by the hordes of the Mandi on January 26, 1885, much to the political embarrassment of Gladstone.

The Church's one foundation

AURELIA

The Chur-ch's one foun-da-tion Is Je-sus Christ her Lord;

She is his new cre-a-tion By wa-ter and the word:

From heav'n he came and sought her To be his ho-ly bride;

With his own blood he bought her And for her life he died.

2. Elect from every nation,
   Yet one o'er all the earth,
   Her charter of salvation,
   One Lord, one faith, one birth;
   One holy Name she blesses,
   Partakes one holy food,
   And to one hope she presses,
   With every grace endued.

3. Though with a scornful wonder
   Men see her sore opprest,
   By schisms rent asunder,
   By heresies distrest;
   Yet saints their watch are keeping,
   Their cry goes up, "How long?"
   And soon the night of weeping
   Shall be the morn of song.

4. 'Mid toil and tribulation,
   And tumult of her war,
   She waits the consummation
   Of peace for evermore;
   Till with the vision glorious
   Her longing eyes are blest,
   And the great Church victorious
   Shall be the Church at rest.

5. Yet she on earth hath union
   With God, the Three in One,
   And mystic sweet communion
   With those whose rest is won.
   O happy ones and holy!
   Lord, give us grace that we
   Like them, the meek and lowly,
   On high may dwell with thee.

THE CHURCH'S ONE
FOUNDATION

———————————— ✄ ————————————

On June 23, 1902, the coronation of King Edward VII, scheduled for three days later, was indefinitely postponed because of his acute appendicitis. Lady Mary Lygon, lady-in-waiting to the king's daughter-in-law, the future Queen Mary, wrote: "I have never felt anything like the physical and mental oppression of the day in London. It was hot and airless and muggy—the decorations flapped about in an ominous manner—gloom and consternation were in every face." The king's recovery, in spite of rumors that his age and girth made his condition precarious, occasioned special celebration, reminiscent of the service of thanksgiving in St. Paul's Cathedral on February 27, 1872, when he, as prince of Wales, had recovered from another threatening illness. Some of the music of that first celebration was provided by Samuel Sebastian Wesley (1810–1876), the natural son of Charles Wesley's son, Samuel. The two Samuels were each reckoned to be the finest organists of their respective generations.

It was widely and wrongly alleged that the younger Samuel's tune for the 1872 ceremony, "Aurelia," was a pastiche of some "secular twaddle," such as the folk tune "Auld Robin Gray." The composer himself refuted claims that he had drawn from a little part song by the romantic Catholic convert Robert Lucas Pearsall (1795–1856). He thought there may have been a similarity with some quotation of the violinist and opera composer Louis Spohr (1784–1859), who, according to Stainer, had once been thought superior to Beethoven; but Wesley added that Spohr had been accused of snatching from Mozart.

The tune had first been written for Alexander Ewing's translation of "Jerusalem the Golden," by Bernard of Cluny, and was published as such in Charles Kemble's *Selection of Psalms and Hymns* in 1854, which Wesley edited. Wesley was organist of several parishes. He is commemorated by a window in Gloucester Cathedral and a tablet in Exeter Cathedral, where his tenure was marked by violent — and substantive — battles against the clergy. When Gladstone offered him the choice of a knighthood from Queen Victoria or a pension, he took the money.

Samuel John Stone (1839–1900) followed his father as vicar of St. Paul's, Haggerston, until becoming rector of All Hallows on the Wall, London, in 1890. When Salisbury Cathedral wanted to use "The Church's one foundation" for processions, it was expanded to ten stanzas from the five we have in the appendix to the 1868 edition of *Hymns Ancient and Modern*, for which he was a committee member. It had seven stanzas when it was first published in 1866 in Stone's *Lyra Fidelium: Twelve Hymns on the Twelve Articles of the Apostles' Creed*. There it was used to address the ninth article: "The Holy Catholic Church; The Communion of Saints." The *Lyra* had been occasioned by the excommunication in 1866 of John William Colenso (1814–1883), Anglican bishop of Natal, by the metropolitan Robert Gray of Cape Town. Gray, like Stone, was a High Churchman who denounced Colenso's toleration of polygamy and the heretical sacramental theology of his *Commentary on the Epistle to the Romans* in 1861. In a blatant example of Erastianism, similar to the notorious Gorham Case of 1847, which drove the future Cardinal Manning to conversion, the Judicial Committee of the Privy Counsel sustained Colenso's claims, and an ensuing schism in South Africa was not repaired until 1911. This then was the efficient cause of the schisms and heresies referred to in the third stanza, which, when sung by Catholics to Wesley's tune, take on a more universal tone and sturdier proportions.

Savior, again to thy dear Name we raise

ELLERS

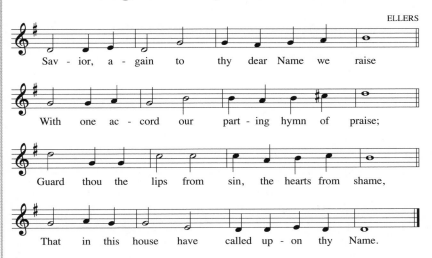

Sav - ior, a - gain to thy dear Name we raise

With one ac - cord our part - ing hymn of praise;

Guard thou the lips from sin, the hearts from shame,

That in this house have called up - on thy Name.

2. Grant us thy peace, Lord, through the coming night
   Turn thou for us its darkness into light;
   From harm and danger keep thy children free,
   For dark and light are both alike to thee.

3. Grant us thy peace throughout our earthly life;
   Peace to thy Church from error and from strife;
   Peace to our land, the fruit of truth and love;
   Peace in each heart, thy Spirit from above:

4. Thy peace in life, the balm of every pain;
   Thy peace in death, the hope to rise again;
   Then, when thy voice shall bid our conflict cease,
   Call us, O Lord, to thine eternal peace.

SAVIOR, AGAIN TO THY DEAR NAME WE RAISE

---------------------------------- ℘ ----------------------------------

One of the lilting and poignant hymns for Evensong is this by John Ellerton (1826–1893), Anglican vicar and promoter of the Society for Promoting Christian Knowledge. It was written for a choral festival in 1866. Ellerton also wrote another of the finest evening hymns, "The day Thou gavest, Lord, is ended," in 1870 and, lest he neglect the other side of day, translated Fortunatus's "Welcome, happy morning" sometime shortly before 1868. Although born in London, Ellerton went on from Cambridge University to serve parishes in Brighton, Cheshire, Surrey, and Essex, where he spent his last years as a paralytic. Throughout his life he enjoyed writing hymns for children, publishing *Hymns for Schools and Bible Classes* in 1859 and coauthoring *The Children's Hymn Book* in 1881. His evangelistic fervor gave birth to the *London Mission Hymn Book* of 1884. As a musical scholar of merit, he was regularly consulted by the editors of virtually all the major hymnals of the day. And as a man of equally meritorious piety, he had the rare distinction of being mourned and memorialized by his curate, Henry Housman, in *John Ellerton, Being a Collection of His Writings on Hymnology, Together with a Sketch of His Life and Works* in 1896.

"Savior, again" was published in the appendix of *Hymns Ancient and Modern*, in the same 1868 edition that included Stone's "The Church's one foundation." The first version, that of 1866, was written as a personal meditation on the blessing that concludes the Prayer Book's Order for Daily Evening Prayer. Over the years it was slightly altered to a more public and communal expression. Thus, for example, the original words of the third stanza were: "Grant us thy peace upon our homeward way,/ With thee began, with thee shall end the day." One year after the publication of "Savior, again to thy dear name we raise" in 1868, the present tune was composed for it by Edward John Hopkins (1818–1901). Born in London, Hopkins joined in 1826 that long line of choristers of the Chapel Royal and went on to a career as one of England's leading organists, becoming a member of the Royal Academy of Musicians in 1851 and receiving honorary degrees from the Archbishop of Canterbury and Trinity College, Toronto. Like his contemporary William Henry Monk, he taught music to the blind. The "Honorary Societies of the Temple," which elected him organist in 1843, are those establishments of the Inns of Court occupying what had been the London headquarters of the Knights Templar since 1185. The Temple Church is built in the round on the model of the Holy Sepulcher in Jerusalem, providing interesting, if challenging, acoustics. Hopkins continued to perform publicly until what was then considered the great age of seventy-eight.

While his contributions to organ building were universally respected, there is a division of opinion about the influence of the arbitrary system of pointing in *The Cathedral Psalter*, which he edited along with Stainer and others. Later editors have tried to correct those instances in which the words were subservient to the music, a problem more pronounced in more modern forms of chanting, such as that of the Jesuit Joseph Gelineau. That is not a problem in this utterly simple tune for the evening hymn.

Immortal, invisible, God only wise

ST. DENIO

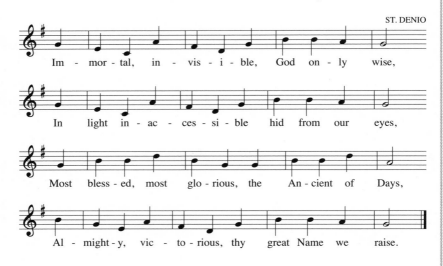

Im - mor - tal, in - vis - i - ble, God on - ly wise,

In light in - ac - ces - si - ble hid from our eyes,

Most bless - ed, most glo - rious, the An - cient of Days,

Al - might - y, vic - to - rious, thy great Name we raise.

2. Unresting, unhasting, and silent as light,
   Nor wanting, nor wasting, thou rulest in might;
   Thy justice like mountains high soaring above
   Thy clouds, which are fountains of goodness and love.

3. To all life thou givest, to both great and small;
   In all life thou livest, the true life of all;
   We blossom and flourish, like leaves on the tree,
   Then wither and perish; but naught changeth thee.

4. Great Father of glory, pure Father of light,
   Thine angels adore thee, all veiling their sight;
   All laud we would render: O help us to see
   'Tis only the splendor of light hideth thee.

Immortal, invisible, God only wise

—— ※ ——

Ieuan Qwyllt, known in a less adventurous tongue as John Roberts, was one of the most influential preservers and rehabilitators of the Welsh choral tradition. His own tune "Moab," featured in his celebrated tune book *Llyfr Tonau Cynulleidfaol*, was considered "one of the seven greatest tunes in the world" by the composer, lecturer, and Vice-Chancellor of the University of Sheffield Sir William Henry Hadow (1859–1937), who edited *The Oxford Dictionary of Music*. Qwyllt was born in Tanrhywfelen, Pennllwyn, close by Aberystwyth, in 1822 and died in Caernarvon in 1877. As a minister of the Welsh Calvinist Methodist Church, Qwyllt worked diligently with area coal miners, for whom he edited a journal, *Gwaladgarwr*. Among other benefactions, he introduced the workers and their families and their village choral societies to the wider chorale repertoire of Bach and Handel, while establishing the native kind of musical festivals, Cymanfau Ganu, which continue to the present day. With equal energy, and the prudence born of experience, he also founded the Snowdon Temperance Union. Qwyllt translated, under the title *Swn y liwbili*, the hymnbook that the American revivalists Moody and Sankey had published in 1873 for one of their preaching tours in Britain to supplement what they thought were English hymns too staid for their style of evangelism.

In 1839, having arranged the tune "Llanfair," which probably was written by Robert Williams in 1817, Ieuan Qwyllt wrote "St. Denio," sometimes called "Joanna," which he first called "Palestina." It was based on the ballad "Can Mlynedd i'nawr," which means "A Hundred Years from Now," and was published in 1839 in his *Caniadau y Cyssegr*. It seems to have been set with this hymn of Walter Chalmers Smith (1824–1908) for the first time in the *Hymnal 1940* with which I grew up. We sang it so often that I soon knew it by heart.

Smith was a minister of the Free (Scottish) Church, having been born in Aberdeen, and, after a pastorate from 1850 to 1857 in London, he returned to Edinburgh, where he lived until his retirement. He was moderator of the Free Church in 1893 and died in Perthshire. Thus he was born in the year of the discovery of the Great Salt Lake in Utah and died a few weeks before the Ford Motor Company introduced the Model T. His hymn, of course, is based on 1 Timothy 1:17, which Saint Paul wrote to his legate Timothy in Ephesus, possibly from Troas, in A.D. 65. The line is similar to the doxologies of Galatians 1:5 and Romans 9:5 and may actually be Paul's citation of a Christian hymn already well known. So Chalmers builds a hymn upon a hymn. In the Greek text the first adjective is "incorruptible," but, like the Vulgate, the King James Version, to which even Chalmers would have had recourse, translates it "immortal." If no hymn is immortal, this one comes close.

Alleluia! sing to Jesus

HYFRYDOL

Al - le - lu - ia! sing to Je - sus! His the

scep - ter, his the throne; Al - le - lu - ia!

his the tri - umph, His the vic - to - ry a - lone;

Hark! the songs of peace - ful Si - on Thun - der

like a might - y flood; Je - sus out of ev - 'ry

na - tion Hath re - deemed us by his blood.

2. Alleluia! not as orphans
   Are we left in sorrow now;
   Alleluia! he is near us,
   Faith believes, nor questions how;
   Though the cloud from sight received him,
   When the forty days were o'er,
   Shall our hearts forget his promise,
   "I am with you evermore"?

3. Alleluia! Bread of Angels,
   Thou on earth our food, our stay!
   Alleluia! here the sinful
   Flee to thee from day to day;
   Intercessor, friend of sinners,
   Earth's redeemer, plead for me,
   Where the songs of all the sinless
   Sweep across the crystal sea.

4. Alleluia! King eternal,
   Thee the Lord of lords we own;
   Alleluia! born of Mary,
   Earth thy footstool, heaven thy throne;
   Thou, within the veil hast entered,
   Robed in flesh, our great High Priest;
   Thou on earth both Priest and Victim
   In the Eucharistic feast.

ALLELUIA! SING TO JESUS

⁂

The author of this text and the composer of its majestic tune were self-educated exemplars of the noble amateur in the finest Victorian tradition. William Chatterton Dix (1837–1898) was born in Bristol, England, and, like Charles Ives (1874–1954), was in the insurance business. His specialty was marine insurance, but his abiding love was music and classical literature. While his formal training did not go beyond the Bristol Grammar School, he taught himself to translate Greek hymns. His own Anglican hymns include such other favorites as the Christmas poem "What child is this, who, laid to rest" and the one for Epiphany, "As with gladness men of old," which he wrote from his sickbed at the age of twenty-one. This hymn for the Ascension was written in 1866 and published in the 1868 edition of his *Altar Songs, Verses on the Holy Eucharist*. It paraphrases the song of the twenty-four elders before the throne of the Lamb in Revelation 5:9: "Thou hast redeemed us to God by thy blood out of every nation."

Rowland Hugh Prichard (1811–1878) was as precocious as Dix, having written the tune "Hyfrydol" at the age of twenty. It first appeared in the hymnal *Haleliwiah Drachefn* in 1855. Born near Bala in Graienyn, he worked the looms in a factory of the Welsh Flannel Manufacturing Company. By the age of thirty-three he had written enough to publish a collection of his own tunes under the title *Cyfaill y Cantorion*. The lives of Welsh choral singers from the factories and mines read like an unsentimental propaedeutic for the 1940 novel, and later film, *How Green Was My Valley*, by Richard Llewellyn. At the close of a mission I preached in New York City, Maureen O'Hara, who had starred in that film, told me that the singing miners in it were authentic, having traveled from Wales to shoot the scenes in California. There is another tune, one written specifically for Dix's hymn by Samuel Sebastian Wesley in 1868 and called "Alleluia." But "Hyfrydol" seemed to be the preferred one in my parish, in part perhaps because it is easily sung, especially by male voices: the range of all its phrases save for the last do not go beyond a fifth. Choirboys, inevitably, called it "Hydrofoil."

Immortal Love, for ever full

BISHOPTHORPE

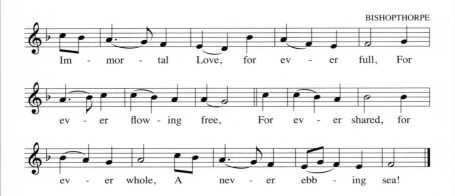

Im - mor - tal Love, for ev - er full, For
ev - er flow - ing free, For ev - er shared, for
ev - er whole, A nev - er ebb - ing sea!

2. Our outward lips confess the Name
   All other names above;
   Love only knoweth whence it came,
   And comprehendeth love.

3. We may not climb the heavenly
     steeps
   To bring the Lord Christ down;
   In vain we search the lowest deeps,
   For him no depths can drown:

4. But warm, sweet, tender, even yet
   A present help is he;
   And faith has still its Olivet,
   And love its Galilee.

5. The healing of his seamless dress
   Is by our beds of pain;
   We touch him in life's throng and
     press,
   And we are whole again.

6. Through him the first fond prayers
     are said
   Our lips of childhood frame;
   The last low whispers of our dead
   Are burdened with his Name.

7. O Lord, and Master of us all,
   Whate'er our name or sign,
   We own thy sway, we hear thy call,
   We test our lives by thine.

IMMORTAL LOVE,
FOR EVER FULL

"Immortal Love," first entitled "Our Master," is a brilliant exercise in emotion that never condescends to bathos. Among the lines of religious verse that any decent poet should honestly envy is the couplet: "And faith has still its Olivet,/ And love its Galilee." John Greenleaf Whittier wrote it in 1856 during his seclusion in Amesbury, Massachusetts—that is, nine years before that other of his most cherished hymns, "Eternal Goodness." Both came out in Whittier's *Tent on the Beach, and Other Poems* in 1867. The first two stanzas are the first two of the original, the third is the fifth of the original, and the last four had been stanzas thirteen through sixteen.

The perfect balance of sense and sentiment is matched by the music, "Bishopthorpe," which is sometimes but less often called "Repentance" or "Charmouth." It was selected for Whittier's poem as one of the 561 hymns in the standard *Hymnal* of the Episcopal Church in 1916. The earliest published record dates to 1790 and is found in the *Psalms of David* compiled by Edward Miller, which volume also included the tune "Rockingham," to which is set "When I survey the wondrous Cross," written in 1707 by Isaac Watts. There is fairly general agreement, including testimony of Miller himself, that Jeremiah Clark wrote it. The purist Robert Bridges reproduced it in 1920 in the second edition of his *Yattendon Hymnal*, using an earlier copy written in three parts discovered in the Foundling Hospital in London, where also Clark's tune "Bromley" was discovered.

The Foundling Hospital, established as an orphanage in 1739, used music both for educating the children and in fund-raising concerts. Handel donated an organ to its chapel and wrote the anthem "Blessed are they that consider the poor" for a benefit concert there in 1749. When Whittier wrote of the "first fond prayers" that "our lips of childhood frame," he could not have known it would be set to the Foundling tune, but he certainly would have found it apposite.

Ten thousand times ten thousand

ALFORD

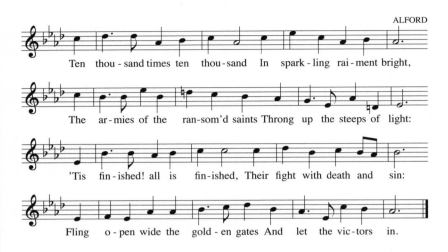

Ten thou-sand times ten thou-sand In spark-ling rai-ment bright,

The ar-mies of the ran-som'd saints Throng up the steeps of light:

'Tis fin-ished! all is fin-ished, Their fight with death and sin:

Fling o-pen wide the gold-en gates And let the vic-tors in.

2. What rush of alleluias
   Fills all the earth and sky!
   What ringing of a thousand harps
   Bespeaks the triumph nigh!
   O day for which creation
   And all its tribes were made!
   O joy, for all its former woes
   A thousand-fold repaid!

3. O then what raptured greetings
   On Canaan's happy shore!
   What knitting severed friend-
      ships up,
   Where partings are no more!
   Then eyes with joy shall sparkle
   That brimmed with tears of late;
   Orphans no longer fatherless,
   Nor widows desolate.

4. Bring near thy great salvation,
   Thou Lamb for sinners slain,
   Fill up the roll of thine elect,
   Then take thy power and reign!
   Appear, Desire of nations!
   Thine exiles long for home:
   Show in the heavens thy promised
      sign!
   Thou Prince and Savior, come!

Ten thousand times ten thousand

While T. S. Eliot is justly credited with advertising the metaphysical poetry of John Donne (1571–1630), much of the spadework in his revival was done by Henry Alford (1810–1871), who published an edition of Donne's works when he was a twenty-nine-year-old vicar of Wymeswold in Warwickshire. Having studied at Trinity College, Cambridge, he spent eighteen years in that parish, and, after four years in a large London parish, he became dean of Canterbury. In that position, he served under two ambiguous archbishops: Charles Thomas Longley (1794–1868), who opposed both Puseyite ritualism and the theological modernism of Colenso, and Archibald Campbell Tait, who obstructed the Tractarians even more vociferously while supporting Gladstone's efforts to disestablish the Church of Ireland.

A poet himself, Alford wrote and translated numerous hymns, was founding editor of the *Contemporary Review*, and should be especially esteemed for the felicitously entitled book *A Plea for the Queen's English*. His updated combination of classical erudition, Scripture scholarship, and pious hymnody, in the mold of Rabanus Maurus of the eighth and ninth centuries, made him worthy of ranking with John Mason Neale, Francis Pott, and Ronald Knox. Well into the twentieth century, Alford's four-volume commentary on the Greek New Testament (1844–1861) was a standard introduction to German higher criticism for the English-speaking world. It cannot be supposed that the author of this heavenly hymn so florid in patristic allusion and diction would have supported Archbishop Tait's attempts to suppress the Athanasian Creed.

In 1870, a fourth stanza was added to the first three, which had been published in 1867 in the journal *Good Words*. The following year, the entire hymn fittingly was sung at the author's funeral. John Bacchus Dykes wrote the music for it, named for Alford. It first appeared in print in *Hymns Ancient and Modern* in 1875, the year before Dykes's own death. In vigor, it is comparable to his "Gerontius," written for Newman's hymn, and in mood it matches "O Quanta Qualia," which he adapted from plainchant for Neale's translation of Abelard.

O Sion, haste

O Si-on, haste, thy mis-sion high ful - fill - ing, To tell to
all the world that God is Light; That he who made all
na - tions is not will - ing One soul should per - ish,
Refrain
lost in shades of night: Pub - lish glad ti - dings: Ti - dings of
peace, Ti - dings of Je - sus, Re - demp - tion and re - lease.

2. Proclaim to every people, tongue, and nation
   That God, in whom they live and move, is Love:
   Tell how he stooped to save his lost creation,
   And died on earth that man might live above. *Refrain*

3. Give of thy sons to bear the message glorious;
   Give of thy wealth to speed them on their way;
   Pour out thy soul for them in prayer victorious
   Till God shall bring his kingdom's joyful day. *Refrain*

4. He comes again! O Sion, ere thou meet him,
   Make known to every heart his saving grace;
   Let none whom he hath ransomed fail to greet him,
   Through thy neglect, unfit to see his face. *Refrain*

O SION, HASTE

One of the enduring and most stirring missionary hymns was written by a rather quiet literary woman, whose own mission was to her immediate family. Mary Ann Thomson was born in London in 1834 and died in 1923 in Philadelphia, where her husband, John, had long been head of the Free Library. His tenure saw the library's growth to the point of planning the vast buildings modeled after the palaces of the Place de la Concorde. According to her own account, Mrs. Thomson, who had written numerous other hymns generally forgotten today, completed this one three years after she had started it in 1868 while nursing one of her children who had typhoid fever. That was the year Henry Smart published his tune for "Hark, hark my soul!," which Father Faber had written in 1854.

Mary Ann Thomson especially admired Smart's music and intended her verses for the same tune, "Pilgrims." As it turned out, her hymn eventually was published, but to music by James Walch (1837–1901). Walch was an organist in Lancashire who played in Congregational and Anglican churches. After several years as a local orchestra conductor in Bolton, near his birthplace of Egerton, he started a music business in Barrow-in-Furness. The tune "Tidings" dates to 1875 or possibly 1876, that is, a year or so before he started in trade. Another of his melodies, "Sawley," written in 1860, is often used for "Jesus, the very thought of Thee," which is a translation by Edward Caswall of a twelfth-century Latin hymn.

Thomson, for reasons unspecified, was under the wrong impression that Walch had written the tune for her text. In fact, he had intended it for Faber's hymn, whose other tune by Smart had been Thomson's inspiration. So it is rather curious that she wrote her words for a tune that was never used with her text; and the tune used for her words was meant for the text she would replace. Faber and Thomson both follow the meter scheme 11, 10, 11, 10 with refrain, but switching the melodies would be ill-advised. The hymn and tune have been staples of Anglican hymnody since 1892, although along the way the original second and third stanzas were deleted; the whole text is bound to be suppressed by relativists who scorn the missionary imperative. Among the neglected lines are:

> Behold how many thousands still are lying
>> Bound in the darksome prison-house of sin,
> With none to tell them of the Saviour's dying,
>> Or of the life he died for them to win.

The last line of the present third stanza is an alteration of the confident—and valid—line: "And all thou spendest Jesus will repay." An elderly friend of mine remembered singing that, and we both agreed that it was handsomely practical and Pauline: perhaps too much so for the ascetically delicate. Several of Thomson's poems appeared in *The Living Church*, a long-lived Episcopal journal in which I published my first theological essay—a brief piece on historical revisionism in the liturgy—when I was about twenty-five. Its appearance doubly pleased me when a senior cleric, not knowing that I was its author, advised me to read it as a corrective for the wrong notions of young ordinands such as myself.

The day thou gavest, Lord, is ended

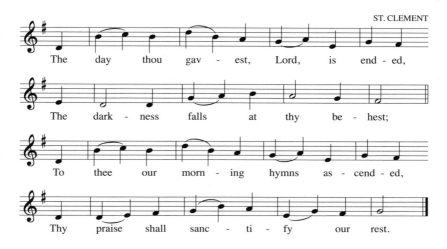

ST. CLEMENT

The day thou gav - est, Lord, is end - ed,

The dark - ness falls at thy be - hest;

To thee our morn - ing hymns as - cend - ed,

Thy praise shall sanc - ti - fy our rest.

2. We thank thee that thy Church, unsleeping
   While earth rolls onward into light,
   Through all the world her watch is keeping,
   And rests not now by day or night.

3. As o'er each continent and island
   The dawn leads on another day,
   The voice of prayer is never silent,
   Nor dies the strain of praise away.

4. The sun that bids us rest is waking
   Our brethren 'neath the western sky,
   And hour by hour fresh lips are making
   Thy wondrous doings heard on high.

5. So be it, Lord; thy throne shall never,
   Like earth's proud empires, pass away.
   Thy kingdom stands, and grows for ever
   'Till all thy creatures own thy sway.

THE DAY THOU GAVEST, LORD, IS ENDED

Close to perfection is this matching of words to the music of Sir Arthur Sullivan's friend Clement Cotterhill Scholefield, who wrote "St. Nicholas" for that other evening hymn "O Brightness of the immortal Father's face." Sullivan's generous spirit and critical acumen may have recognized in Scholefield's quiet lyricism something that, when applied to twilight praise, might have made his own style seem positively hurdy-gurdyish. Scholefield wrote both while curate in London at St. Peter's in South Kensington. While "St. Nicholas" was for Edward Eddis's translation of a Greek hymn of the third century, this present one was penned afresh by John Ellerton, Scholefield's inspired colleague in the Anglican parish ministry. Although it appeared slightly revised from the original in the 1874 hymnbook of the Society for Promoting Christian Knowledge, it was not published for general use in the United States until the *Hymnal* of 1916: rather strange this, given its quality.

Ellerton intended it for use in foreign mission fields, as one may detect from the wistful — almost homesick — sentiments: "The sun that bids us rest is waking/ Our brethren 'neath the western sky." The words and song have been wafted on the night air from Kenya to the Punjab and Samoa and wherever, *pace* Browning, "the quiet-coloured end of evening smiles." A marvelous pathos stirred when it was sung at the lowering of the Union Jack in ceremonies returning Hong Kong to China in 1997. But there is nothing strained about the sentiment, which is almost a requiem for time itself, nor is there any jingoism in its politics: "So be it, Lord; thy throne shall never,/ Like earth's proud empires, pass away." Here, perhaps even more poignant for its plaintive motion, is but another version of Isaac Watts' "O God, our help in ages past" and Rudyard Kipling's "God of our fathers, known of old."

The day thou gavest, Lord, is ended

Possibly this would have become more quickly favored had it not been recommended sung with a sixteenth-century melody, "Command-ments," to which Psalm 140 and the Decalogue had been set in the Geneva Psalter in 1551. Sturdy and distinguished as it is, it lacks the elegant voice that makes "St. Clement" some sort of cradle song for the whole cosmos, and all in a very domestic and unassuming way, like the prayer of John Henry Newman in a sermon of 1834: "May He support us all the day long, till the shades lengthen, and the evening comes, and the busy world is hushed, and the fever of life is over, and our work is done! Then in His mercy may He give us a safe lodging, and a holy rest, and peace at the last."

God of the prophets, bless the prophets' sons

TOULON

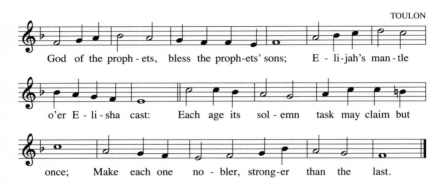

God of the proph - ets, bless the proph-ets' sons; E - li-jah's man - tle o'er E - li - sha cast: Each age its sol - emn task may claim but once; Make each one no - bler, strong-er than the last.

2. Anoint them prophets! Make their ears attent
To thy divinest speech; their hearts awake
To human need; their lips make eloquent
For righteousness that shall all evil break.

3. Anoint them priests! Strong intercessors they
For pardon, and for charity and peace!
O that with them, the world, so far astray,
Might pass into Christ's life of sacrifice!

4. Anoint them kings! Aye, kingly kings, O Lord!
Anoint them with the Spirit of thy Son:
Theirs not a jeweled crown, a blood-stained sword;
Theirs by the love of Christ a kingdom won.

5. Make them apostles, heralds of thy cross;
Forth may they go to tell all realms thy grace:
Inspired of thee, may they count all but loss,
And stand at last with joy before thy face.

GOD OF THE PROPHETS,
BLESS THE PROPHETS' SONS

———————— ⅋ ————————

On the surface, there could hardly be a hymn giving more palpable evidence of the Protestant Reformationist itch than this. In a long life that spanned from the presidency of Andrew Jackson to that of Warren G. Harding (and musically from the youth of Stephen Foster to the first appearance of Louis Armstrong in King Oliver's Jazz Band), its author, Dennis Wortman (1835–1922), was a Reformed Church pastor in New York and Philadelphia, a delegate to the World's Evangelical Alliance in Amsterdam in 1867, and, in 1901, president of the General Synod of the Reformed Church in America. Having graduated in 1857 from Amherst, he belonged to the class of 1860 at the Reformed Church Theological Seminary in New Brunswick, New Jersey. This hymn was commissioned by his class, as a "Prayer for Young Ministers," for the seminary's centenary celebration in October 1884.

The music is even older in Reformationist lineage: "Toulon" is an abbreviated version of "Old Hundred-Twenty-Fourth," which was written, or at least adapted, by Louis Bourgeois (ca. 1523–1600) before 1551 for the Geneva Psalter. Bourgeois was a Huguenot who, from 1541 until his return to his native Paris in 1557, received the patronage of Calvin as choirmaster of St. Peter's Church in Geneva. Although he disappeared from the historical record after 1561, his influence on Protestant choral music was approached in his day only by Claude Goudimel (1505–1572), who was killed in Lyons in the St. Bartholomew's Day Massacre. The tune was sung by the Calvinists of Geneva in 1602 to celebrate the "Escalade," their repulsion of the Duke of Savoy's army; and it was doubtless sung by the passengers on the *Mayflower* and consequently in the Massachusetts Bay Colony, for it was the setting for Psalm 8 in their Psalter. The Ainsworth Psalter used by the Pilgrims was named for its compiler, Henry

Ainsworth (1571–ca. 1623), a Hebrew and Oriental scholar who had been their minister in Amsterdam.

These Bible-conscious people knew the scriptural lineage of the three-fold offices of prophet, priest, and king, which they thought were accomplished in their notion of Reformed ministry. So vividly had Protestant theology appropriated and interpreted the *tre munera* that, for instance, a report of a subcommittee of the United States Bishops' Ad Hoc Committee on Priestly Life and Ministry in 1971 said the terminology lacked "deep roots" in the Catholic tradition. That report was properly rejected because Vatican II (see, for example, *Lumen Gentium*, no. 20) had already traced its patristic and conciliar credentials. It was the Church's meditation as early as Clement of Rome in the first century and Eusebius of Caesarea early in the fourth century and was explained as stoutly by Aquinas, albeit to a different end, as by Calvin. The Council of Trent had debated the significance of the order of the three. Wortman's "Prayer for Young Ministers" gives the order, beginning with the prophetic or teaching office, according to a tradition more Catholic than he would have allowed.

It was the Catholic Church that first fully understood how Christ the High Priest fulfills all three: for while Melchizedek was king and priest, and David was prophet and king, and Jeremiah was priest and prophet, Christ himself is prophet and priest and king and makes His apostolic ministers stewards of His titles *in persona Christi*. This sturdy ordination hymn, the gift of zealous people who in their zeal had dug up their own roots, is a sort of prophecy that comes to pass in the Sacrament of Holy Orders.

Ye who own the faith of Jesus

DEN DES VATERS SINN GEBOREN

Ye who own the faith of Je-sus Sing the won-ders that were done,

When the love of God the Fa-ther O'er our sin the

vic - t'ry won, When he made the Vir - gin Mar - y

Refrain

Moth - er of his on - ly Son. Hail, Mar - y, full of grace.

2. Blessèd were the chosen people
   Out of whom the Lord did come,
   Blessèd was the land of promise
   Fashioned for his earthly home;
   But more blessèd far the Mother
   She who bare him in her womb.

3. Wherefore let all faithful people
   Tell the honor of her name,
   Let the Church in her foreshadowed
   Part in her thanksgiving claim;
   What Christ's Mother sang in gladness
   Let Christ's people sing the same.

4. Let us weave our supplications,
   She with us and we with her,
   For the advancement of the faithful,
   For each faithful worshipper,
   For the doubting, for the sinful,
   For each heedless wanderer.

5. May the Mother's intercessions
   On our homes a blessing win,
   That the children all be prospered,
   Strong and fair and pure within,
   Following our Lord's own footsteps,
   Firm in faith and free from sin.

6. For the sick and for the agèd,
   For our dear ones far away,
   For the hearts that mourn in secret,
   All who need our prayers today,
   For the faithful gone before us,
   May the holy Virgin pray.

7. Praise, O Mary, praise the Father,
   Praise thy Savior and thy Son,
   Praise the everlasting Spirit,
   Who hath made thee ark and throne
   O'er all creatures high exalted,
   Lowly praise the Three in One.

YE WHO OWN THE
FAITH OF JESUS

———————— ❧ ————————

Of all the literary proponents of the German Pietist movement, none
excelled Johann Anastasius Freylinghausen (1670–1739) of Brunswick in Germany, not even Joachim Neander, who was born twenty
years earlier but lived only thirty years. A widely loved preacher, Freylinghausen wrote the words for forty-four hymns and half as many melodies, which were included two years after his death in a vast collection
of hymns that he had edited in two separate works in 1704 and 1714.
Together they included 1,498 hymns and 327 tunes. One of his compositions is the setting for this great and boldly Tractarian processional hymn
by Vincent Stuckey Stratton Coles (1845–1929).

This High Anglican divine was born in the year his fellow hymnodists Newman and Oakely were received into the Catholic Church.
Coles, educated at Eton and Balliol College, Oxford, always remained
an Anglican, as had his father, the rector of Shepton Beauchamp in
Somerset, to whose title he succeeded. But he did much to promote
Catholic thought within the Church of England, expressly so as librar-
ian (that is, research scholar) and principal of Pusey House in Oxford
from 1884 to 1897 and 1897 to 1909 respectively. His influence on
university undergraduates as a preacher and lecturer was a later parallel to the afternoon sermons of Newman in the University Church of
St. Mary the Virgin. From 1910 to 1920 he was warden of the religious
Community of the Epiphany in Truro.

Coles would pattern himself after Edward Bouverie Pusey, who became
Regius professor of Hebrew in 1828 and served as such and as canon of
Christ Church Cathedral until his death in 1882. Pusey, who had studied
at Gottingen and Berlin would have known the works of Freylinghausen. (One thinks of that charmed circle of geniuses in Christ Church,
including Pusey's own rather gruff personality and the timid Lewis Carroll

looking out from their cloister, seemingly irrelevant, and yet influencing the world in ways rarely matched certainly by academics of any age.)

Pusey had written the eighteenth of the Tracts for the Times in 1833 and became the symbolic leader of the Oxford movement after Newman "poped," as his former fellow religionists were wont to put it. "Puseyites" became a term of opprobrium for the Tractarians. In his *Eirenicon* of 1865, written to that other hymnodist John Keble, Pusey hoped for visible union between Anglicanism and Roman Catholicism, once the Catholics shed what he considered to be excessive Marian devotion.

All the more ironic, then (although not beyond the normal limits of Pusey's reasonable piety), are the lovely Marian expressions of the processional hymn Coles wrote in honor of the Blessed Virgin. It has been sung countless times in Ninian Comper's glorious chapel of Pusey House. That institution on St. Giles Street was built as a memorial to house Pusey's important library. I once lived there and later returned to it when it became associated with my college in the university. I had the opportunity many times to play the hymn in the chapel on a portative organ manufactured somewhat incongruously in Vermont. They were indelible moments, just down the cloister from a chamber housing, among other eclectic items, the death mask of Dr. Pusey. Perhaps more importantly, the building overlooked the friary of the Dominicans, into whose chapel I could peek from an upper floor.

Sing of Mary, pure and lowly

PLEADING SAVIOR

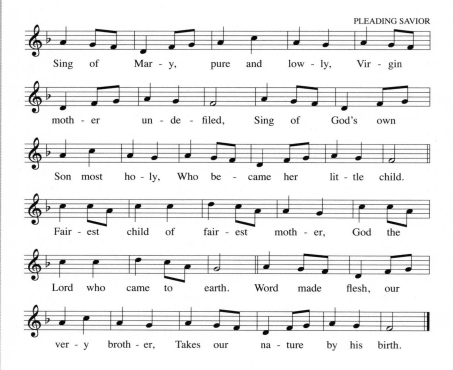

Sing of Mar - y, pure and low - ly, Vir - gin

moth - er un - de - filed, Sing of God's own

Son most ho - ly, Who be - came her lit - tle child.

Fair - est child of fair - est moth - er, God the

Lord who came to earth. Word made flesh, our

ver - y broth - er, Takes our na - ture by his birth.

2. Sing of Jesus, son of Mary,
   In the home at Nazareth.
   Toil and labor cannot weary
   Love enduring unto death.
   Constant was the love he gave her,
   Though he went forth from her side.
   Forth to preach, and heal, and suffer,
   Till on Calvary he died.

3. Sing of Mary, Sing of Jesus,
   Holy Mother's holier son.
   From his throne in heaven he sees us,
   Thither calls us every one,
   Where he welcomes home his Mother
   To a place at his right hand,
   There his faithful servants gather,
   There the crownèd victors stand.

4. Joyful Mother, full of gladness
   In thine arms thy Lord was borne
   Mournful Mother, full of sadness,
   All thy heart with pain was torn.
   Glorious Mother, now rewarded
   With a crown at Jesus' hand,
   Age to age thy name recorded
   Shall be blest in every land.

5. Glory be to God the Father;
   Glory be to God the Son;
   Glory be to God the Spirit;
   Glory to the Three in One.
   From the heart of blessed Mary,
   From all saints the song ascends,
   And the Church the strain re-echoes
   Unto earth's remotest ends.

SING OF MARY, PURE
AND LOWLY

———————————— ✄ ————————————

Rarely are the words and tune of a hymn so incongruous in their origins
as these lines set to "Pleading Savior." The tune got its name from
the opening of the hymn it first accompanied in 1855 in the original edition of the Congregational hymnal called the *Plymouth Collection*. This
vast collection of nearly fourteen hundred hymns was largely the work
of the indefatigable and controversial minister of the Pilgrim Church
in Brooklyn, New York, Henry Ward Beecher. His father, Lyman, had
been a principal player in fomenting the nativist riots against the Ur-
suline nuns of Boston in 1834, preaching on August 10 against "The
Devil and the Pope of Rome." The Beecher family dedicated much of
its rhetorical energy and literary talent to abolitionism (Lincoln visited
and prayed in Henry's Brooklyn parsonage). The cause was famously
dramatized by Henry's sister Harriet in *Uncle Tom's Cabin*, though Henry's
advocacy of female suffrage was opposed with equal force by his sister
Catherine (1800–1878), who balanced her antisuffrage sentiments with
promotion of higher education for women. Henry, of course, figured in
a sensational adultery trial in 1875; Harriet had already caused a different kind of uproar when she accused the late Lord Byron of incest. In a
quieter vein, their nephew Charles Emerson Beecher (1856–1904) was
the Yale paleontologist who pioneered the study of trilobites. Henry's
brother Charles helped with the hymnal, along with the organist of the
Plymouth Church, John Zundel (1815–1882) of Germany, who had been
organist of the Lutheran church in St. Petersburg and bandmaster of the
Imperial Horse Guards.

The eclectic feminism of the Beechers could not have anticipated the
high Marianism of the words. While the poem that inspired it appeared
without the name of its author in a parish pamphlet in the English village
of Ilkeston in Derbyshire probably in 1914, it was rewritten by Roland

Sing of Mary, pure and lowly

Ford Palmer (1891–1985). Born in England, Palmer migrated to Canada and attended the University of Toronto. Ordained to the Anglican priesthood in 1917, he entered the novitiate of the Society of St. John the Evangelist in Cambridge, Massachusetts, and eventually became superior of that society in Canada. The S.S.J.E. was an Anglican religious order for men, the first founded in England since the Reformation. The idea of "Protestant monks" was most unfamiliar, and when some of them set up in a parish on Cherry Street in Philadelphia, walking outdoors in their cassocks, a lady in the neighborhood complained to the Protestant Episcopal bishop that some of his clergymen were practicing celibacy in the streets.

Ten years before his death, I visited with Father Palmer in British Columbia, where his gracious and very gentle aspect became strongly saddened about the changes and degradations in his Church. He was honored to have written this hymn and pleased that it was sung; but he spent more time on other subjects, including his several spiritual books. His tendencies were very Catholic and would have been more vitally so were he alive now. He had originally written two stanzas, to follow the present second, that were neglected along the way because they were too daringly Catholic. Consequently, most people today are unaware of them. One (originally the third) implies the Assumption, and the other refers to the Mysteries of the Holy Rosary. Catholic voices could recover these lines, which I have included here.

Hail to the brightness

WESLEY

Hail to the bright-ness of Si - on's glad morn-ing!

Joy to the lands that in dark - ness have lain!

Hushed be the ac - cents of sor - row and mourn - ing,

Si - on in tri - umph be - gins her mild reign.

2. Hail to the brightness of Sion's glad morning,
   Long by the prophets of Israel foretold!
   Hail to the millions from bondage returning,
   Gentiles and Jews the blest vision behold.

3. Lo, in the desert rich flowers are springing,
   Streams ever copious are gliding along;
   Loud from the mountaintops echoes are ringing,
   Wastes rise in verdure and mingle in song.

4. See, from all lands, from the isles of the ocean,
   Praise to Jehovah ascending on high;
   Fallen are the engines of war and commotion,
   Shouts of salvation are rending the sky.

HAIL TO THE BRIGHTNESS

It did seem to me a good fortune when some years ago I happened upon this luminous work in a frayed copy of *The Hymnal for Young People*. The editors, in 1928, advertised that it contained the "high points of Christian aspiration and thought through eighteen centuries" and was guided by two principles: "their worth as lyric poetry and their fitness to express the attitudes which are normal to the religion of young life." Standards were higher then, although many of that hymnal's selections apparently were considered beneath the canons of my own boyhood songbooks. This was foolish, for that attitude neglected this hymn, which has to be, by any measure, one of the best evangelical expressions of its period for all periods. The whole hymn resonates with the stimulus of the American frontier, and the tune "Wesley" is deceptively sophisticated, ringing out like an admixture of Appalachia and Vienna.

Its exclusion from most traditional repertoires is curious, inasmuch as its author and composer are so familiar and widely respected. Thomas Hastings wrote it in 1830, the year in which Lowell Mason supplied the music. Hastings was a rare case of an equally competent writer and composer. He wrote the tune "Toplady" for "Rock of Ages" at approximately the same time. A real pioneer woodsman in Oneida County, New York, he had to make a special effort to teach himself the basics of composition. His literary gifts seem to have been cultivated almost exclusively in the school of the Bible. Hastings was an albino and consequently had poor eyesight, which made his work all the more heroic. In this, if in little else, he resembles Edvard Grieg (1843–1907). He was, nevertheless, already involved in assembling a hymn anthology at the age of eighteen.

Two years after writing this hymn, Hastings removed to New York City and collaborated with Mason, who was still in Boston founding in that same year the Boston Academy of Music. *Spiritual Songs for Social Worship*, one of their many joint efforts, had a major influence particularly among Presbyterian congregations. As Mason's *Carmina Sacra* sold over half a million copies, so Hastings published fifty volumes of music, providing the words for nearly six hundred hymns and approximately one thousand tunes. Hastings died in New York on May 15, 1872, just three months before Mason's death in Orange, New Jersey. Were this lyrically energetic composition the only work of these two prolific men, it would be sufficient to earn them a lasting tribute and happy place in the desired annals.

ACKNOWLEDGMENTS

The Author and EWTN Publishing, Inc. gratefully acknowledge permission to reprint the following hymns and melodies:

Words to the following hymns from *The English Hymnal*, used by permission of Oxford University Press:

> "Hail thee, festival day," translated by M. F. Bell (1862–1947)
> "He who would valiant be," by Percy Dearmer (1862–1936), after John Bunyan (1628–1688)
> "Ye who own the faith of Jesus," by V. S. S. Coles (1845–1929)

Words to the following hymn from the *Yattendon Hymnal*, used by permission of Oxford University Press:

> "O sacred head, sore wounded," by Robert Bridges (1844–1930)

Melodies to the following hymns from *The English Hymnal*, used by permission of Oxford University Press:

> MONKS GATE, coll. and adpt. Ralph Vaughan Williams (1872–1958)
> SALVE FESTA DIES, by Ralph Vaughan Williams (1872–1958)
> SINE NOMINE, by Ralph Vaughan Williams (1872–1958)

Index of First Lines

Index of Melodies

INDEX OF NAMES

Harding, James B., 212
Hardy, Thomas, 169
Haschka, Lorenz Leopold, 202
Hassler, Hans Leo, 64
Hastings, Thomas, 157, 200, 311, 312
Haydn, Franz Joseph, 93, 166, 167, 169, 202
Heber, Reginald, 211, 212, 214, 215, 220, 223, 224, 226, 227
Helmore, Thomas, 29, 257, 274
Hemerken, Thomas, 98
Hemy, Henri Frederick, 76, 259
Henrici, Christian Friedrich (Picander), 64
Henry VIII (king of England), 26, 44, 96, 130
Herbert, George, 43, 118, 119, 248
Hippolytus, Saint, 169
Hooker, Brian, 158
Hopkins, Edward John, 283
Hopkins, Gerard Manley, 86, 229
Hopkins, John, 151
How, William Walsham, 267, 268
Hughes, John, 191

Irving, Edward, 12

Jacopone da Todi, 87
James of Jerusalem, Saint, 17
Jeffreys, George, 124
John Chrysostom, Saint, 17, 271
John Damascene, Saint, 43, 44, 49
Johnson, Samuel, 148
Jones, Edward, 223
Joseph the Hymnographer, Saint, 49

Julian, John, 49, 50

Keble, John, 99, 217, 218, 233, 236, 305
Ken, Thomas, 140
Kipling, Rudyard, 298
Knox, Ronald Arbuthnott, 35, 80, 81, 133, 223, 256, 293
Knox, Wilfred, 256

Leo III, Saint (pope), 59
Leo X (pope), 130
Leo XIII (pope), 49, 80
Lewis, C. S., 3
Lindsey, Theophilus, 244
Llewellyn, Richard, 288
Logue, Michael, 253
Luke, Jemima Thompson, 251
Lutkin, Peter Christian, 112
Lyon, Meyer, 105
Lyte, Henry Francis, 229, 232, 233, 241

Madan, Martin, 145, 197
Mant, Richard, 238
Marot, Clément, 130
Martin, George Clement, 43
Mason, Jackson, 67
Mason, John, 133
Mason, Lowell, 133, 134, 200, 205, 215, 245, 311
Mendelssohn, Felix, 122, 184, 223, 230, 257, 274
Miller, Edward, 161, 291
Miller, Robert B., 173
Milton, John, 6, 115, 205, 247

Hail to the brightness